The Information Retrieval Series   Volume 34

Chirag Shah

Collaborative Information Seeking

The Art and Science of Making
the Whole Greater than the Sum of All

 Springer

Chirag Shah
School of Communication & Information
The State University of New Jersey
New Brunswick, NJ, USA

ISSN 1387-5264   The Information Retrieval Series
ISBN 978-3-642-28812-8   ISBN 978-3-642-28813-5 (eBook)
DOI 10.1007/978-3-642-28813-5
Springer Heidelberg New York Dordrecht London

Library of Congress Control Number: 2012942855

ACM Computing Classification (1998): H.3, K.4

Printed on acid-free paper

Springer is part of Springer Science+Business Media (www.springer.com)

To my late father and eternal role model—
Rajendrakumar Shah

Foreword

Information seeking is a term that describes a collection of fundamental human processes that enable survival and growth. Some elements of information seeking are involuntary and continuous elements of consciousness, but most studies of information seeking focus on conscious processes that tend to be grouped under the name 'search'. In the 20th century, industrialization led to an informated society, which in turn has made search for information one of the basic skills of 21st century modernity. Information work is seldom solitary and most information is selectively shared at different stages of the information life cycle. Not only do people collaborate to create or analyze information, but they often collaborate on the seeking processes. This book focuses on theory, systems, and evaluation for the evolving study of collaborative information seeking.

Research and development in the information, library, and computer science domains led to great advances in search services. Today, the easy cases of search are well-served by search engines, e.g., known item searches, single facet searches, and searches for pointers to content. If the answer to a question can be expressed by a single info object (e.g., a page, a figure) then search engines can find that object. What remains problematic for these cases are assessing the veracity of the source and the appropriate interpretation and the use of information objects. However, there is much research to be done on search for open-ended, exploratory problems where answers require many information objects and points of view. The answer to a thesis question, which medical treatment strategy to select, how to invest for your retirement, which university to attend, the effects of social media on adolescent behavior, or similar questions, require people to invest more time, marshal more systems and services, and orchestrate the interaction of multiple subprocesses. Increasingly, the actions of other people add new dimensions to the multiple steps associated with multi-session, collaborative information seeking. This kind of information seeking requires a lot more support than current search engines provide.

The subtleties of human–information interaction done alone are complex: mapping needs to words (query tokens or displayed menu metadata), managing information tools and services, scanning candidate result snippets to evaluate whether to invest further examination, consuming documents to assess relevance and construct meaning, synthesizing these assessments over multiple consumptions to reach some conclusion or decision, and monitoring the process over perhaps long time intervals. Doing these activities with other people introduces possibilities for improved effectiveness but adds considerable collaborative load costs to share, achieve mutual understanding, form consensus, and monitor or document the collaborative information seeking process. We are only beginning to understand the tradeoffs that accrue between effectiveness and efficiency as people increasingly are able to seek information together. In this volume, Chirag Shah provides both a framework for thinking about and studying collaborative information seeking, and a roadmap for building systems that improve both effectiveness and efficiency.

Chapel Hill, NC, USA   Gary Marchionini

Preface

We live in a society where information is, without a doubt, a powerful force. This statement may sound like a cliche, but it always amazes me how often we forget. May be that's the purpose (or should be) of the technology that surrounds such information. The other aspect of information technology that amazes me is the fact that it is so new, considering human history. The clock that tells us the precise time of the day dates back only to the sixteenth century. The base 10 numbering system is only 500 years old, and mechanical devices used to calculate and present information have existed for only a couple of centuries. Of course, today when we say "information technology", we are probably thinking about computers and other digital devices, and they are merely a few decades old.

What intrigues me the most is how we have been able to integrate such new concepts and technologies with long-standing human behavior. Take for example, working in groups and living as a society. This behavior has proven to be extremely important for the survival and prosperity of our species. Back in the days of hunting together to today's office work, mankind has understood the need to work and thrive together. It is this behavior—the one of collaborating with each other—that has made it possible to achieve great feats in the history. How else can one man (or woman)[1] build the pyramids[2] or crack the human genetics code.

Of course, not all problems call for people working together. While Einstein had help and drew inspirations from others, he did come up with many significant findings himself. Leonardo de Vinci and Picasso, similarly, worked alone. Claude Shannon, considered to be the father of digital information age, was known to have worked in solitude behind closed doors. But let's put geniuses aside and talk about the remaining 99.99 % of us (which of course, still includes a lot of smart people). We do, often need to work in collaboration. I'm sure even Einstein needed help placing his furniture in his Princeton house; he was a genius, not a superhuman!

---

[1] I'm not going to worry about being politically correct in this book and assume that the savvy reader understands he or she being equal.

[2] Though the ancient Egyptian workers were forced to work on pyramid construction on such "forced collaboration". More on this later.

This book is about those times when people work in collaboration—an eternal human behavior, in the light of new and innovative technologies in the information age that we live in. More precisely, it is concerned about situations pertaining to information retrieval/seeking/sense-making where people are collaborating or should be collaborating.

One may ask—Why this book? Why now? There is a simple two-fold answer to both these questions. Using technology to understand and support collaborative behavior has been around for a while—what is known as Computer-Supported Cooperative Work (CSCW), but it is in the recent years that we have seen more specialized attention given to applying CSCW methods and frameworks for information seeking situations. On the other hand, the field of Information Retrieval (IR, or broadly speaking IS, information seeking) has found (or re-realized) the importance of considering social and collaborative aspects of search, synthesis, and information use.

This has led to a newly developed interest in the field that is still emerging at the intersection of several other well-established fields, including CSCW, IR, HCI, and social media/networking. This book as an attempt to introduce the relatively young domain of collaborative information seeking (CIS) research by discussing how it came to be, what it currently offers, and where it is headed next. The best part is that we all get to define and contribute to this future.

Personally, my journey on this path started during the summer of 2007 when I was an intern at FXPAL, working with Gene Golovchinsky and Jeremy Pickens. Back then, we worked on something called Collaborative Exploratory Search (CES), and argued that IR systems need to have "smart" components that could mediate collaborative activities and produce results that are "better" than any individual IR process, and we succeeded with at least one kind of situation (time-limited, recall-oriented task with two people collaborating under assumed roles). We did continue this work further by identifying more situations and defining other roles, but as I returned to UNC and resumed working on my dissertation, I started moving in the direction of user-mediated collaboration. My dissertation provided a framework (among other things) for studying and supporting user-focused CIS. I have carried on working on various aspects of CIS (both user and system sides) as a faculty at Rutgers University. In the meantime, I have also participated in a number of professional events around CIS, including half a dozen workshops—two of which I co-organized.

This book is a culmination of all of these experiences, and while they have made me biased on the topic, I have tried my best to include others' views as well. In the end, my hope is that those working in this domain, and the larger field of IR see this book as a record of modern day CIS research that has tried to incorporate many view-points and contributions to inform those looking for a comprehensive treatment of this topic, along with the wonderful opportunities (and challenges) it presents.

New Brunswick, NJ, USA   Chirag Shah

Acknowledgements

I would like to thank all of the following people and organizations for their contributions to my research relating to this book. Without them, this work would not exist.

- Gene Golovchinsky and Jeremy Pickens at FXPAL, California, for introducing me to the area of collaborative exploratory search during my internship in summer 2007.
- The National Science Foundation, for funding my dissertation studies and research with IIS grant # 0812363.
- Yahoo! for providing funding for the development of Coagmento through Campus Innovation Award (2011–2012).
- Rutgers University PhD students Roberto Gonzalez-Ibanez and Muge Haseki, who have not only been working with me on various issues of collaborative information seeking (CIS), but also contributed to parts of this book. Specifically, Roberto wrote a section on affective dimension of CIS, and Muge did Appendix D on computer-mediated communication (CMC).
- My PhD advisor Gary Marchionini, for his constant encouragement and guidance on all of my scholarly endeavors at UNC. Without his kindness, support, and trust in my work, I could not have been able to even embark upon this journey presented here.
- The rest of my dissertation committee—Diane Kelly, Barbara Wildemuth, and late Deborah Barreau from UNC Chapel Hill, and Susan Dumais from Microsoft Research.
- My colleagues at Rutgers University, especially Nick Belkin, Paul Kantor, Michael Lesk, Marie Radford, and Mark Aakhus who enriched my understanding of CIS and the fields of information and communication through many conversations and mentoring sessions.
- A number of external advisors who have either commented on different drafts of my work (articles, proposals, this manuscript) or had very helpful discussions with me on this topic—Madhu Reddy from Penn State; Michael Twidale from UIUC; Rob Capra from UNC Chapel Hill; Jonathan Foster from University of Sheffield; Preben Hansen from Swedish Institute of Computer Science; Susan

Dumais, Merrie Morris, Ryen White, Paul Bennett, and Jaime Teevan from Microsoft Research; and Dan Russell and Ed Chi from Google.

- My late father Rajendrakumar, mother Sneha, and sister Shweta, for their constant love, kindness, and support, even when they are all in different continents.
- And last, but not the least, my wife Lori, for being absolutely supportive of my research and sacrificing her time with me so that I could work on this book. Even in the darkest hour of toil and frustration, she had faith in me and my efforts. Lori also provided valuable feedback on early drafts of this book, as well as beta versions of Coagmento. Without her, this work could not have been possible.

Contents

Part I   Introduction

1   Introduction 3
   1.1   Collaboration in Information Seeking Situations 3
   1.2   Information Retrieval, Seeking, and Collaboration 4
      1.2.1   Collaboration to Help Information Seeking 4
      1.2.2   Information Seeking to Help Collaboration 5
   1.3   CIS Scenarios 6
      1.3.1   What/How We Already Do with Regard to CIS 6
      1.3.2   What/How We Would Like to do During CIS 7
   1.4   Structure of the Book 8
   References 9

2   Collaboration 11
   2.1   Definitions and Models of Collaboration 11
   2.2   Principles of Collaboration 16
   2.3   Process of Collaboration 17
   2.4   Limitations of Collaboration 18
   2.5   Collaboration in the Context of Information-Intensive Tasks 20
   2.6   How the Concept of Collaboration Relates to CIS 21
   References 23

3   Collaborative Information Seeking (CIS) in Context 25
   3.1   Introduction 25
   3.2   Collaborative Information Retrieval (CIR) and Co-search 26
   3.3   Co-browsing or Collaborative Navigation 28
   3.4   Social Search 30
   3.5   Collaborative Filtering 32
   References 36

Part II   Conceptual Understanding of CIS

4   Frameworks for CIS Research and Development 41
    4.1   Introduction 41
    4.2   Space and Time Aspects of CIS 41
    4.3   User–Source–Time Configuration for CIS 42
    4.4   Control, Communication, and Awareness in a CIS Environment . . 44
        4.4.1   Control 45
        4.4.2   Communication 46
        4.4.3   Awareness 46
        4.4.4   Importance of Control, Communication, and Awareness in
                CIS Systems 49
    4.5   Nature and Level of Mediation 50
        4.5.1   System/Algorithmically Mediated Collaboration 50
        4.5.2   User/Interface Mediated Collaboration 51
    4.6   Dimensions of Collaborative Systems 51
    4.7   Summary 56
    References 57

5   Toward a Model for CIS 61
    5.1   Models for Collaboration 61
    5.2   Models for Information Seeking 63
    5.3   Models for User and System Interaction 68
        5.3.1   Degree of Involvement 72
        5.3.2   Explicitness of Collaboration 73
    5.4   Toward a Cognitive Model for CIS 74
        5.4.1   Capturing Affective Dimension of CIS 74
        5.4.2   Extending Information Seeking Processes (ISP) Model for
                Collaboration 77
    5.5   Summary 82
    References 83

Part III   CIS Systems, Applications, and Implications

6   Systems and Tools for CIS 89
    6.1   Costs, Challenges, and Design Implications for CIS Systems . . . 89
    6.2   System-Mediated Collaboration 91
        6.2.1   Cerchiamo 91
        6.2.2   Querium 92
    6.3   User-Mediated Collaboration 93
        6.3.1   Ariadne 93
        6.3.2   SearchTogether 95
    6.4   A Case Study in Designing a CIS Solution with Coagmento 96
        6.4.1   Design 96
        6.4.2   Development 104
        6.4.3   Deployment 109

6.5   Future Development 112
References 113

7   Evaluation 115
   7.1   Challenges for Evaluating CIS Systems and Situations 115
   7.2   Evaluation Methodologies 116
      7.2.1   Evaluating Usability with User Studies 116
      7.2.2   System-Based Training-Testing 117
      7.2.3   Qualitative Evaluation 117
      7.2.4   Task or Application Based Evaluation 117
   7.3   System Measures 118
      7.3.1   Precision, Recall, and F-measure 118
      7.3.2   Coverage 119
      7.3.3   Effectiveness 120
      7.3.4   Likelihood of Discovery 120
      7.3.5   Diversity 121
   7.4   User Measures 121
      7.4.1   Collaborative Aptitude 121
      7.4.2   Usability 123
      7.4.3   Cognitive Load 124
      7.4.4   Engagement 124
      7.4.5   Awareness 125
      7.4.6   Affects/Emotions 125
   7.5   Case Study 126
      7.5.1   Subjects 127
      7.5.2   System 127
      7.5.3   Session Workflow 128
      7.5.4   Conditions 128
      7.5.5   Task 129
      7.5.6   Results and Discussion 130
      7.5.7   Conclusion 134
   7.6   Summary 135
   References 135

8   Conclusion 139
   8.1   CIS—Looking Back, Looking Forward 139
   8.2   Theoretical Issues 139
   8.3   Experimental and Practical Issues 141
   8.4   Summary 143
   References 143

Appendix A   Ten Stories of Five *C*s 145
   A.1   Introduction 145
   A.2   A Model of Collaboration 145
   A.3   Scenarios 147
      A.3.1   Paying Taxes 147
      A.3.2   What's for Dinner? 148

A.3.3   School Elections 149
A.3.4   Group Project 149
A.3.5   VidArch 150
A.3.6   Searching in a Library 151
A.3.7   Planning a Trip 152
A.3.8   Discovery of SARS Virus 153
A.3.9   Factory Line 154
A.3.10 May Day Parade 155
A.4   Conclusion 156
References 157

**Appendix B   Brief Overview of Computer-Supported Cooperative
Work (CSCW)** 159
B.1   Organizing CSCW Systems and Environments 159
B.2   Control, Communication, and Awareness in CSCW 160
B.2.1   Control 160
B.2.2   Communication 162
B.2.3   Awareness 162
B.3   Groupware Systems 164
B.4   Summary 165
References 166

**Appendix C   Brief Overview of Computer-Supported Collaborative
Learning (CSCL)** 169
C.1   Theories 169
C.2   Practice and Applications 170
C.3   Summary 171
References 171

**Appendix D   Brief Overview of Computer-Mediated Communication
(CMC)** 173
D.1   Social Presence Theory 173
D.2   Media Richness Theory 174
D.3   Social Information Processing (SIP) Theory 175
D.4   Social Identification/De-individuation (SIDE) Theory 176
D.5   Hyperpersonal Communication Model 176
D.6   Summary 177
References 177

Glossary 179

Index 183

List of Abbreviations

CES   Collaborative Exploratory Search
CIB   Collaborative Information Behavior
CIR   Collaborative Information Retrieval
CIS   Collaborative Information Seeking
CMC   Computer-Mediated Communication
CS   Computer Science
CSCL   Computer-Supported Cooperative Learning
CSCW   Computer-Supported Cooperative Work
HCI   Human–Computer Interaction
IR   Information Retrieval
IS   Information Seeking
LIS   Library & Information Science
PIM   Personal Information Management

List of Figures

Fig. 1.1   Contextual depiction of Collaborative Information Seeking (CIS) .   5

Fig. 2.1   A set-based model of collaboration. An inner set is essential to or supports the outer set 13

Fig. 2.2   Distinguishing communication, contribution, coordination, cooperation, and collaboration using different variables. A variable is represented with a *bar* going minimum to maximum from left to right 15

Fig. 3.1   Depiction of CIS and related topics using the dimensions of human–system and explicit–implicit collaboration 26

Fig. 3.2   A typical scenario of information seeking in an IR environment . . 33

Fig. 3.3   Content-based information filtering 33

Fig. 3.4   Collaborative information filtering 34

Fig. 4.1   Space–time dimensions for library activities [15]. Permit pending . 42

Fig. 4.2   Various collaborative activities and systems along space and time dimensions 43

Fig. 4.3   A framework for CIS environments (part 1 of 2) 52

Fig. 4.4   A framework for CIS environments (part 2 of 2) 53

Fig. 5.1   Steps to collaboration (http://www.empowerment.state.ia.us/files/ annual_reports/2001/Collaboration.pdf) 62

Fig. 5.2   A set-based model of collaboration. An inner set is essential to or supports the outer set 62

Fig. 5.3   Four layer model of information seeking centered around information access and organization 65

Fig. 5.4   Extension of the four layer model of information access and organization 66

Fig. 5.5   A model for Collaborative Information Seeking (CIS) extended from the model in Fig. 5.3 68

Fig. 5.6   Saracevic's model of stratified interaction 70

Fig. 5.7   Looking at collaboration with the amount of user and system involvement 72

Fig. 5.8   Looking at collaboration with the amount of explicitness or
            intention from user and system   73
Fig. 5.9   Collaborative ISP stages for session-1   79
Fig. 5.10   Positive/negative feelings, and affective relevance for session-1   . .   80
Fig. 5.11   Collaborative ISP stages for session-2   80
Fig. 5.12   Positive/negative feelings, and affective relevance for session-2   . .   81
Fig. 6.1   Cerchiamo's architecture. Printed with permission   92
Fig. 6.2   Querium interface: (1) top area for new queries, (2) navigation
            sidebar, (3) main results, and (4) document view. Printed with
            permission   93
Fig. 6.3   A search visualization in Ariadne. Printed with permission   94
Fig. 6.4   Screenshot of SearchTogether. (a) Integrated messaging, (b) query
            awareness, (c) current results, (d) recommendation queue, (e)–(g)
            search buttons, (h) page-specific metadata, (i) toolbar, (j) browser.
            Printed with permission   95
Fig. 6.5   Coagmento v1: design version   98
Fig. 6.6   Toolbar provided on top of the document being viewed with
            Coagmento   99
Fig. 6.7   Coagmento v2: development version   105
Fig. 6.8   Snippets collection window   105
Fig. 6.9   Annotations window   106
Fig. 6.10   Participants during a study session   107
Fig. 6.11   Coagmento v3: deployment   109
Fig. 7.1   A framework for IR-focused system-based evaluation measures   . .   119
Fig. 7.2   A version of Coagmento used for the study   127
Fig. 7.3   Study session workflow   128
Fig. 7.4   Experimental setup for four different conditions   129
Fig. 7.5   Depiction of coverage by various conditions (drawn to scale)   132
Fig. 7.6   Query distance for $C2_{ARTIFICIAL}$, $C4_{SAME\_ROOM}$, and $C5_{REMOTE}$
            using Lavenshtein algorithm   133
Fig. 8.1   CIS as an interdisciplinary field, along with some of the issues
            stemming from different parts of it   140
Fig. A.1   A model for collaboration   146
Fig. B.1   CSCW/groupware matrix showing how different collaborative
            activities and systems fit across time and space dimensions.
            Courtesy of Momo54 (http://en.wikipedia.org/wiki/User:Momo54)   160

List of Tables

Table 2.1 Various group activities and examples 20
Table 4.1 CIS in the context of user–source–time dimensions 43
Table 4.2 Differentiating between intent and activeness 54
Table 5.1 Information seeking strategies (Belkin et al., 1995) 71
Table 5.2 Summary of participants' feelings and affective relevance
           through ISP stages 82
Table 6.1 Summary of responses by 84 participants on ease of use and
           satisfaction questionnaire for the lab study 108
Table 6.2 Summary of responses by 19 participants on ease of use and
           satisfaction questionnaire for the field study 110
Table 6.3 Summary of responses by 8 participants on ease of use and
           satisfaction questionnaire for the participatory design phase II
           study 111
Table 7.1 Experimental conditions 129
Table 7.2 Summary of various universes used in our analysis 130

Part I
Introduction

2

This part provides an introduction to the subject matter, including the core concepts of collaboration and information seeking (IS), as well as discussion on related notions such as information retrieval (IR) and sense-making, and how they all connect.

"Two are better than one, because they have a good return for their work: If one falls down, his friend can help him up. But pity the man who falls and has no one to help him up! Though one may be overpowered, two can defend themselves. A cord of three strands is not quickly broken."

King Solomon

Chapter 1
Introduction

Abstract This chapter's purpose is two-fold: introduce the notions of collaboration and information seeking/retrieval, and provide a context in which these concepts will be discussed throughout the book. It is achieved by concisely yet clearly
indicating what is meant by collaboration here, how information seeking and information retrieval (IR) are seen to be related, and what it means to collaborate in
information seeking. An attempt is also made to situate collaborative information
seeking (CIS) with related concepts such as collaborative information behavior and
collaborative sense-making. Several examples and scenarios are presented to clarify
how CIS situations arise and why we should care about them.

1.1 Collaboration in Information Seeking Situations

Two heads are better than one. How often have we heard this? And yet, when it
comes to accessing or assessing information, somehow the merits of working together are lost. While it is natural for us to work in collaboration for difficult or
complex tasks [1], many situations involving search, retrieval, and synthesis of information are not typically conceived as such processes.

The apparent paradox can be seen in many daily scenarios. Imagine you are planning a vacation with your family (example often used by Morris [3, 4] as well as
Golovchinsky and Pickens [2, 5]). There are many parts of this complex project
that revolves around looking for relevant information, comparing and synthesizing
various pieces of it from multiple sources, and finally making decisions. It is not
atypical for your spouse and other family members to be involved in some or all of
these parts. This is an example of people working together in information seeking
task. But how often do we really think about such a project as collaborative information seeking (CIS)? No wonder we lack proper support for carrying out such
tasks!

Other day-to-day life examples include co-authors working on a scholarly article,
an engaged couple doing wedding planning, and a recruitment committee working
on their new hiring project [6, 7]. Notice that these examples go beyond simply
searching together; they include information lookup, sharing, synthesis, and decision making. In addition, they all have an end-goal that is mutually beneficial to
the parties involved. Such CIS projects typically last several sessions and the par-

C. Shah, *Collaborative Information Seeking*, The Information Retrieval Series 34,
DOI 10.1007/978-3-642-28813-5_1, © Springer-Verlag Berlin Heidelberg 2012

ticipants are joined with an intention to contribute and benefit. Not surprisingly the whole process is highly interactive. And so, our focus in this book will be on collaborative processes that are intentional, interactive, and possibly mutually beneficial.

1.2 Information Retrieval, Seeking, and Collaboration

It is an understatement to say that we live in an information age; information affects us in more profound ways than we often realize. We are not just talking about finding a relevant book in a library or a useful document from a digital repository; we are referring to a large array of situations that require us to inquire for and retrieve information to solve problems. The problem could be curiosity as to whether or not it will rain today, or a dire need to figure out the treatment options for one's mother's recent diagnosis of type II diabetes; it could be finding the driving directions to the beach, or collecting evidence to support one's legal case. It is hard to imagine a day without intentionally or unintentionally looking for and/or encountering information that help us carry out various tasks. This activity of looking for information for performing tasks and solving problems is broadly referred to as information seeking here, which includes not only searching and retrieving, but also browsing, sharing, assessing, and synthesizing information. Thus, information retrieval is seen as a subset of information seeking. It is important to note that sense-making is often viewed as an integral part of information seeking—the activity of information seeking being done to make sense of something, or sense-making helping the process of information seeking.

Collaboration, on the other hand, is a separate activity that could be (and is) studied outside of information retrieval/seeking/sense-making fields. Collaboration is an activity of multiple parties coming together to work toward a mutually beneficial common goal. Think about tug-of-war, where every individual in your team is contributing his/her strength to pull the rope in one direction for the goal of winning the game. In this example, it is probable that your team has a captain, but when it comes to actually working on the collaborative task (pulling the rope), everyone is contributing more or less the same. Thus, the real authority lies in the collaboration rather than in individuals.

So how does collaboration connect to information seeking (or broadly speaking information behavior)? There are two ways of looking at it.

1.2.1 Collaboration to Help Information Seeking

Collaboration is used for solving problems that are too difficult or complex for an individual. Information seeking could be such a problem. Take for example, searching for a house to buy. This project is quite complex in nature and typically involves multiple parties, including the buyers (e.g., a husband and a wife), the real estate

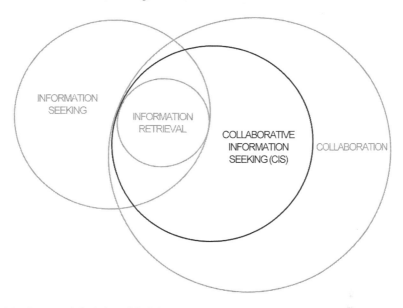

Fig. 1.1   Contextual depiction of Collaborative Information Seeking (CIS)

agent, and the mortgage consultant. They all have the same mutually beneficial goal. Thus, this information seeking project is inherently collaborative, making it an example of CIS.

1.2.2 Information Seeking to Help Collaboration

Another way to look at the connection between collaboration with information seeking is that often a collaborative project requires information seeking. Think about the example of a family vacation. The whole project is collaborative, and a part of it (planning) is focused on information seeking.

To summarize, one could come to CIS from an information seeking project or a collaborative project. It is often difficult to distinguish these two kinds of scenarios, and for the most part it will not affect the discussion in this book. However, it is important to point out these intertwined relationships among information retrieval/seeking and collaboration for conceptual understanding. Figure 1.1 is a simplistic view of these connections. In the following section, we will look at a few scenarios to clarify further how the interconnections of collaborative and information seeking activities work to create CIS situations.

1.3 CIS Scenarios

Going beyond examples, let us consider a few scenarios where people work in collaboration in information seeking situations. We will divide them in two categories: what/how we already do, and what/how we would like to do CIS. These scenarios will not only help us ground our understanding of how and why CIS is important to study and address, but also give us clues to solving some of its issues as we will see later in this book.

1.3.1 What/How We Already Do with Regard to CIS

These are scenarios that portray typical situations in CIS.

Scenario-1: Working on Tax Preparation   Joe goes to his tax attorney Carol to work on his taxes this year. During their first meeting, Carol obtains a handful of information from Joe and starts filling out the forms. Later she gives a call to Joe to discuss the tax benefits and returns. Joe thinks he should be able to claim more. He returns to Carol with more documents that can be used to file more exemptions. Meanwhile, Carol finds a couple of spots where she can squeeze in for more returns. Finally they both are happy with the outcome and file the tax returns.

In this whole process, both Joe and Carol are working to solve the same problem. They both have the same interest about the outcome of the process, even though the rewards will be different for each one. At times, Joe cooperated with Carol giving her all the information she wanted and at times, Carol cooperated with Joe's higher expectations for tax returns. They both did certain tasks independently, but then they had to coordinate to put everything together. Joe contributed to the project by providing all the relevant information. Carol contributed by applying her expertise to handle such problems. Throughout the process, both parties had some way of communicating with each other for interactions.

Scenario-2: Researching History   Mark walks up to a reference librarian Susanne in a public library. He is studying 20th century American poets and trying to find all the material that could be relevant. Susanne helps him to locate the section of the library, where Mark can find the books on poetry. However, that would not be enough. Mark describes the scope of his study and that gives Susanne information to start suggesting specific books to Mark. After skimming through those books over a couple of day's time, Mark thinks he has a lot more material than he needed. He returns to Susanne with this concern, and she suggests for him to look at a book on Anthology of American Poets. This book not only helps Mark directly, but also lets Susanne refine her suggestions as she also flips through it. Finally, Mark has good material on this topic that is not too general and covers most of the information that he would like to have.

Working on this collaborative task required both Mark and Susanne to interact with each other (communication) person-to-person at a certain place and time (co-ordination). The starting point of this collaboration was Susanne agreeing to help Mark (cooperation). While Susanne seems to have done most of the work (contribution), she also learned a certain number of things in the process. Finally, while the rewards of this process were different for both the parties, it is important to note that they both worked together to solve the same problem.

1.3.2 What/How We Would Like to do During CIS

Having seen two scenarios of how people work in CIS project, let us now turn our attention to situations where one could benefit from doing CIS and/or having CIS solutions specially designed for the given context.[1]

Scenario-1: Managing Scientific Project   Gail is a neuroscientist who leads a multi-campus team working on new techniques for using viruses as vectors for neuronal therapies. Gail also consults for a large biotech company. She scans a dozen journals regularly, participates in online forums, and has a post-doctoral fellow who regularly conducts systematic searches of the biomedical literature. Her research group maintains a database of papers and much of her time is spent re-finding and integrating new ideas she gains from preprints, discussions with colleagues, and results from her lab work. She needs seamless tools that support search across diverse kinds of public and personal information streams and allow flexible organization and analysis.

Gail often relies on her clinical colleagues to identify and interpret newly-published research results. She often wishes that they could share particular search sessions, as well as the summaries she currently receives. Gail can often direct less experienced colleagues to search on topics they did not initially consider. Sometimes in meetings, Gail and her colleagues discuss particular searches and run additional searches during the discussion.

Gail can access the biotech company's library of technical reports and pre-prints through a secure web portal. While this is a useful resource, she is frequently confused by the organization of the sub-collections and by the company-specific terminology and metadata. Having online access to a reference librarian during search sessions would make her more productive.

Scenario-2: John the Accountant   John is an accountant in his forties who recently underwent successful surgery for colon cancer. He knows that he will have a long life as a cancer survivor as long as he maintains a healthy life style. He continues to learn about the disease, has joined online support groups, and desires tools

---

[1]These are derived from the scenarios created for the ResultsSpace project at UNC Chapel Hill. Details can be found at http://www.ils.unc.edu/resultsspace/.

that allow him to find and organize information about colon cancer. As part of his support group, he often offers encouragement and advice to others.

John joined an online community to identify a group of peers—fellow cancer survivors, researchers, doctors, and other motivated and knowledgeable people— with whom he can coordinate his ongoing investigations. Searching independently, they form a trusted search community that will make automatically generated recommendations more reliable by increasing the likelihood of matching information needs. They can also form synchronous collaborations in small groups to explore and share information about new developments and to track ongoing research in the field.

John has been lobbying his insurance company and hospital to expand their post-treatment counseling services to obtain online search help from registered nurses (RNs) who specialize in particular diseases. Working through a dedicated portal, John should be able to get feedback from his RN counselor on the results he is finding on this own and with his peers. The RN would have access to John's medical record (the details of which may not be available to John in a useful form) that she could use to identify information relevant to John's condition.

Finally, John would like a tool to manage his information set related to his cancer both to maintain a record of what he has learned, and to publish a subset of that, along with his commentary, to help his family and friends understand his condition, and perhaps to draw them into his circle of collaborators.

Scenario-3: Market Research   Alan's client is a cell phone manufacture Aztech who wants to make changes to a existing phone AZ10 in their product line. They would like to gather information from a variety of sources about the user interface and design of previous versions of this phone, related phones in their product line, and competitor's products. Alan and his team need to search the web for relevant reviews, comments and reactions. They plan to divide the search work primarily between Alan and Steve, but Mary, their boss, would also like to review their findings. After finding the information, they need to look for themes and synthesize these into a report to deliver to the client. The client would also like to look at the original information sources and comments that Alan and his team make. The project team on the client side would also like to conduct exploratory searches on the data collected since their questions may change or evolve.

1.4 Structure of the Book

Having introduced the topic of the book in this chapter, we are now ready to dive deeper into both theoretical and practical aspects of this emerging topic. Following is the organization of this book.

The first part of the book, which includes the current chapter, will continue with more and detailed discussions on collaboration and information seeking, as well as related concepts, terminology, and frameworks. The goal of this part is to orient the reader in CIS with a comprehensive treatment of its underlying concepts.

In the second part of the book (Chaps. 4 and 5), the discussion will be focused on CIS as a standalone domain. A series of frameworks, theories, and models will be introduced to provide a conceptual ground for CIS.

The final part of this book (Chaps. 6–8) will describe several systems and applications of CIS, along with important issues of evaluation and broader implications of CIS research on IR and HCI fields. The appendices at the end of the book provide brief overviews of related fields and research concentrations such as computer-supported cooperative work (CSCW), computer-supported collaborative learning (CSCL), and computer-mediated communication (CMC).

References

1. Peter J. Denning. Mastering the mess. *Communications of the ACM*, 50(4):21–25, 2007.
2. Gene Golovchinsky, Jeremy Pickens and Maribeth Back. A taxonomy of collaboration in online information seeking. In *Proceedings of JCDL 2008 Workshop on Collaborative Exploratory Search*, Pittsburgh, PA, June 2008.
3. Meredith Ringel Morris. Interfaces for collaborative exploratory web search: motivations and directions for multi-user design. In *Proceedings of ACM SIGCHI Conference on Human Factors in Computing Systems 2007 Workshop on Exploratory Search and HCI: Designing and Evaluating Interfaces to Support Exploratory Search Interaction*, pages 9–12, April 2007.
4. Meredith Ringel Morris and Eric Horvitz. SearchTogether: an interface for collaborative web search. In *ACM Symposium on User Interface Software and Technology (UIST)*, pages 3–12, Newport, RI, October 2007.
5. Jeremy Pickens and Gene Golovchinsky. Collaborative exploratory search. In *Proceedings of Workshop on Human–Computer Interaction and Information Retrieval*, pages 21–22, MIT CSAIL, Cambridge, MA, October 2007.
6. Chirag Shah. Toward Collaborative Information Seeking (CIS). In *Proceedings of JCDL 2008 Workshop on Collaborative Exploratory Search*, Pittsburgh, PA, 2008.
7. Chirag Shah. Working in collaboration—what, why, and how? In *Proceedings of Collaborative Information Retrieval Workshop at CSCW 2010*, Savannah, GA, 2010.

Chapter 2
Collaboration

Abstract Collaboration, a commonly known and understood concept in many domains, is discussed in this chapter to shed some light on its different aspects and how they correspond to information seeking in collaboration. In particular, this chapter will present several definitions and models, as well as principles, process, and limitations of collaboration that are derived from various fields. Finally, the reader will be introduced to the concept of collaboration in the context of information seeking, along with several examples.

2.1 Definitions and Models of Collaboration

We seem to have an intuitive understanding of what it means to collaborate, but a closer look may surprise us. As its Latin roots 'com' and 'laborate' suggest, *collaboration* indicates, "to work together". The Latin roots *com* and *laborare* suggest that collaboration has something to do with working together. However, this seems very close to the meanings of 'cooperation' and 'coordination'. The definitions of these three terms from the New Oxford American Dictionary are given below for reference.

coordination [noun]

1. the process or state of coordinating or being coordinated.

   - the organization of the different elements of a complex body or activity so as to enable them to work together effectively: *both countries agreed to intensify efforts at economic policy coordination.*
   - cooperative effort resulting in an effective relationship: *action groups work in coordination with local groups to end rain forest destruction.*
   - the ability to use different parts of the body together smoothly and efficiently: *changing from one foot position to another requires coordination and balance.*

2. Chemistry the linking of atoms by coordinate bonds

ORIGIN mid 17th cent. (in the sense [placing in the same rank]): from French or from late Latin *coordinatio(n-)*, based on Latin *ordo, ordin- 'order.'*

C. Shah, *Collaborative Information Seeking*, The Information Retrieval Series 34,
DOI 10.1007/978-3-642-28813-5_2, © Springer-Verlag Berlin Heidelberg 2012

cooperation (also co-operation) [noun]

1. the process of working together to the same end: *they worked in close coopera-tion with the AAA.*

   • assistance, esp. by ready compliance with requests: *we would like to ask for your cooperation in the survey.*
   • Economics: the formation and operation of cooperatives.

ORIGIN late Middle English: from Latin *cooperatio(n-)*, from the verb *cooperari* (see COOPERATE); later reinforced by French *coopération.*

collaboration [noun]

1. the action of working with someone to produce or create something: *he wrote on art and architecture in collaboration with John Betjeman.*

   • something produced or created in this way: *his recent opera was a collabora-tion with Lessing.*

2. traitorous cooperation with an enemy: *he faces charges of collaboration.*

DERIVATIVES
collaborationist [noun & adjective (sense 2)].
ORIGIN mid 19th cent.: from Latin *collaboratio(n-)*, from *collaborare* 'work to-gether.'

London [10] interpreted the meaning of 'collaboration' as *working together syn-ergistically* (p. 8). Gray [8] defined collaboration as "a process of joint decision-making among key stakeholders of a problem domain about the future of that do-main" (p. 11). Roberts and Bradley [16] called collaboration "an interactive process having a shared transmutational purpose" (p. 209).

We often find people using the term 'collaboration' in various contexts and inter-changeably with terms such as 'coordination' and 'cooperation'. It is very important that we first ground the meaning of the term 'collaboration' before addressing var-ious issues regarding collaboration. Denning and Yaholkovsky [4] suggested that coordination and cooperation are weaker forms of working together, and that all of these activities require sharing some information with each other. Taylor-Powell et al. [19] added another component to this contribution, as they realized that in order to have an effective collaboration, each member of the group should make an individual contribution to the collaboration. Using communication, contribution, coordination, and cooperation as essential steps toward collaboration, they showed how a true collaboration requires a tighter form of integration.[1]

Based on these two works, a model of collaboration is synthesized and presented in Fig. 2.1. This model has five sets: *communication* (information exchange), *contri-bution, coordination, cooperation,* and *collaboration.* Considering notions of sets,

---

[1] Available at http://www.empowerment.state.ia.us/files/annual_reports/2001/Collaboration.pdf.

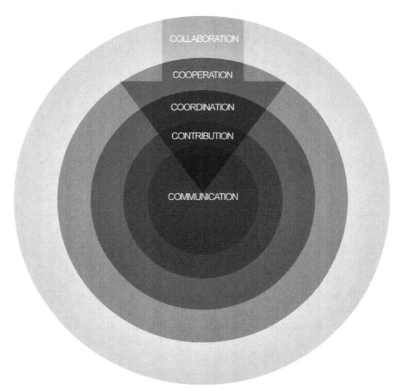

Fig. 2.1 A set-based model of collaboration. An inner set is essential to or supports the outer set

the model shows which activity is supporting which other. For instance, coordination is a subset of collaboration, which indicates that, for a meaningful collaboration, we need to have some way of coordinating people and events. Collaboration is a superset of cooperation, which means in order to have a true collaboration, we need something more than cooperation. These five sets are described below in more detail. To help explain these concepts, various activities in the context of a library will also be listed.

- *Communication*. This is a process of sending or exchanging information, which is one of the core requirements for carrying out collaboration, or maintaining any kind of productive relationship for that matter. For instance, there is a message on the local public library's bulletin board about a book sale for charity the coming weekend. This is a way for the library to communicate with the visitors, which may result in some coordinated event.
- *Contribution*. This is an informal relationship by which individuals help each other in achieving their personal goals. For instance, Mark has some old books that he no longer needs, but they could be of use to others. He, therefore, asks the library if they would take those books. Upon the library's approval (communication), Mark donates the books to the library.

- *Coordination*. This is a process of connecting different agents together for a harmonious action. This often involves bringing people or systems under an umbrella at the same time and place. During this process, the involved agents may share resources, responsibilities, and goals. For instance, Mark decides to study with his fellow student Richard in the library. They both get together at the library on a set day and study their own material. They both are in a way helping each other by keeping each other company (contribution), but they do not share a specific goal that they are working toward together.
- *Cooperation*. This is a relationship in which different agents with similar interests take part in planning activities, negotiating roles, and sharing resources to achieve joint goals. In addition to coordination, cooperation involves all the agents following some rules of interaction. For instance, if the reference librarian, Carol, had simply pointed Mark to the relevant section for his query, she has cooperated with him, but they did not collaborate. What extends several cooperative acts to collaboration is an active session of interaction in which both the parties worked together to solve a problem.
- *Collaboration*. This is a process involving various agents that may see different aspects of a problem. They engage in a process through which they can go beyond their own individual expertise and vision by constructively exploring their differences and searching for common solutions. In contrast to cooperation, collaboration involves creating a solution that is more than merely the sum of each party's contribution. The authority in such a process is vested in the collaboration rather than in an individual entity.

For instance, Mark walks up to a reference librarian, Carol, in a public library. He is studying 20th century American poets and trying to find all the material that could be relevant. Carol helps him to locate the section of the library, where Mark can find the books on poetry. However, that would not be enough to be considered collaboration. Mark describes the scope of his study and that gives Carol information to start suggesting specific books to Mark. After skimming through those books over a couple of day's time, Mark thinks he has a lot more material than he needed. He returns to Carol with this concern, and she suggests that he look at a book that is an anthology of American poets. This book not only helps Mark directly, but also lets Carol refine her suggestions as she also flips through it. Finally, Mark has good material on this topic that is not too general and covers most of the information that he would like to have.

Working on this collaborative task required both Mark and Carol to interact with each other (communication) person-to-person at a certain place and time (coordination). The starting point of this collaboration was Carol agreeing to help Mark (cooperation). While Carol seems to have done most of the work (contribution), she also learned a certain number of things in the process. Finally, while the rewards of this process were different for both the parties, it is important to note that they both worked together to solve the same problem.

In addition to this, we can hope that this solution is also a better one, since often a group of entities are found to create a much better solution than any individual entity by itself [18]. Chrislip and Larson [3] defined collaboration as a

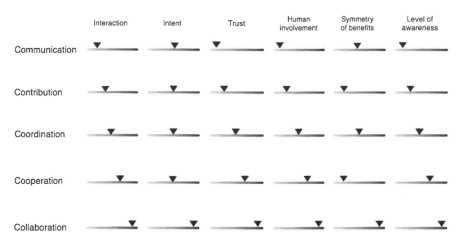

Fig. 2.2 Distinguishing communication, contribution, coordination, cooperation, and collaboration using different variables. A variable is represented with a *bar* going minimum to maximum from left to right

"mutually beneficial relationship between two or more parties [agents] who work toward common goals by sharing responsibility, authority, and accountability for achieving results" (p. 5). Similarly, according to Gray [8], collaboration is "a process through which parties [agents] who see different aspects of a problem can constructively explore their differences and search for solutions that go beyond their own limited vision of what is possible" (p. 5).

The difference among these five activities can be summarized using the following variables, which are also depicted in Fig. 2.2.

1. *Interaction*. While communication is at the center of other activities, it is possible to have a very little amount of interaction while simply communicating. For instance, a system administrator sending an email to a user for his overused disk quota may not require any further interaction. The administrator may not even personally know or see the user. A typical collaboration, on the other hand, requires a high level of interaction among the participants.
2. *Intent*. Similar to interaction, a collaborative project requires much stronger intent compared to those tasks that are merely coordinating events or one entity cooperating with another.
3. *Trust*. In order to have an effective and mutually beneficial collaboration, the participants need to establish a good amount of trust among them. Such is not a requirement for simply coordinating or cooperating.
4. *Human involvement*. A process of communication may not require much human involvement. For instance, posting a message on a noticeboard is an act of communication, but it does not require the poster or the readers of that message being involved with each other. Collaboration, on the other hand, requires the participants to be actively engaged in the project at hand.

5. *Symmetry of benefits*. The kind of collaboration considered here is by definition mutually beneficial. Thus, it benefits everyone involved in the process. The
   amount of benefit may vary depending on participants' roles and responsibilities.
   In contrast, in a cooperative process, one party helps the other party in fulfilling
   their goals. A student gathering relevant literature for his supervisor is an act of
   cooperation, contributing to the supervisor's goal. Co-authorship, on the other
   hand, is an act of collaboration, benefiting all the participants.
6. *Level of awareness*. For an interactive, intentional, and mutually beneficial collaboration to be successful, it is imperative that all the participants be aware of
   each other's actions and contributions. This also helps in establishing a level of
   trust among the participants. Provision of such awareness may not be a requirement for coordination or cooperation.

2.2 Principles of Collaboration

Let us now look at the principles or conditions for an effective collaboration. Most
researchers agree that an effective collaboration must be *democratic* and *inclusive*,
that is, it must be free of hierarchies of any kind and it must include all parties who
have a stake in the problem [10]. Note that such democratic collaboration may still
have asymmetric roles for different collaborators.

Regarding *democracy* in collaboration, Flora et al. [7] pointed out, "without
community empowerment and broad participation in agenda setting, the decision-
making process of discussion, debate, and compromise is relatively meaningless"
(p. 273). Osborne and Gaebler [14] also expressed their views against hierarchies
by noting that centralized and hierarchical associations tend to be divided up into
many layers and boxes. They recognized a difficulty in carrying out communication
across units and between layers, thus inhibiting the real potential of collaboration.

There is also a general agreement about *inclusiveness* in collaboration. Theobald
[20], for instance, argued that all the leadership of a community must be involved,
whether participants fit traditional definitions of leaders or not. Chrislip and Larson
[3] concurred, reporting that all the successful collaborations they studied involved
many participants from several factors, such as government, business, and community groups, as opposed to few participants predominantly from one sector.

Gray [8] further claimed that collaboration could only be meaningful if the stakeholders are interdependent. She explained, "collaboration establishes a give and take
among the stakeholders that is designed to produce solutions that none of them
working independently could achieve" (p. 25).

To spell out what situations could create a meaningful collaboration, Surowiecki
[18] presented four conditions for a successful collaboration.

1. *Diversity of opinion*. Each person should have some private information, even if
   it is just an eccentric interpretation of known facts.
2. *Independence*. People's opinions are not determined by the opinions of those
   around them.

3. *Decentralization.* People are able to specialize and draw on local knowledge.
4. *Aggregation.* Some mechanism exists for turning private judgments into a collective decision.

Collaboration, in many situations, is a process that ties people of varying opinions and abilities together. However, the process may not necessarily lead to agreement on all issues. For instance, Gray [8] acknowledged that not all collaborations lead to consensus, but added that, when agreements for action are reached, they are always done so by consensus. Denning and Yaholkovsky [4] also noted that it is solidarity, not software, that generates collaboration.

2.3 Process of Collaboration

Following is a list of points compiled by London [10] from a combination of sources, including Chrislip and Larson [3], Straus and Williams [17], Portnoy [15], and Gray [8], that one needs to consider before starting a collaborative process.

1. What are the structural relationships between the parties and the possible power issues inherent in the collaborative arrangement?
2. Is there a clear understanding among all the parties of the respective goals of the other participants?
3. What form of leadership is required to facilitate the process?
4. Does the project have some form of integrating structure, such as a cross-section of steering committees, to facilitate and coordinate decision-making and implementation?
5. Will the project be more effective with a neutral, third party mediator?
6. Should the media be involved?
7. Does the project have enough time, money, and staff support?

Such questions and considerations are useful to understand as collaboration may induce costs, and we many want to make sure that the given problem and circumstances do call for collaboration.

Let us now look at what collaboration involves. Collaboration is typically a complex process involving a number of phases, a variety of interactions, and other subprocesses. Gray [8] identified three major phases of collaboration.

1. *Pre-negotiation or problem-setting phase.* This phase is often the most difficult, and involves six issues to be addressed.
   a. The parties must arrive at a shared definition of the problem, including how it relates to the interdependence of the various stakeholders.
   b. The parties must make a commitment to collaborate.
   c. Other stakeholders must be identified whose involvement may be necessary for the success of the endeavor.
   d. The parties must acknowledge and accept the legitimacy of the other participants.

    e. The parties must decide what type of convener or leader can bring the parties together.

    f. The parties must determine what resources are needed for the collaboration to proceed.

2. *Direction-setting phase.* During this phase, the parties need to identify the interests, which brought them together, determine how they differ from the interests of the others, set directions, and establish shared goals. This phase is characterized by six steps.

    a. Establishing ground rules

    b. Setting the agenda

    c. Organizing sub-groups (especially if the number of issues to be discussed is large or the number of stakeholders exceeds the twelve to fifteen member limit for effective group functioning)

    d. Undertaking a joint information search to establish and consider the essential facts of the issue involved

    e. Exploring the pros and cons of various alternatives

    f. Reaching agreement and settling for a course of action

3. *Implementation phase.* During this final phase, the participants go through the following steps.

    a. Participating groups or organizations deal with their constituencies.

    b. Parties garner the support of those who will be charged with implementing the agreement.

    c. Structures for implementation are established.

    d. The agreement is monitored and compliance is ensured.

Similar to these three phases of Gray, Denning and Yaholkovsky [4] provided three main stages of solving a complex problem: design, collaboration, and follow-through. The authors defined the collaboration stage as a set of five specific sub-stages: (1) declare, (2) connect, (3) listen to and learn all perspectives, (4) allow a "we" to develop, and (5) create together.

Individual collaborative process will depend on various factors such as the nature of collaboration, the number of people or parties involved, the timeframe, and the resources at hand.

2.4 Limitations of Collaboration

It was noted earlier that in many situations, collaboration is a natural choice, especially for solving problems that are hard [4]. However, one must also need to understand the costs and benefits associated with a collaborative process in order to evaluate the usefulness and the effectiveness of that collaboration.

London [10] identified the following limitations of a collaborative process.

1. Collaboration is a notoriously time-consuming process and is not suitable for problems that require quick and decisive action.

2. Power inequalities among the parties can derail the process.
3. The norms of consensus and joint decision-making sometimes require that the common good take precedence over the interests of a few.
4. Collaboration works best in small groups and often breaks down in groups that are too large.
5. Collaboration is meaningless without the power to implement final decisions.

Gray [8] listed five circumstances under which it is best not to collaborate:[2] (1) when one party has unchallenged power to influence the final outcome; (2) when the conflict is rooted in deep-seated ideological differences; (3) when the power is unevenly distributed; and (4) when constitutional issues are involved or legal precedents are sought, and (5) when a legitimate convener cannot be found.

Sometimes we see collaboration forced on a group of people. Examples of such forced collaborations include the merger of two companies or instructor-enforced class groups. In such situations, the collaboration may start with acts of cooperation, where the participants are merely following a set of rules working with others in the group. Later, such cooperative events may result in collaboration as the participants take active part (intention) in driving the process of working together for a common goal. However, collaboration may still not be successful if the participants do not trust each other or if the power and benefits are unbalanced [8, 10].

Collaboration can also have limited advantages if the costs and benefits are unevenly distributed among the participants. As one of the eight challenges of groupware system development, Grudin [9] talked about disparities in benefits and responsibilities among the participants. He claimed that it is almost impossible to have a groupware system in which every participant does the same amount of work and/or benefits the same. His examples show how some participants of a groupware system have to do additional work while not getting equivalent benefits. Due to such inequality, the groupware application may become less and less useful and may even stop being used.

While the kind of collaboration that is considered here (intentional and mutually beneficial) is slightly different than Grudin's notion of groupware, and the discussed CIS systems are considerably different than the groupware systems Grudin talked about, several of the issues he raised and the recommendations he made are relevant.

For the above-mentioned challenge, Grudin's recommendation for the system developer was to make sure that the system benefits all the participants. At the same time, he identified the difficulties in doing so, because, while the managers or higher authorities are gaining more benefits, they are the decision makers. Pleasing the upper management personnel is equally important, if not more, as pleasing the rest of the participants who have to do additional work.

Part of the problem in disparity of benefits is also due to the highly asymmetric roles in such kind of collaborations. Having diversity in collaboration could be very useful for a successful collaboration [18], but as Aneiros and Estivill-Castro [1] argued, roles according to positions (manager vs. knowledge workers), can create

---

[2]The author's observations and claims are based on her studies in the civic collaboration domain.

Table 2.1 Various group activities and examples

Activity	Definition	Examples
Communication	Exchanging information between two agents	Email, chat
Contribution	Offering of an individual agent to others	Online support groups, social Q&A
Coordination	Connecting different agents in a harmonious action	Conference call, net meeting
Cooperation	Agents following some rules of interaction	Wikipedia, Second Life
Collaboration	Working together synergistically to achieve a common goal	Brainstorming, co-authorship

several constraints while seeking information collaboratively. They advised against such a master/slave model of collaboration and proposed a way of unconstrained co-browsing with asymmetric roles.

2.5 Collaboration in the Context of Information-Intensive Tasks

To understand the model of collaboration presented earlier (Fig. 2.1) in the context of information science, these five sets are listed in Table 2.1 with examples. Sending an email or conversing on an IM client is a form of communication. Of course, this communication could be a part of a collaborative project (see that communication is a subset of collaboration in Fig. 2.1). In fact, email is one of the most commonly used methods of communication in a collaborative project [12]. While communication tools can be used to send one agent's contribution to another, there are specialized tools and places for doing so. Among these, online support groups and social Q&A sites, such as Yahoo! Answers, are very popular. The asker and answerer (contributor) on these sites are not truly collaborating; one agent (user) is merely helping the other with his information need. To make such a process more effective and explicit, people use conference calls or net meetings. This requires co-ordinating the agents (people as well as systems). Once again, such a coordinated event could be a part of a collaborative project. If we take coordinated contribution with a set of rules that the participating agents need to follow, we can find examples of cooperation. On Wikipedia, the participants not only contribute in a coordinated fashion, but there are also rules for this participation and contribution that the users need to follow. In case of a disagreement, there are guidelines that suggest how to make this interaction work. Beyond cooperative activities, collaboration involves a group of agents working toward a common goal with explicit interactions. Imagine co-authoring an article. The authors involved in this project not only contribute and coordinate with other authors, but they also follow some sort of rules that guide the aggregation of contributions and their mutual interactions. The authors also interact with each other to create this common product, which may be greater than the summation of their individual contributions.

Let us look back to the terms 'coordination' and 'cooperation', and see how they fit around this understanding of collaboration. Austin and Baldwin [2] noted that while there are obvious similarities between cooperation and collaboration, the former involves pre-established interests, while the latter involves collectively defined goals. Malone [11] defined coordination as "the additional information processing performed when multiple, connected actors pursue goals that a single actor pursuing the same goals would not perform" (p. 5). While this definition is close to the one we have seen about collaboration, one can argue that it still fits in the model described in Fig. 2.1 since it says nothing about creating solutions. For instance, organizing a meeting involves coordinating among the attendees, but it is not a collaborative activity.

From the definitions and models described above, we can conclude that, in order to have a successful collaboration while seeking information, we need to create a supportive environment where:

1. The participants of a team come with different backgrounds and expertise.
2. The participants have opportunities to explore information on their own without being influenced by the others, at least during a portion of the whole information seeking process.
3. The participants should be able to evaluate the discovered information without always consulting others in the group.
4. There has to be a way to aggregate individual contributions to arrive at the collective goal.

One important aspect of the above requirements that is missing is the kind of task. There may not be much point in collaborating for simple fact-finding information tasks. As Morris and Horvitz [13] hypothesized, tasks that are exploratory in nature are likely to benefit from collaboration.

2.6 How the Concept of Collaboration Relates to CIS

The notion of collaboration and the requirements to have a successful collaboration presented in the previous section will now be taken to propose (1) a set of conditions under which collaboratively seeking information is useful, and (2) a set of guidelines for building a successful CIS environment.

The conditions under which collaboratively seeking information is useful are given below. They are not very different from those of any other kind of collaborative process.

1. *Common goal and/or mutual benefits*
   This is covered in the definition of the kind of collaboration that is under consideration here. Often, it is the common goal and/or the possibility of mutual benefits that brings people together for collaboration. For the most part, this is not

a function of a system. A system can provide support for people with common goals who want to collaborate and reap the benefits of that collaboration, but does not typically initiate the collaboration. On the other hand, a few systems provide a functionality of connecting the visitors to the same websites in order for them to have a possible collaboration, such as the one given by [5]. These systems are based on the assumptions that the people browsing the same websites may have the same information needs.

2. *Complex task*

   Morris and Horvitz [13] showed that there are not many benefits for collaborating on simple tasks, such as fact-finding. Denning and Yaholkovsky [4] also recognized the benefit of collaborating while solving "messy" or "wicked" problems. While listing the conditions under which it is not useful to collaborate, London [10] argued that if a task is simple enough, there is no point in collaborating. This may imply that the task should be exploratory in nature, and may span several sessions.

3. *High benefits to overhead ratio*

   Often, a simple divide and conquer strategy could make collaboration successful. However, such a process may have its overhead. London [10] noted that collaboration is only useful if such an overhead is acceptable for the given situation. Fidel et al. [6] showed that collaboration induces additional cognitive load, what they referred to as the *collaboration load*. The collaboration in question has to meet or exceed the benefits expectations for it to be viable with the cognitive load that it brings.

4. *Insufficient knowledge or skills*

   A common reason to collaborate is the insufficient knowledge or skills an individual possesses for solving a complex problem. In such cases, the participants can collaborate so that they can achieve something bigger or better than what they each could do individually. In other words, the whole can be bigger than the sum of all.

The guidelines for building a successful CIS environment, following the discussion of the model in Fig. 2.1, and derived from the discussion in this section, are given below.

1. A CIS system should provide effective ways for the participants to communicate with each other.
2. A CIS system should allow (and encourage) each participant to make individual contributions to the collaborative.
3. A CIS system should coordinate participant actions, information requests, and responses to have an active and interactive collaboration. This collaboration could be synchronous or asynchronous, and co-located or remote.
4. Participants need to agree to and follow a set of rules to carry out a productive collaboration. For instance, if they have a disagreement on the relevancy of an information object, they should discuss and negotiate; they should arrive at a mutually agreeable solution rather than continuing to dispute it. The system needs to support such a discussion and negotiation process among the participants.

5. A CIS system should provide a mechanism to let the participants not only explore their individual differences, but also negotiate roles and responsibilities. There may be a situation in which one participant leads the group and others follow (cooperate), but the real strength of collaboration lies in having the authority vested in the collective.

References

1. Maria Aneiros and Vladimir Estivill-Castro. Usability of real-time unconstrained WWW-co-browsing for educational settings. In *Proceedings of the IEEE/WIC International Conference on Web Intelligence*, pages 105–111, Compiegne University of Technology, France, September 2005.
2. Ann E. Austin and Roger G. Baldwin. *Faculty Collaboration: Enhancing the Quality of Scholarship and Teaching*. J-B ASHE Higher Education Report Series (AEHE). Jossey-Bass, San Francisco, 1991.
3. David D. Chrislip and Carl E. Larson. *Collaborative Leadership: How Citizens and Civic Leaders Can Make a Difference*. Jossey-Bass, San Francisco, 1994.
4. Peter J. Denning and Peter Yaholkovsky. Getting to "We". *Communications of the ACM*, 51(4):19–24, 2008.
5. Judith S. Donath and Niel Robertson. The sociable web. In *Proceedings of the World Wide Web (WWW) Conference*. CERN, Geneva, Switzerland, 1994.
6. Raya Fidel, Annelise Mark Pejtersen, Bryan Cleal and Harry Bruce. A multidimensional approach to the study of human–information interaction: a case study of collaborative information retrieval. *Journal of the American Society for Information Science and Technology*, 55(11):939–953, 2004.
7. Cornelia Butler Flora, Jan L. Flora and Susan Fey. *Rural Communities: Legacy and Change*. Westview, Boulder, 2004.
8. Barbara Gray. *Collaborating: Finding Common Ground for Multiparty Problems*. Jossey-Bass, San Francisco, 1989.
9. Jonathan Grudin. Groupware and social dynamics: eight challenges for developers. *Communications of the ACM*, 37(1):92–105, 1994.
10. Scott London. Collaboration and community. http://scottlondon.com/reports/ppcc.html, November 1995.
11. Thomas W. Malone. What is coordination theory? Technical Report SSM WP # 2051-88, Massachusetts Institute of Technology, Boston, MA, February 1988.
12. Meredith Ringel Morris. A survey of collaborative web search practices. In *Proceedings of ACM SIGCHI Conference on Human Factors in Computing Systems*, pages 1657–1660, Florence, Italy, 2008.
13. Meredith Ringel Morris and Eric Horvitz. SearchTogether: An Interface for Collaborative Web Search. In *ACM Symposium on User Interface Software and Technology (UIST)*, pages 3–12, Newport, RI, October 2007.
14. David Osborne and Ted Gaebler. *Reinventing Government*. Addison-Wesley, Reading, 1992.
15. Fern Portnoy. Collaboration: go for it. *Foundation News*, pages 59–61, 1986.
16. Nancy C. Roberts and Raymond Trevor Bradley. Stakeholder collaboration and innovation: a study of public policy initiation at the state level. *The Journal of Applied Behavioral Science*, 27(2):209, 1991.
17. David Straus and David Williams. *Collaborative Problem Solving in Local Agenda Setting Processes*. Lincoln Institute of Land Policy, Cambridge, 1986.
18. James Surowiecki. *Wisdom of Crowds: Why the Many Are Smarter than the Few and How Collective Wisdom Shapes Business, Economies, Societies and Nations*. Doubleday, New York, 2004.

19. Ellen Taylor-Powell, Boyd Rossing and Jean Geran. Evaluating collaboratives: reaching the potential. Technical report, University of Wisconsin-Extension, Madison, Wisconsin, July 1998.
20. Robert Theobald. *The Rapids of Change*. Knowledge Systems, Indianapolis, 1987.

Chapter 3
Collaborative Information Seeking (CIS) in Context

Abstract The field of collaborative information seeking (CIS) has been going through a fundamental shift, so much that it is almost emerging as a new field altogether. One of the challenges that such an invigorating process brings to a field is how to define its key elements, and CIS is no exception. Researchers have brought forth their works in this domain under the labels of collaborative information retrieval, collaborative information behavior, co-browsing, and collaborative or collective search, among others. Often a subset of these terms are used interchangeably, but one could also see them as subdomains in their own right. This chapter introduces the reader to several of the most commonly used terms and definitions. Corresponding works for these terms are summarized to provide a comprehensive overview of recent developments in this field. In addition to the literature, the chapter also uses discussions and derived lessons from half a dozen recent workshops and other events on CIS and related topics. The landscape of CIS is constantly evolving, but the present chapter should provide a firm ground for one to observe and participate in the development of this emerging field.

3.1 Introduction

It is often difficult for researchers and practitioners in this field to agree on a definition for CIS. Even if they do come to a common understanding of this term, there is still the question of how it relates to many other seemingly similar terms. The literature is filled with usages such as collaborative search [52], collaborative information retrieval [8, 16, 29], social searching [12, 14], concurrent search [4], collaborative exploratory search [44, 45], co-browsing [13, 20, 23], collaborative navigation [36, 37], collaborative information behavior [47], collaborative information synthesis [9], and of course collaborative information seeking [17, 24, 51]. Many definitions and conceptual understandings exist in the literature. I have referred to CIS as a process of information seeking "that is defined explicitly among the participants, interactive, and mutually beneficial".

Here we will attempt to classify various related works into categories with the labels such as CIR, co-browsing, and social search. We will also briefly explore a relevant topic of collaborative filtering. Figure 3.1 is a depiction of various concepts

C. Shah, *Collaborative Information Seeking*, The Information Retrieval Series 34,
DOI 10.1007/978-3-642-28813-5_3, © Springer-Verlag Berlin Heidelberg 2012

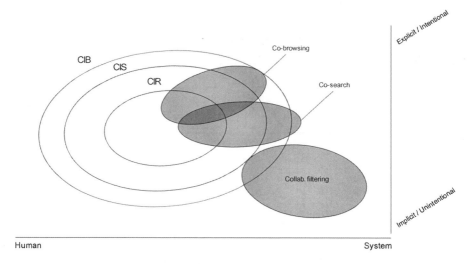

Fig. 3.1 Depiction of CIS and related topics using the dimensions of human–system and explicit–implicit collaboration

around CIS. As seen, these concepts are placed on dimensions of human–system and explicit–implicit collaboration.

3.2 Collaborative Information Retrieval (CIR) and Co-search

The discussion will now be narrowed down to those scenarios in collaborative setup where the goal is to seek information together for a common information need. As discussed earlier, if/when the problem of IR is difficult to solve, a carefully executed collaboration can help. Smyth et al. [52] argued that one way of making it possible to connect users to the information that is difficult to find is to incorporate collaboration in the search phase of an information seeking process. They showed how collaborative search could act as a front-end for existing search engines and re-rank results based on the learned preferences of a community of users. They attempted to demonstrate this concept by implementing the I-Spy system [18]. I-Spy captures the queries and the related results for a given workgroup and uses that information to provide filtered, and presumably more relevant, information to the user. Thus, I-Spy acts more as a collaborative filtering process than as synchronous collaborative searching.

While I-Spy attempts to extend content-based filtering techniques by incorporating communities, several collaborative IR systems have been developed by extending a traditional IR model to incorporate multiple users. However, such extension is often ineffective or non-trivial. For instance, Hyldegard [28], with her studies of information seeking and retrieval in a group-based education setting, found that even though people in a collaborative group to some extent demonstrated similar cognitive experiences as the individuals in Kuhlthau's Information Search Process (ISP) model [35], these experiences did not only result from information seeking activities, but also from work-task activities and intragroup interactions. Her further work also indicated [29] that group based problem solving is a dynamic process that shifts between a group perspective and an individual perspective. Such a finding calls for a thorough investigation into collaborative information seeking that is not simply an extension of a traditional IR system for multiple users. As Olson et al. ([43], p. 347) suggested, "The development of schemes to support group work, whether behavioral methods or new technologies like groupware, should be based on detailed knowledge about how groups work, what they do well, and what they have trouble with."

Unlike co-browsing, where the applications are aimed toward web browsing, works on collaborative IR are often focused on specialized domains for searching. For instance, Twidale and Nichols [53] presented the Ariadne system, which allowed a user to collaborate with an information expert remotely and synchronously over a library catalogue. The idea behind Ariadne was to allow the patron (naive user) to collaborate with a reference librarian (search expert) for an information need in a library situation. The authors identified the importance of supporting social aspects of searching for information and showed how it can be addressed using their system. However, Ariadne did not have support for asynchronous collaboration.

Morris and Horvitz [42] presented the SearchTogether system that allowed a group of remote users to collaborate synchronously or asynchronously. This system was based on supporting awareness, division of labor, and persistence for collaboration. Their rationale for facilitating awareness was that it could enable lightweight collaboration by reducing overhead involved in explicitly asking other group members to provide that information. Awareness was provided using per-user query histories, page-specific metadata, and annotations. Division of labor was implemented using integrated IM as well as a recommendation mechanism, by which a participant can recommend a page to another participant. SearchTogether also provided "Split Search" and "Multi-Engine Search" options for automatic division of labor. Finally, persistence was implemented by storing not only all session states, but also automatically creating a shared artifact that summarizes the findings of a collaborative search.

MUSE [34] supports synchronous, remote collaboration between two people searching a medical database. MUSE lets its users perform standard single-user searches, with a provision of chat and the ability to share metadata about the current database results with the other user. S^3 [42] is not so much of a CIS system, but it has an important component of being able to share the retrieved results asynchronously among a set of users.

A stream of research came out of the CIR group at University of Washington, studying the situations where members of a work-team are seeking, searching, and using information collaboratively and showing how such a process can be realized in a multi-team setting. This started with Fidel et al.'s work [15], where the authors defined collaborative IR (CIR) "as any activity that collectively resolves an information problem taken by members of a work-team regardless of the nature of the actual retrieval of information." They employed a cognitive work analysis framework to guide a field study examining social, organizational, cognitive, and individual characteristics of information seekers, and then focusing to address collaborative situations [16]). From their studies involving two design teams working in collaboration, they found [10] that (1) the nature of the task and the structure and the culture of the organization in which tasks are performed are important factors that determine CIR behavior, and (2) not all information behavior takes place collaboratively even in teams that carry out CIR. In their further work on this line, the authors found [46] that (1) any information retrieval activity (identifying information needs, formulating queries, retrieving information, evaluating it, and applying it to address the need) may be performed by an individual on behalf of the team, by an ad-hoc group, or by the team working together in a meeting, and (2) technologies intended to support teamwork could be more effective by recognizing and supporting collaboration in the activities that comprise information retrieval and their coordination. This suggests that a successful CIR/CIS system should not try to lock the users down in a certain kind of framework imposed by that system; it should rather let the participants choose their own way of collaborating, and provide enough support for carrying out that collaboration.

The efforts of connecting multiple users for information seeking (retrieval or browsing) continue to produce systems either by reinventing the wheel of traditional IR, or by extending existing IR systems to accommodate more than one user. None of these systems have been adopted widely in practice. Several reasons can be found for the lack of wider visibility of collaborative systems, among which are the cognitive load involved in using these systems, the learning curve to start using these environments, and the lack of proper integration of information seeking to other parts of the collaboration.

3.3 Co-browsing or Collaborative Navigation

Co-browsing or social navigation is the process of allowing a set of participants navigate or browse, and share information with a possible intermediate interface. Root [50] introduced the idea of social browsing to support distributed cooperative work with unplanned and informal social interaction. He described a "social interface", which provided direct, low-cost access to other people through the use of multimedia communications channels. The design of his conceptual system, called CRUISER,[1] incorporated three basic concepts: social browsing, a virtual workspace, and interaction protocols. His premise was that by integrating all of our digital media into a richly interconnected workspace, we could significantly extend and enrich the available context of our workgroup activities.

---

[1] "Cruising" was the stereotypical teenage activity of the 50s and early 60s. The term refers to the practice of piling into somebody's car and visiting the chain of gathering places frequented by other peer group members, or simply driving around in search of almost any sort of social encounter [39].

Root's idea of facilitating informal and effortless interaction among a group of people was carried over later by Donath and Robertson [12] with *The Social Web* that allowed a user to know that others were currently viewing the same webpage and communicate with those people. They believed that users accessing the same page are likely to be in search of the same type of information and share similar interests. Providing them with the ability to communicate with each other can facilitate information searches and help foster community.

Cabri et al. [11] presented a system for synchronous cooperative browsing that permitted users within a workgroup to share information and cooperate toward a common goal. This was done using a proxy without changing the browsers on user ends. Gerosa et al. [20] presented a similar idea of proxy-based co-browsing with the application of e-learning. They called this *Symmetric Synchronous Collaborative Navigation*, a form of social navigation, where users virtually share a web browser. They presented a symmetric, proxy-based architecture implemented without the need for a special browser or other software. Once again, the motivation behind such lightweight interfaces was to allow the users to emerge into a collaborative environment with as little effort as possible. Esenther [13] emphasized having a lightweight real-time collaborative web browsing service and providing an instant co-browsing facility. Their system was targeted to casual (non-technical) users and allowed remote participants to easily synchronize pointing, scrolling and browsing of uploaded content in their web browsers.

Another example of collaborative browsing application is *AntWorld* [40], a tool developed to make it easier for the members of a common-interest user group to collaborate in searching the web. *AntWorld* harnesses the expertise of the members of a common interest group as displayed by their evaluation of documents encountered while searching. It stores users judgments about the documents they find and uses this information to guide other users to pages they may find useful.

Sometimes it is not just the webpages that people want to browse and share, but other objects such as bookmarks. Keller et al. [32] presented *WebTagger*, a social bookmarking service similar to del.icio.us (http://delicious.com), which allowed a group of users to tag and share webpages. *WebTagger* enables users to supply feedback on the utility of the resources that they bookmarked relative to their information needs, and provides dynamically-updated ranking of resources based on incremental user feedback.

Several other systems used their own interfaces rather than relying on a web browser. For instance, *GroupWeb* [22] is a browser that allows group members to visually share and navigate World Wide webpages in real time. Its groupware features include document and view slaving for synchronizing information sharing, telepointers for enacting gestures, and "what you see is what I see" views to handle display differences. *GroupWeb* also incorporated a groupware text editor that lets groups create and attach annotations to pages. Similarly, *GroupScape* [21] was a multiuser HTML browser to support synchronous groupware applications and browsing of HTML documents on the web.

Yet another architecture to support multiuser browsing is *CoVitesse* [37], a groupware interface that enables collaborative navigation on the web based on a collaborative task model. This system represented users navigating collaboratively in an information space made of results of a query submitted to a search engine. In contrast to these systems, which are primarily designed for remotely located participants, *CoSearch* [2] is implemented to provide multi-device support for collaborative browsing among co-located participants.

Some of the applications allow the users of that system to play different roles during their social or collaborative browsing for information. For instance, Pickens et al. [45] proposed the roles of *Prospector* and *Miner* in a collaborative video search environment, the former one responsible for seeking out various areas where relevant information could be found, and the latter one responsible for digging deeper in a given sub-domain with high likelihood or useful information. A collaborative navigation system proposed by Gerosa et al. [20] had the provision where each user could take the lead and guide others in visiting websites. However, Aneiros and Estivill-Castro [3] advocated against controlled co-browsing where one user guides the browsing process for the others (what they referred as the *master/slave model*) and proposed to use a model with unconstrained collaborative web browsing. They argued that such unconstrained collaborative web navigation is essential to allow natural information flow among multiple users.

3.4 Social Search

In case of interactions relating to searching for information, Evans and Chi [14], discussed how social interactions could help in searching together. They called this *social search*. Such social ties leading to social search can be extended to stronger ties leading to collaborative search.

Let us talk about how ties in information seeking environments such as transferring weaker ties to stronger ones to encourage possible collaboration has been used several other places too. For instance, there are co-browsing applications that let visitors of the same webpage be aware of each other, hoping they may want to collaborate as they have the same information need [12].

Sometimes the stronger ties are formed not to do collaboration, but for a possible filtering of information. Most of the collaborative filtering systems depend on converting weaker ties (e.g., being the users of the same system and interested in similar objects) to stronger ties (e.g., connecting the users based on their behavior, and having them influenced by each other). For instance, a Netflix user can have social (weaker) ties with his friends on Netflix network, but when Netflix's collaborative filtering system starts making recommendations based on one's social network, and when the users in the network start using those recommendations and/or start interacting with their peers based on their similar interests, the weaker ties of social network become stronger and more specific.

In summary, a social network typically exhibits weaker ties among the participants, based on their interactions, intentions, and objectives. A collaborative network, on the other hand, shows stronger ties. A social tie can be useful and converted to a collaborative tie. The reverse can happen too. Often participants without social ties are put in a collaborative project. While working on such a project, the participants may develop a social tie as well. Based on this, it can be seen that one tie (social or collaborative) does not subsume the other; they both can be complementary to each other.

While a social network differs from a collaborative group based on the strength of the ties (which was proposed to be measured by objectives, intentions, and interactions), it can be useful for creating and understanding the other. There have been several works on social networks, and since a social tie can be converted to a collaborative tie, we can learn a lot about collaborative groups by looking at those works done on social network analysis.

As we saw, several of the early works on social network analysis explored the notion of homophily. One of their key findings was that the people tend to create social ties with those who match their interests. While this may not be a surprise, it tells us that in order to have a tie, the participants need to have something in common, and the more the commonalities, the stronger a tie can be. For instance, two users of Twitter may not have any tie at all, but when one discovers the other to be interesting or relevant in some way, he/she can decide to follow that person's Tweets. This creates a stronger tie. Such a tie can eventually be useful for creating possible collaborations. In our personal experience, we have seen several collaborations happened through blogs and feeds subscriptions (stronger ties).

Another line of research in social network analysis looked at the influence of the peers on a network. Works, such as Berelson et al. [6], showed that people are easily and frequently influenced by their peers on the same social network. Such behavior was more predominant in younger generations. Today, online social networking services, such as MySpace and Facebook, make such influences even easier and more frequent.

Considering that a weak form of tie in a social network can be transferred to a stronger tie creating collaboration among the participants, and the participants can be influenced by that weak tie, we can study the motivations (why) and scenarios (what, when) of collaboration by looking at the influences in social networks.

It is also important to note here that one of the interesting factors to study in collaboration is the social aspect of it. Social interactions happening due to the collaboration can be engaging, enriching, and entertaining.

Moving our attention to the technologies that facilitate social or collaborative ties, it should be noted that with the advent of technology involving social networking, people are increasingly becoming familiar and encouraged to share information about themselves, as well as explore other people's information. Such information exchange is used not only for connecting people or providing recommendations, but also for accomplishing a variety of tasks as we saw earlier. The analysis of social networks, on the other hand, has been a well-studied domain for nearly a century and is being adapted to the newly emerged online social networking sites.

What is of interest here is the realization that some of the aspects of CIS, particularly communication, are analyzed extensively in social networking research. In addition to this, research in CIS can also benefit from the understanding developed from social network analysis about how and why people work with each other, the costs and benefits of such collaborations, and user behavior in these ties or networks.

Collaboration can also be considered a stronger form of social tie that, according to the definition presented here, involves a group of people working together for a common goal. Often the seeds for such collaboration are planted at the level of social interactions. As Karamuftuoglu [30] argued, knowledge production, as a part of IR, is fundamentally a collaborative labor, which is facilitated by community interactions. This argument allows us to look at the analysis of social network from a different perspective in which social searching, which is a weaker form of searching together [14], can lead to collaborative searching, which is a tighter and more specialized form of searching together.

3.5 Collaborative Filtering

Information filtering refers to a variety of processes involving the delivery of information to people who need it [5]. In other words, information filtering is a process through which information is derived based on relevance to a user as well as his preferences or past behavior. The manifestation of relevance, preferences, or the past behavior can be limited to the given user or can be extended to map to the same attributes about other users.

To clarify this point, let us plot various scenarios of information seeking. Figure 3.2 shows a typical information seeking scene for a single user. The need for information is expressed and executed, and the found results are returned to the user. The user then evaluates the results and keeps the ones that are relevant to him.

Now, if we had a "smart" system, it will monitor this user's behavior over time and use it in new information seeking processes (Fig. 3.3). The behavior refers to the kind of queries that the user submits, the results that he views, and the information that he saves. In other words, this smart system learns the user's information seeking model and uses it to aid in future information seeking processes. An example is online movie renting services such as Blockbuster and Netflix. Based on the kind of movies a user has rented in the past, as well as the ratings that he assigned, the system recommends new movies to him. In recommender systems literature, such an approach is referred to as the content-based recommendations [1]. In such systems, the utility $u(c, s)$ of item s for user c is estimated based on the utilities $u(c, s_i)$ assigned by user c to items $s_i \in S$ that are "similar" to item s. In our example of online movie renting, in order to recommend movies to user c, the system tries to understand the commonalities among the movies user c has rated highly in the past (specific actors, directors, genres, subject matter, etc.).

In conjunction with the system learning the user behavior, the user himself can also provide his preferences by setting up his profile. The system can then filter the information based on the user profile.

Now let us extend the above scenario to incorporate multiple users. Such a scenario is depicted in Fig. 3.4. As we can see, now the system uses the information

Part III
CIS Systems, Applications, and Implications

This part will describe several systems and applications of CIS, along with important issues of evaluation and broader implications of CIS research on IR and HCI fields. The appendices that follow provide brief overviews of related fields and research concentrations such as computer-supported cooperative work (CSCW), computer-supported collaborative learning (CSCL), and computer-mediated communication (CMC).

> *"Individual commitment to a group effort—that is what makes a team work, a company work, a society work, a civilization work."*
>
> Vince Lombardi

Chapter 6
Systems and Tools for CIS

Abstract In this chapter, we will review several tools, some new and some old, that help achieve CIS goals. We will start out the chapter reviewing some of the fundamental challenges of designing CIS systems. Then we will divide up our discussion on CIS systems into two categories: system-mediated collaboration, and user-mediated collaboration. Under the former category, we will review Cerchiamo and Querium, and under the latter category, we will review Ariadne, SearchTogether, and Coagmento. We will also walk through designing, developing, and deploying Coagmento system through formative evaluation process as a case study.

6.1 Costs, Challenges, and Design Implications for CIS Systems

There are several costs associated with using a system that supports collaborative information behavior, some of which are listed below. Understanding these costs is vital for a good system design, and it is possible that each system designer may have to address these costs in different ways.

1. *Cost of learning.* This is the cost associated with learning a new system. A CIS system is likely to be complex and one may need to be educated about the functionalities and scope of each of its components.
2. *Adaptation/adoption cost.* Knowing how to use a system does not necessarily mean the users will adopt it in the long run. One of the findings from the pilot runs of Coagmento (discussed later in detail) and reported in [10], is that the subjects failed to see why someone would use such a system instead of using Google, IM, and email. The subjects successfully learned the system, but they did not see how they could adopt it, leaving more familiar and already adopted systems such as Google, IM, and email. There is a cost associated with such adoption or adapting to such a new system.
3. *Cognitive load.* Many projects have attempted to address the issue of cognitive load induced by a system. Part of the cognitive load is in learning and then adapting to the system, which are presented before. The other aspect of cognitive load for a CIS system will be induced during the actual usage of it. As presented in the guidelines of a successful CIS system, four kinds of awareness are essential to provide. While such awareness is useful, it can also be overwhelming.

C. Shah, *Collaborative Information Seeking*, The Information Retrieval Series 34,   89
DOI 10.1007/978-3-642-28813-5_6, © Springer-Verlag Berlin Heidelberg 2012

4. *Collaborative cost.* Often referred to as the collaborative load, this is a kind of cognitive load that is unique to the CIS environment, and comes from being a part of a group. For instance, a participant in a collaborative project may have to pay attention to the group's history in addition to the personal history, inducing additional cognitive load.

In addition to dealing with these costs, a CIS system designer faces several challenges. Grudin [4] recognized eight challenges for designing groupware systems.

1. Bringing a balance in work and benefit. More than often, the users of a groupware system do not all get the same benefits for the amount of work they have to do. The designer has to address the needs and the work distribution for all the users.
2. Building a critical mass. If a groupware cannot achieve "critical mass" of users to be useful, it can fail as it is never to any one individual's advantage to use it.
3. Entertaining to normal social processes. A groupware system may sometimes hinder the social and political norms that its users have. A good system design adapts to an existing social structure rather than imposing one.
4. Handling errors. A system needs to be prepared to handle a wide range of exceptions and support improvisations that characterize much of the group activities.
5. Providing unobtrusive accessibility. Features that support group processes may be used relatively infrequently, and one needs to design a system that provides unobtrusive accessibility and integration of them with more heavily used features.
6. Evaluation. Due to its often-complex design, multi-faceted and multi-user interface, and a variety of user and system interactions, evaluating a groupware system can be a huge challenge.
7. Addressing intuition. Decision makers in a production environment rely heavily on informed intuition. Most product development experience is based on single-user applications, and transferring it to a multi-user groupware application can be a challenge.
8. Adaptation. Groupware systems require more careful implementation and introduction in the workplace than product developers usually confront.

Based on the costs and challenges presented above, the following five design guidelines can be useful for CIS system designers.

1. Understand real needs. Just because some software has the supportive tools for CIS, does not mean it will actually be used to help a user's CIS. The designers need to understand various aspects of the target domain, educate the users and managers, and design a system that can provide a good balance of costs and benefits to each user.
2. Keep it simple. The design of the interface needs to be very intuitive and easy to use. As we saw before, there are costs associated with learning a new system as well as adopting it. The users may feel more comfortable if the system appears very user friendly. This will help in lowering the costs for learning and continual usage of the system.

3. Make it accessible. Similar to Grudin [4], the CIR group of University of Washington [1] recommended that instead of designing a collaborative system that the users have to get used to, one should design a system that fits the way the users are used to working. While several of the components of a CIS system may be new to a typical user, we should try to minimize imposing a rigidly structured system on a new user. Instead, the system should have many components that the user is already familiar with and know how to use, and allow the user to explore other innovative tools provided.
4. Provide the right tools. As we discussed earlier, support for control, communication, and awareness (group, workspace, contextual, and peripheral) are very crucial to a good CIS system. It is important to provide the tools that implement these features in an unobtrusive manner. Often, it may be useful to extend a single-user application that is already adopted and add collaboration features to it.
5. Allow private working. One of the requirements of a successful collaboration is independence [14]. The participants should be able to work by themselves without the pressure of being "watched" or requiring anyone's opinions. Eventually, of course, we expect the participants to share their findings and have interactions that can lead to better solutions, but one should have the ability to work on his/her own at times. This can help in reducing the cost of cognitive load induced by the system as well as the collaboration, and bring in the benefit of individual contributions.

6.2 System-Mediated Collaboration

This section will introduce a couple of recent CIS systems that provide system-based mediation.

6.2.1 Cerchiamo

Cerchiamo, developed at Fuji Xerox Palo Alto Lab (FXPAL), allows teams of searchers to explore document collections synchronously. Working with Cerchiamo, team members use independent interfaces to run queries, browse results, and make relevance judgments. The system mediates the team members' search activity by passing and reordering search results and suggested query terms based on the teams' actions. The combination of synchronous influence with independent interaction allows team members to be more effective and efficient in performing search tasks.

This is an algorithmically-mediated system in which both users, acting in each of their prescribed roles, influence each other in real-time. This influence is seamless, integrated and bi-directional. Neither user must actively disengage from his or her current search activities in order to share information with the search partner. The

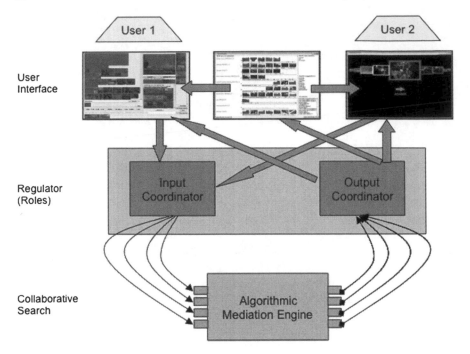

Fig. 6.1 Cerchiamo's architecture. Printed with permission

underlying search algorithm takes into account the search activities of both users and redistributes information and adjusts underlying retrieval algorithm parameters based on both users' roles. Cerchiamo's architecture is shown in Fig. 6.1. The reader is referred to [2] for more details.

6.2.2 Querium

Another system-mediated tool for collaborative search from FXPAL is Querium [3] (see Fig. 6.2). It is a session-based search framework that keeps track of queries, documents, and other activities that occur in a search session to help people reflect on what they have done and to allow them to pivot among documents, queries, and terms to discover new information. Querium can be configured to use a range of collections, including DocuBrowse, and the TREC newspaper corpus. Querium uses Reverted Indexing to find documents similar to documents that a user has identified as useful.

Querium allows users to perform the following actions:

- Search based on keywords
- Search based on groups of one or more documents
- Fuse results from multiple queries into a single list

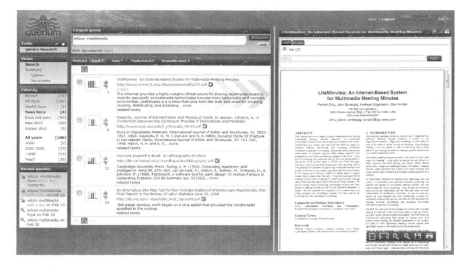

Fig. 6.2 Querium interface: (*1*) top area for new queries, (*2*) navigation sidebar, (*3*) main results, and (*4*) document view. Printed with permission

- Sort and filter results based on document metadata and on (retrieval) process metadata
- Integrate inputs from multiple searchers working on a shared information need to implement collaborative search

6.3 User-Mediated Collaboration

This section will introduce a couple of recent CIS systems that provide user-based mediation.

6.3.1 Ariadne

Twidale et al. [16] developed Ariadne to support the collaborative learning of database browsing skills. In addition to enhancing the opportunities and effectiveness of the collaborative learning that already occurred, Ariadne was designed to provide the facilities that would allow collaborations to persist as people increasingly searched information remotely and had less opportunity for spontaneous face-to-face collaboration.

Ariadne was developed in the days when Telnet-based access to library catalogues was a common practice. Building on top of this command-line interface, Ariadne could capture the users' input and the database's output, and form them

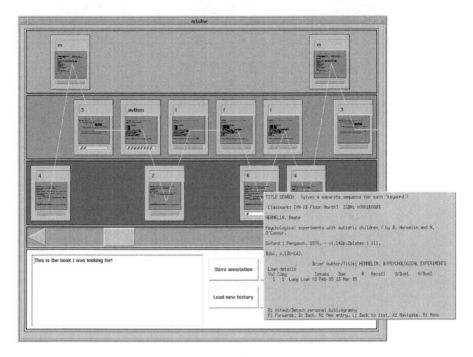

Fig. 6.3 A search visualization in Ariadne. Printed with permission

into a search history that consisted of a series of command-output pairs. Such a separation of capture and display allowed Ariadne to work with various forms of data capture methods.

To support complex browsing processes in collaboration, Ariadne presented a visualization of the search process (Fig. 6.3). This visualization consisted of thumbnails of screens, looking like playing cards, which represented command-output pairs. Any such card can be expanded to reveal its details. The horizontal axis on Ariadne's display represented time, and the vertical axis showed information on the semantics of the action it represented: the top row for the top level menus, the middle row for specifying a search, and the bottom row for looking at particular book details.

This visualization of the search process in Ariadne makes it possible to annotate, discuss with colleagues around the screen, and distribute to remote collaborators for asynchronous commenting easily and effectively. As we saw in the previous section, having access to one's history as well as the history of one's collaborators are very crucial to effective collaboration. Ariadne implements these requirements with the features that let one visualize, save, and share a search process. In fact, the authors found one of the advantages of search visualization was the ability to recap previous searching sessions easily in a multi-session exploratory searching.

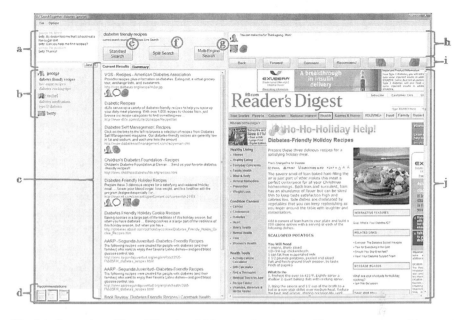

Fig. 6.4 Screenshot of SearchTogether. (*a*) Integrated messaging, (*b*) query awareness, (*c*) current results, (*d*) recommendation queue, (*e*)–(*g*) search buttons, (*h*) page-specific metadata, (*i*) toolbar, (*j*) browser. Printed with permission

6.3.2 SearchTogether

More recently, one of the collaborative information seeking tools that have caught a lot of attention is SearchTogether, developed by Morris and Horvitz [7]. The design of this tool was motivated by a survey that the researchers did with 204 knowledge workers [6], in which they discovered the following.

- A majority of respondents wanted to collaborate while searching on the Web.
- The most common ways of collaborating in information seeking tasks are sending emails back and forth, using IM to exchange links and query terms, and using phone calls while looking at a Web browser.
- Some of the most popular Web searching tasks on which people like to collaborate are planning travels or social events, making expensive purchases, researching medical conditions, and looking for information related to a common project.

Based on the survey responses, and the current and desired practices for collaborative search, the authors of SearchTogether identified three key features for supporting people's collaborative information behavior while searching on the Web: awareness, division of labor, and persistence. Let us look at how these three features are implemented. A snapshot of the SearchTogether client is shown in Fig. 6.4.

As we saw before, awareness is one of the most critical elements of a collaborative system. SearchTogether instantiates awareness in several ways, one of which is per-user query histories. This is done by showing each group member's screen name, his/her photo and queries in the "Query Awareness" region (Fig. 6.4b). The access to the query histories is immediate and interactive, as clicking on a query brings back the results of that query from when it was executed. The authors identified query awareness as a very important feature in collaborative searching, which allows group members to not only share their query terms, but also learn better query formulation techniques from one another.

Another component of SearchTogether that facilitates awareness is the display of page-specific metadata (Fig. 6.4h). This region includes several pieces of information about the displayed page, including group members who viewed the given page, and their comments and ratings. The authors claim that such visitation information can help one either choose to avoid a page already visited by someone in the group to reduce the duplication of efforts, or perhaps choose to visit such pages, as they provide a sign of promising leads as indicated by the presence of comments and/or ratings.

Division of labor in SearchTogether is implemented in three ways: (1) "Split Search" allows one to split the search results among all online group members in a round-robin fashion, (2) "Multi-Engine Search" takes a query and runs it on n different search engines, where n is the number of online group members, (3) manual division of labor can be facilitated using integrated IM.

Despite the anticipated benefits that the authors anticipated, the automatic division of labor features, implemented using split search and multi-engine search were not heavily used during their user studies. The lack of usage of these features does not indicate their failure; it shows their misfit for the given situation. Performing automatic split implies that the person doing the split is the group leader. While such a scenario is possible in many business and management situations, it did not come up during the lab studies.

Finally, the persistence feature in SearchTogether is instantiated by storing all the objects and actions, including IM conversations, query histories, recommendation queues, and page-specific metadata. Such data about all the group members are available to each member when he/she logs in. This allows one to easily carry a multi-session collaborative project.

6.4 A Case Study in Designing a CIS Solution with Coagmento

6.4.1 Design

To provide an effective solution for CIS, we spent significant efforts on the design phase. This section provides details about how we derived design specifications for Coagmento, built a preliminary interface, tested it with pilot runs, obtained feedback using cognitive walkthroughs, and enhanced the design specifications using participatory design sessions.

6.4.1.1 Personal Interviews

As Grudin [4] pointed out, "many expensive failures in developing and marketing software that is designed to support groups are not due to technical problems; they result from not understanding the unique demands this class of software imposes on developers and users" (p. 93). Such views are reaffirmed by recent works such as [10]. Keeping this in mind, we interviewed a number of people who work and/or teach in information intensive domains, asking questions about their past and present collaborative projects. The details of this study are reported in [12]. Here, we will report only those findings that are relevant to the system design.

We discovered that email and face-to-face meetings are some of the most popular methods of collaboration. These methods represent two extremes of the classical model of collaborative methods [9, 15], where email fits on the remote and asynchronous end, and meetings fit on the co-located and synchronous end. However, due to the changing structure of work environments and habits (people working on multiple projects with different sets of collaborators, across multiple sessions, and with multiple devices), the need to fill in the gap between these extremes is more apparent than ever.

While most of the respondents wished for better tools for collaboration, they agreed they would have a hard time departing from familiar tools, such as email and IM, even though these tools were not explicitly designed to support collaboration. Even if people know about tools such as del.icio.us (http://delicious.com), they still send website links to each other over email. System designers and developers face a grave implication due to this fact; they need to provide seamless integration of tools that support collaboration within a user's existing working environment rather than making him choose between his tried-and-tested method and a new tool. This finding reflects the views of Grudin [4], where he suggested extending an existing single-user system, with which a user is already familiar, with groupware features to minimize the cognitive load and maximize the adoption rate. As one of the respondent admitted in our interviews, "We focus on results, and not how to do it."

6.4.1.2 Preliminary Design of Coagmento

In order to come up with initial design specifications for Coagmento, two works are particularly helpful: one based on a general notion of collaboration, and the other more specific to designing a collaborative system. Surowiecki [14] lists four conditions for a successful collaboration: (1) diversity of opinion, (2) independence, (3) decentralization, and (4) aggregation. Morris and Horvitz [7] presented the SearchTogether system based on supporting (1) awareness, (2) division of labor, and (3) persistence for collaboration. Based on these works and the responses from the personal interviews, the following set of guidelines for designing a user-centered CIS system are inferred.

1. The system should provide an effective way for users to communicate with each other.

Query-box

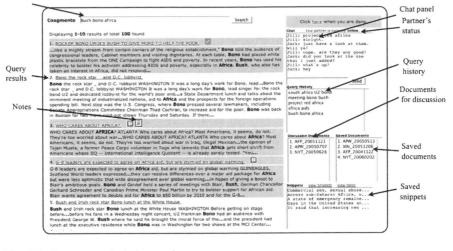

Fig. 6.5 Coagmento v1: design version

2. The system should allow (and encourage) each user to make individual contributions to the collaboration.
3. The system should coordinate user actions, information requests, and responses to support an active and interactive collaboration. This collaboration could be synchronous or asynchronous, and co-located or remote.
4. Users need to agree to and follow a set of rules to carry out a productive collaboration. For instance, if they have a disagreement on the relevancy of an information object, they should discuss and negotiate; they should arrive at a mutually agreeable solution rather than continuing to dispute it. The system needs to support discussion and negotiation processes among the users.
5. The system should provide a mechanism to let the users not only explore their individual differences, but also negotiate roles and responsibilities. There may be a situation in which one user leads the group and others follow (cooperate), but the real strength of collaboration lies in having the authority vested in the collective.

Using the above guidelines, a prototype system called Coagmento was developed that allows two people to work together for seeking information. Collaborators can work synchronously or asynchronously, and they may be co-located or remotely connected. This version of Coagmento was designed to work with a specific collection rather than the open web. The main screen of Coagmento is shown in Fig. 6.5. Let us now see how the above listed characteristics are realized in Coagmento.

- Coagmento includes a search interface, chat, and document space (the same space where the results are displayed in the figure), as well as various marking facilities (discussed later)—all in one place.
- All of these tools are presented on a single interface and readily accessible. There is no need to switch to different windows or tabs as in SearchTogether.

Fig. 6.6 Toolbar provided on top of the document being viewed with Coagmento

- Coagmento displays the partnership information and provides visual feedback based on one's partner's as well as one's own actions. For instance, if a document is already viewed by either of the persons in a pair, it will be highlighted anywhere it appears in a rank-list for both of them.
- Coagmento keeps a log of all the queries used during a search session. The list of these queries is presented on the interface. Unlike SearchTogether, clicking on a query executes fresh results, and not its history.
- The users of Coagmento can save any document that they find useful or flag it to be discussed with their partners (Fig. 6.6). Once again, these two lists are readily available on the interface and clicking on the name of a document there brings up that document to view.
- If a user is working alone, he may not see much use in writing notes about everything that is saved as he may have an intuitive understanding about the relevance of those results. While working with a partner, on the other hand, the user may need to convey what and why aspects about the usefulness of a document. Coagmento allows a user to add notes to any document (Fig. 6.6). Morris and Horvitz [7] found such a feature useful, but they also realized that they needed a way for users to simply highlight and save portions of pages. Coagmento provides a way to 'snip' a passage while viewing a document that the user found useful (Fig. 6.6). This is done by highlighting any text on any displayed page and clicking on the 'Snip' button on the toolbar.
- Coagmento saves the state information. This means a user can leave a session and when he comes back, he will find the session as it was, with some possible updates in case his partner kept working while he was gone. This allows the users to collaborate in either synchronous or asynchronous mode. There is an indication on the interface to let a user know if his partner is online or not.

Based on the description above, it should be clear that in principle, Coagmento builds on the framework of other tools such as SearchTogether, and extends them in certain ways. One aspect of SearchTogether that Coagmento does not implement fully is the division of labor. There are three ways in which this feature is realized in SearchTogether: (1) chat, (2) recommendations, and (3) split search. Coagmento has a chat feature, which can be used to talk about the distribution of the work. As far as the recommendations feature is concerned, the authors of SearchTogether found it underutilized. They concluded that rather than providing a "recommend" option, providing a "share this" option would allow a better way of sending pages back and forth. Coagmento does this through its "discuss this document" feature. For the SearchTogether system, it was found that the automatic division of labor features such as split search were not heavily used. The usefulness of such features needs further investigation.

6.4.1.3 Cognitive Walkthroughs

To obtain feedback on various functions that Coagmento offered, we provided cognitive walkthroughs to 11 different participants from age 25 to 58 and with diverse
backgrounds. These participants were graduate students and faculty members in
the fields of information science, library science, social science, and journalism. In
general, the participants were mature researchers and/or academicians in their respective fields. A majority of these participants also taught various courses relating
to information and library science, and media and journalism. They, therefore, could
talk not only from their personal experiences, but also from those of their students.
Further details of this study can be found in [13]. The findings from this study can
be summarized as follows.

- Ability to effectively collect and share information is highly desired from a CIS
  system. People typically do this using traditional tried-and-tested tools such as
  email and IM, without realizing that there could be more effective ways of doing
  it in collaborative projects. Coagmento allows the users to easily collect and share
  snippets of information, which most participants reported to be a unique feature.
  However, one may not want to use a CIS system such as Coagmento just because it has a couple of unique features. As noted before, we need to understand
  the larger context and environment in which people collaborate for information
  seeking projects.
- It was a pleasant discovery that the participants saw Coagmento's use even in non-
  collaborative projects. Such appropriation is important to have for a successful
  groupware system, as Grudin [4] noted.
- The participants asked to see more information on the interface, including time
  stamps. This was important feedback, yet at the same time created a design challenge. How much information is enough and how much is too much? Should we
  show day, date, as well as time in hour, minutes, and seconds? We need to develop
  systems that allow the users to choose this. Having a configurable interface can
  let the users work through its features without getting overwhelmed.

Based on the lessons learned from the demonstrative walkthroughs, Coagmento
was enhanced primarily to support a real life testing of the system. The TREC ciQA
(Complex Interactive QA) 2007 data-set was used as the collection for this version
of Coagmento. This data-set had nearly one million documents from various news
sources. The collection was indexed using the Lemur Toolkit, and a modified In-
dri search service served the requests in the background. The following subsection
describes a few pilot runs done with this system.

6.4.1.4 Pilot Runs

To test the effectiveness of Coagmento in terms of providing appropriate functionalities for people working together while seeking information, three pilot runs were

conducted during three different undergraduate classes at UNC Chapel Hill. To-gether, these three pilot runs had 36 participants, paired randomly in 18 groups.

At the start of a run, usernames and passwords were handed out in a random order to the participants. That way, they were not able to pick their partners, although they might already know each other. At first, a brief overview of Coagmento was presented. Then they were allowed to login to the system. Following is the outline of the entire experiment.

1. Each participant was given the following drill task.

> You are reporters at New York Times. You are working on a story that could show a possible link between President Bush and Bono, the U2 Rock Star. In order to do this, you are first investigating what common interests they both have. May be they are involved in the same project or cause, or they like the same baseball team! It's your job to find out as many such common interests as you can. Find relevant documents and collect the snippets that have the related information on this topic.

When the users first login, they were presented with this drill task. They were also given a printed copy of this task, so that they could refer to it during the task.

2. Once they read the task description on the screen, they could start the task and were taken to the main interface screen of Coagmento.
3. The participants were allowed to try this interface out with the given drill task for about five minutes. One of the first things they did during this time was introducing themselves to their partners and finding out who their partners were. They were encouraged to use every feature of the interface.
4. They were asked to click 'Done' and the system took them out of that task.
5. The users were now presented with a new task.

> You are detectives, specializing in antiquities and historical documents thefts. Your current assignment is to find the evidence for transport of stolen antiquities from Egypt to other countries. Since such evidence often appears when such antiquities are returned to Egypt from other countries, you should search and file news about these goods being returned. Find relevant documents and collect the snippets that have the related information on this topic.

This was the real task and once again they were given a written copy of the task.

6. They were asked to take about 10 minutes to do this task, and allowed about 12 minutes before asking them to declare this task 'Done'.
7. The participants filled in the end of task questionnaire and the exit questionnaire.

At the end of this exercise, an open discussion about this experience and the system was conducted. From log mining and discussions with the participants, it became clear that the participants rarely looked at a document already viewed by their teammates. Given the nature of the system, the participants had to start with a query to get a list of documents to look at. At the level of query formulation, the participants in the same team may use the same or similar queries, but once they get a list of results, they would avoid looking at each other's documents. This has two implications. First, if a task is time-bound, exploratory, and easily dividable, the participants may try not to do overlapping work. They may work individually trying to get as much information as possible, and then combine with their collaborators' individual information to create the group's product. Second, in order to easily know what has already been done by one's self and/or others in the group the interface needs to provide ready support. This reaffirms the value of awareness in collaborative projects.

6.4.1.5 Participatory Design Phase I

To further obtain and revise our design specifications, we organized participatory design sessions in a graduate HCI seminar class at UNC Chapel Hill during the Fall 2008 semester. There were about a dozen graduate students who participated over four sessions, separated by 3–5 weeks. These sessions focused on discussing certain theoretical ideas of collaboration, and coming up with design specifications for an ideal CIS system.

Some of the early discussions during these sessions were focused on definitions of collaboration, describing past experiences with collaborative projects, and identifying difficulties in such situations. Later the discussions were targeted to come up with design specifications for an ideal CIS system.

The participants mentioned several situations in which they were required to or wanted to do collaboration. Given that the participants were graduate students, a common situation was collaborating with co-authors on an article.

One of the issues that the participants reported during such collaborations is coordination. Often, the work is divided among the collaborators in the beginning of the project and a good amount of coordination is required to make sure that everyone is following a common timeline, and that their individual contributions come together in a meaningful product. For instance, in the case of co-authoring an article, the authors have to do their parts, exchange them with each other by a set deadline, and then arrange them to create the final write-up.

Most participants reported using general tools such as email, and specialized tools such as Google Docs for collecting and sharing information with their collaborators. Some of the participants had used RefWorks for collaborative writing projects. While Google Docs was a common choice for writing-related projects, the participants identified several issues with it. They include not being able to attach files, not having search queries captured, and not having time stamp information stored with different actions.

Overall, these participatory design sessions helped us reaffirm some of the issues that were discovered during the literature review and previous design studies, and helped in obtaining a variety of ideas from the participants through highly interactive group discussions.

Two major issues were identified during these sessions for designing a CIS system: (1) the role of awareness, and (2) support for a common workspace. The following suggestions were received for presenting awareness on the interface.

1. A tree or a map to see what path other collaborators took.
2. Personal histories for each of the persons in the group using a zoomable timeline or flowchart.
3. Provide history with different layers like Photoshop. One can then select the layer that he wants to look or work with, but finally they all come together to produce a finished picture.
4. Create switchable overlays of the interface, so one could switch between overlays depending on the requirement at the moment.
5. Provide a histogram of activities.
6. Have multiple tabs on the interface, like a modern browser, allowing one to have multiple views of the same project open and switch between them as needed.
7. Provide feed updates like Twitter or Facebook feeds.

The following suggestions were given with respect to the workspace that the participants would like to see in a CIS system.

1. Ability to choose one's role (e.g., supervisor, reader, information gatherer) and contribute through the workspace based on that role.
2. Sticky notes to remind one's self or give to other collaborators.
3. Use different attributes for/with different objects on the workspace to communicate effectively with each other. Such attributes include color, icons, size, location, gradients, avatars, and sounds.

A fair amount of discussion was also devoted to the issue of searching in groups. The participants concurred that how one searches in collaboration depends on where the search falls in the whole continuum of creativity, and creativity is an individual thing. Given that, a system that lets multiple people search together and share their results, should allow the participants to express their individual creativity and then bridge multiple inputs to create a collaborative product.

Based on these discussions and findings, we enhanced Coagmento, specifically paying attention to awareness and common workspace functions. While other suggestions and realizations from this study were also valuable, we decided to keep them for the future work. This allowed us to develop a complete CIS system that we could test in laboratory. The next section provides details of the development phase.

6.4.2 Development

Based on the findings and experiences with previous studies involving Coagmento, it was once again redesigned. The version of Coagmento used in each of the design studies described so far was website based, which means, that all the participants of a collaborative project had access to the various services such as searching, saving and sharing the results, and chat through a single website. An advantage of this approach is that it gives good control to the researcher over what the users do on this website. However, the biggest disadvantage is that the user is not able use the web as he wishes. Besides, the user may not always want to search. This realization led to redesigning Coagmento with a very different approach, while still offering the same functionalities as before.

The new Coagmento was developed with a client-server architecture, where the client is implemented as a Firefox plug-in that helps multiple people working in collaboration to communicate, and search, share and organize information. The server component stores and provides all the objects and actions collected from the client. Due to this decoupling, Coagmento provides a flexible architecture that allows its users to be co-located or remote, working synchronously or asynchronously, and using different platforms. This version of Coagmento used several of the suggestions and lessons derived from the design studies, while leaving out others due to the limited scope of this work. In particular, Coagmento was redesigned considering the aspects of awareness, communication, and ease of use of sharing while online information seeking.

A screenshot of this new Coagmento is given in Fig. 6.7. As we can see, it includes a toolbar and a sidebar. The toolbar has several buttons that helps one collect information and be aware of the progress in a given collaboration. The toolbar has three major parts:

1. Buttons for collecting information and making annotations. These buttons help one save or remove a webpage, make annotations on a webpage, and highlight and collect text snippets. The windows that pop-up while collecting a snippet and making an annotation from/on a webpage are shown in Figs. 6.8 and 6.9.
2. Page-specific statistics. The middle portion of the toolbar shows various statistics, such as the number of views, annotations, and snippets, for the displayed page. A user can click on a given statistic and obtain more information. For instance, clicking on the number of snippets will bring up a window that shows all the snippets collected by the collaborators from the displayed page.
3. Project-specific statistics. The last portion of the toolbar displays task/project name and various statistics, including number of pages visited and saved, about the current project. Clicking on that portion brings up the workspace where one can view all the collected objects (pages and snippets) brought in by the collaborators for that project.

The sidebar features a chat window, under which there are three tabs with the history of search engine queries, saved pages and snippets. With each of these objects, the user who created or collected that object is shown. Anyone in the group

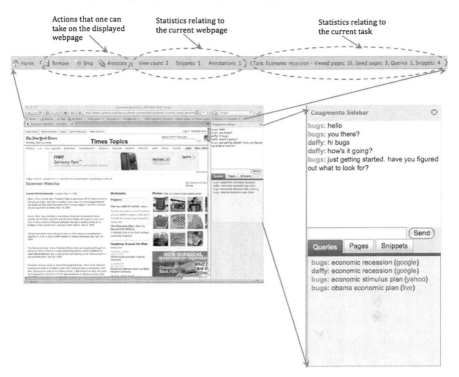

Fig. 6.7 Coagmento v2: development version

Fig. 6.8 Snippets collection
window

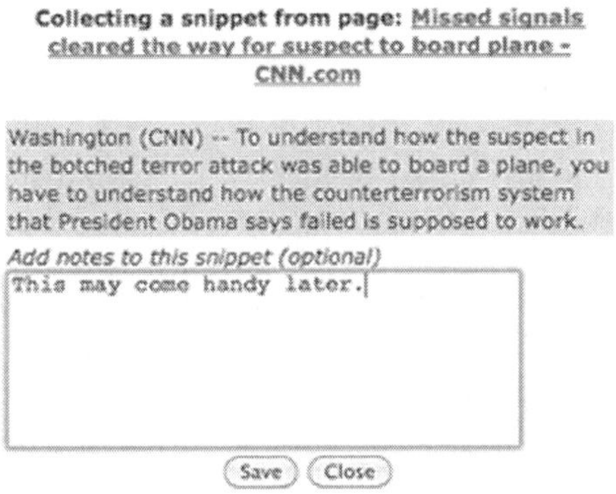

Fig. 6.9 Annotations
window

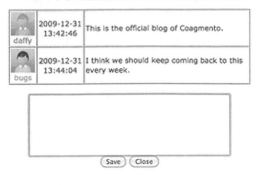

can access an object by clicking on it. For instance, one can click on a query issued by anyone in the group to re-run that query and bring up the results in the main browser window.

6.4.2.1 Laboratory Study

To test various awareness and other functions of Coagmento, we conducted a laboratory study involving 84 participants in 42 pairs recruited from UNC Chapel Hill. These participants were asked to come to the lab for two different sessions, which were one to two weeks apart. The participants were able to choose the day and time convenient to them using the online recruiting system. Since the participants had to sign up in pairs, both the participants in a given pair already knew each other. In addition to this, it was required that the participants in a given pair should have done some collaborative work with each other before; thus, making sure they not only know each other, but also are comfortable working with each other on a collaborative project. The approval of a pair's participation in this study was based on these criteria. Participants were compensated $25 each for their participation in two sessions.

During the first session the participants were shown a video tutorial demonstrating the use of Coagmento and the process of collecting relevant information (snippets of text). After the tutorial, the participants were placed in different rooms so that they could not talk to each other directly or see what the other person was doing (Fig. 6.10). Both the participants used typical mid-end PC workstations, running Windows XP, with Ethernet connectivity and 19″ monitors.

The participants were given two exploratory search tasks, one on economic recession and the other on social networking. They started with the first task, and were asked to switch to the second task after about 20 minutes.

For the second session, the participants were given a refresher of the system and shown how to compile their final report by grouping their collected snippets

Fig. 6.10 Participants during a study session

into different categories for a given task. The categories were presented in the task statement and corresponded to different aspects of the work task. The participants were then asked to take their places in the room other than the one they had used the last time, to take care of any bias the participants may have for the machine or the room they used. They resumed their first task that they had started in the previous session. About 15 minutes later, they were asked to switch to the second task from the first session.

The participants were asked to rate (scale 1 to 7) several factors about the system at the end of each session as shown in the following questionnaire. The questionnaire was derived from the original Computer System Usability Questionnaire [5] removing those statements that were not relevant for this study.

> Q1. Overall, I am satisfied with how easy it is to use this system.
> Q2. I can effectively complete my work using this system.
> Q3. I am able to efficiently complete my work using this system.
> Q4. I feel comfortable using this system.
> Q5. It was easy to learn to use this system.
> Q6. I believe I became productive quickly using this system.
> Q7. It is easy to find the information I need.
> Q8. The information provided for the system is easy to understand.
> Q9. The organization of information on the system screens (toolbar, sidebar) is clear.
> Q10. The interface of this system is pleasant.
> Q11. I like using the interface of this system.
> Q12. This system has all the functions and capabilities I expect it to have.
> Q13. Overall, I am satisfied with this system.

Table 6.1 Summary of
responses by 84 participants
on ease of use and
satisfaction questionnaire for
the lab study

Question	Mean	s.d.
Q1	5.45	1.781
Q2	5.47	1.801
Q3	5.48	1.844
Q4	5.58	1.830
Q5	5.89	1.859
Q6	5.51	1.798
Q7	5.63	1.846
Q8	5.76	1.772
Q9	5.60	1.890
Q10	5.21	1.834
Q11	5.20	1.802
Q12	4.70	1.866
Q13	5.35	1.768

The responses on this questionnaire are summarized in Table 6.1. As we can see, the participants rated each of the statements quite high, indicating good ease of use and satisfaction with the system. In addition to these responses, we let the participants make free-form suggestions about improving Coagmento. Two of the most common features we received the requests for were: having ability to make notes for a project, and receiving notifications of their collaborators' actions in real-time.

We redesigned Coagmento based on these findings, which is presented in the following subsection.

6.4.2.2 Enhanced Coagmento

A re-conceptualized and re-implemented Coagmento is shown in Fig. 6.11. This version of Coagmento has two core components: a plug-in for Firefox browser, and a web-based collaborative space, called CSpace. The plug-in includes a toolbar and a sidebar. Following is a brief description of how different components of Coagmento support collaborative information seeking, synthesis, and sense-making.

Using Coagmento, one could now do the following activities related to information seeking effectively: collect, share, and recommend webpages using the toolbar, re-find and reuse information using the sidebar, and add value (tags, notes, etc.) to found information. Coagmento supports information synthesis by the way of providing a workspace in CSpace, where an individual or group could organize the collected information and compile a report. Coagmento also includes support for alerts or notifications, ability to make recommendations to an individual or the whole group, and a function to monitor and relate information as the group works

Fig. 6.11   Coagmento v3: deployment

through their information seeking process. Such support could help one in their sense-making processes. In addition, Coagmento provides integrated support for communication, note-taking, and collecting text snippets or other objects from web-pages. This new version of constantly improving Coagmento is available from http:// www.coagmento.org/ for free personal or research use.

6.4.3 Deployment

In this section, we will discuss how we deployed Coagmento as a freely available system for anyone to try, and an online field study conducted with it. We will wrap up our discussion by presenting another phase of participatory design sessions, informing us about the next iteration of the design phase.

6.4.3.1 Field Study

Using several email lists, we announced the availability of the new Coagmento [11]. Nearly 100 individuals joined Coagmento as users. We also encouraged these users to sign up as participants for our online field study, and provide us periodic feedback. 24 users agreed to be such participants, but not all of them provided the requested feedback. A summary of the responses on the same questionnaire with 13 statements presented before is provided in Table 6.2.

Table 6.2 Summary of
responses by 19 participants
on ease of use and
satisfaction questionnaire for
the field study

Question	Mean	s.d.
Q1	4.00	1.371
Q2	4.55	1.810
Q3	3.80	1.567
Q4	5.44	1.688
Q5	3.83	1.823
Q6	3.88	1.536
Q7	4.05	1.248
Q8	4.71	1.382
Q9	4.16	1.465
Q10	4.77	1.563
Q11	3.15	1.625
Q12	3.76	1.300
Q13	3.82	1.467

Here we can see that the ratings are not as high as those obtained during the laboratory study, even though the new version of Coagmento includes several enhancements. A part of this disparity can be attributed to the fact that for a lab study, the subjects had to appear in person, and they may have felt more sympathetic to the project while providing their feedback. It is still encouraging to learn that people find this system easy to learn (Q4), even when we could not directly teach them its operation.

6.4.3.2 Participatory Design Phase II

In order to revise our design specifications, we conducted another phase of participatory design sessions during the Fall 2009 semester for the same graduate level HCI seminar, now with a different set of nearly 15 students. This time, we not only discussed general issues relating to CIS system design and implementation, but also specific aspects of Coagmento as available at the time.

We let the participants try the enhanced Coagmento (v3) and provide us feedback. Similar to the previous studies, we asked the participants to rate various aspects of the system for its ease of use and satisfaction. Once again, not everyone that tried the system responded. A summary of the responses that we received is given in Table 6.3.

As we can see, once again, the participants found it relatively easy to learn the system (Q4), and reported reasonably high ratings for other aspects of the system as well. In the free-form field asking them about two aspects that they liked about Coagmento, a majority of the participants identified the ability to save (bookmark) any webpage and collect snippets from anywhere as the biggest positive points.

Table 6.3 Summary of responses by 8 participants on ease of use and satisfaction questionnaire for the participatory design phase II study

Question	Mean	s.d.
Q1	4.75	1.16
Q2	4.38	1.50
Q3	4.50	0.92
Q4	6.00	0.53
Q5	4.13	0.99
Q6	4.50	1.30
Q7	3.88	0.99
Q8	4.50	0.75
Q9	3.63	0.91
Q10	4.50	2.13
Q11	5.00	1.60
Q12	4.25	0.46
Q13	5.50	0.75

One of the participants suggested incorporating a citation builder like Zotero with snippets collection. In general, the participants appreciated having ready access to their history (saved pages, snippets, and queries).

The participants, however, expected several other features not offered by the version of Coagmento they tried. This came up in Q12 (Table 6.3) as well as in the responses to an open-ended question asking them to list a couple of aspects of Coagmento that they did not like. One of the common feature requests that Coagmento did not have was the ability to save snippets from PDF files. This was identified as a highly valuable function in academia, since many scholarly articles appear in PDF format. Another requested feature was the way to organize collected snippets and notes.

In the discussion session followed by online feedback, the following additional issues came up.

- The participants reported experiencing an additional overhead for using Coagmento. They found the installation and learning to use Coagmento to be easy, but incorporating it in existing practices a bit hard. Due to the overhead involved with different actions, starting with login to selecting a project, and finally revisiting the collected information, the participants found themselves not utilizing Coagmento much.
- As a feature, Coagmento allows one to explicitly turn on and off its ability to record one's browsing. While this feature was provided as a way to facilitate privacy, it ended up being an obstacle sometimes as the participants forgot to turn it on. The participants were divided on the issue of making the recording on or off by default.

- Another issue the participants reported facing was of remembering to label a new project. Some of the participants also indicated that it was difficult for them to remember the actual name they gave to a project several days back. In other words, project management was below par and unclear.

Overall, the participatory design sessions provided a platform to engage in interactive discussions with several experienced participants, identify some of the key issues in designing a CIS system, and obtain feedback on an enhanced version of Coagmento.

6.5 Future Development

We have learned several lessons from others' and our own experiences designing and building CIS tools and systems. Following are some of them.

- It does not take long for people to learn such a new kind of collaborative interface. They may still not see the usefulness of all its features, but they can certainly start using them in a matter of a few minutes.
- There are certain tools that an average user is very familiar with and he expects certain kind of behavior from such a tool. In Coagmento, these were search results and chat box. For search results, people tend to compare with their familiar search services, such as Google. They want their results fast, and a lot in number, even if they never go past the first page. Similarly, almost everyone has used some kind of IM and they expect the chat panel to behave just like their favorite IM program.
- It is hard to make people collaborate in unrealistic situations. Most of these users did not see the value in collaborating for such a common task as searching. The cognitive load for using the tools and/or collaborating was probably more than the potential return. However, it is quite possible that the same set of users would be more willing to use these tools the next time as they may have become more comfortable with them.
- People appreciate and desire unique features, such as collecting and sharing snippets of information effectively. However, such features themselves may not be compelling enough to adopt the whole system. One needs to understand these features in a larger context and provide proper support for that context as well. In the case of snippets, it was discovered that, while effectively collecting snippets is a desired feature, the users want to be able to use those snippets in some way. This may involve organizing the snippets and using them to synthesize a report. Thus, without the support for this larger context of being able to utilize the snippets, allowing the users to simply collect the snippets may not be a strong reason for system adoption.
- Shared awareness and workspace were found to be some of the most desired features a CIS system should provide.
- Using a new CIS system is not simply about adopting a new tool, but it is about getting used to a new way of thinking about exploratory and collaborative work

practices. Managing a multi-session collaborative project that already has enough complexity could become even more difficult and confusing while using a completely new interface, as reported by our participatory design participants. It is valuable to provide appropriate support for control, communication, and awareness; but, if it is done without understanding existing practices and cognitive load required to adopt the system, we may end up hurting its usage and adoption.

From the early days of groupware systems to Web 2.0 based online collaborations, the systems to support CIS have come a long way. Several challenges, however, remain to be addressed. The most important of these challenges are not about the technology, but about their right implementation, usage, and sustainability. As Grudin [4] noted, "Many expensive failures in developing and marketing software that are designed to support groups are not due to technical problems. They result from not understanding the unique demands this class of software imposes on developers and users."

Thus, the researchers and developers interested in designing, implementing, and studying the systems to support CIS will have to go beyond understanding the technology; they will need to understand certain fundamental aspects about the target domain, such as decision-making processes, existing practices, and user expectations and interactions in group/social settings. Many studies in the past used empirical observation method (e.g., [8]) to study these aspects and design their systems. While several of their findings are still relevant, new studies with emerging information sources and recent technologies are needed.

One of the biggest challenges that most CIS systems face is the issue of adoption. Before designing or implementing a CIS system, one will need to study the bigger context and see how collaborative features of a CIS system can fit in an existing environment, instead of imposing a rigid structure on the user.

Finally, there is something to be said about the value of innovations. Often, as Steve Jobs said, "People don't know what they want until you show it to them." There is plenty of room in the field of CIS to bring in new and innovative design ideas that can inspire the users and the researchers.

References

1. Raya Fidel, Annelise Mark Pejtersen, Bryan Cleal and Harry Bruce. A multidimensional approach to the study of human–information interaction: a case study of collaborative information retrieval. *Journal of the American Society for Information Science and Technology*, 55(11):939–953, 2004.
2. Gene Golovchinsky, John Adcock, Jeremy Pickens, Pernilla Qvarfordt and Maribeth Back. Cerchiamo: a collaborative exploratory search tool. In *Proceedings of Computer Supported Cooperative Work (CSCW)*, 2008.
3. Gene Golovchinsky. Abdigani Diriye. Session-based search with Querium. In *Workshop on Human-Centered Information Retrieval (HCIR)*, 2011.
4. Jonathan Grudin. Groupware and social dynamics: eight challenges for developers. *Communications of the ACM*, 37(1):92–105, 1994.

5. J.R. Lewis. IBM computer usability satisfaction questionnaires: psychometric evaluation and instructions for use. *International Journal of Human–Computer Interaction*, 7(1):57–58, 1995.

6. Meredith Ringel Morris. A survey of collaborative web search practices. In *Proceedings of ACM SIGCHI Conference on Human Factors in Computing Systems*, pages 1657–1660, Florence, Italy, 2008.

7. Meredith Ringel Morris and Eric Horvitz. SearchTogether: an interface for collaborative web search. In *ACM Symposium on User Interface Software and Technology (UIST)*, pages 3–12, Newport, RI, October 2007.

8. Gary M. Olson, Judith S. Olson, Mark R. Carter and Marianne Storrosten. Small group design meetings: an analysis of collaboration. *Human–Computer Interaction*, 7(4):347–374, 1992.

9. Tom Rodden. A survey of CSCW systems. *Interacting with Computers*, 3(3):319–353, 1991.

10. Chirag Shah. Lessons and challenges for Collaborative Information Seeking (CIS) systems developers. In *GROUP 2009 Workshop on Collaborative Information Behavior*, Sanibel Island, Florida, 2009.

11. Chirag Shah. Coagmento—a collaborative information seeking, synthesis and sense-making framework (an integrated demo). In *Proceedings of Computer Supported Cooperative Work (CSCW)*, Savannah, GA, 2010.

12. Chirag Shah. Designs for systems to support collaborative information behavior. In Jonathan Foster, editor, *Collaborative Information Behavior*, pages 141–159. IGI Global, Hershey, PA, 2010.

13. Chirag Shah. Working in collaboration—what, why, and how. In *Proceedings of Collaborative Information Retrieval Workshop at CSCW 2010* Savannah, GA, 2010.

14. James Surowiecki. *Wisdom of Crowds: Why the Many Are Smarter than the Few and How Collective Wisdom Shapes Business, Economies, Societies and Nations*. Doubleday, New York, 2004.

15. Michael B. Twidale and David M. Nichols. Collaborative browsing and visualisation of the search process. *Aslib Proceedings*, 48(7–8):177–182, 1996.

16. Michael B. Twidale, David M. Nichols and Chris D. Paice. Supporting collaborative learning during information searching. In *Proceedings of Computer Supported Collaborative Learning (CSCL)*, pages 367–374, Bloomington, Indiana, 1995.

Chapter 7
Evaluation

Abstract Evaluating performances of CIS systems and users can be challenging due to the complex interactions that take place among various users and systems processes. While some of the aspects of a CIS system or user could be measured by typical assessment techniques from single-user IR/IS, one often needs to go beyond them to provide a meaningful evaluation. This chapter presents a framework for CIS evaluation with two major parts: system-based and user-based. It outlines several of the relevant assessments employed for IR/IS/CIS works, and provides a comprehensive list of measures, along with suitable methods for deploying them for empirical evaluations.

7.1 Challenges for Evaluating CIS Systems and Situations

Evaluating a CIS environment can be a huge challenge due to its complex design that involves a set of users, integrated systems, and a variety of interactions. One can evaluate a CIS system using typical measures of IR. However, as discussed before, information seeking is not merely about retrieving information, and thus, evaluating a CIS system with its retrieval effectiveness may not be sufficient. While traditional IR evaluations can still be used to measure the retrieval performance of a collaborative filtering system, just as Smyth et al. [22] did, we need additional measures for CIS systems.

Baeza-Yates and Pino [2] presented some initial work on trying to come up with a measure that can extend the evaluation of a single-user IR system for a collaborative environment. While this was based on the retrieval performance, Aneiros and Estivill-Castro [1] came up with the proposal of evaluating the *goodness* of a collaborative system with usability. In addition, Baeza-Yates and Pino [2] treated the performance of a group as the summation of the performances of the individuals in the group. While this may work for simple information seeking and retrieval, we can imagine situations in which this is not true. For instance, if two people working together can find twice as much information as either of them working independently, was that a *good* thing? How about the amount of time they spent cumulatively? The participants may not be able to find twice as many results, but what if they achieved *better understanding* of the problem or the information due to working in collaboration? Then there are other factors, such as *engagement, social interactions,* and *social capital*, which may be important depending upon the application, but are usually not looked at in non-interactive or a single-user IR evaluations.

In this chapter, we will first review a number of methodologies that have been used for CIS evaluation in Sect. 7.2. Then we will talk about specific measures taken primarily from IR, HCI, and CSCW literatures that help in evaluating CIS systems and approaches. These measures will be divided in two categories: system-based (Sect. 7.3), and user-based (Sect. 7.4). Finally, we will look at a case study to understand how these measures listed here can be used to evaluate a CIS system.

7.2 Evaluation Methodologies

To commence our discussion on evaluation in this field, we will first look at a broad overview of how researchers have approached this issue using different methodologies.

7.2.1 Evaluating Usability with User Studies

The majority of the work reported in the literature that has attempted to evaluate the effectiveness of a collaborative system has looked at the usability of the collaborative interface. For instance, Morris and Horvitz [12] tested their SearchTogether system with a user study to evaluate how users utilize various tools offered in their interface and how those tools affect the act of collaboration. The authors used seven pairs of users and let each pair choose their topic of mutual interest to work with. The evaluation was based on the log, observations, and questionnaire data. While they showed the effectiveness of their interface in letting people search together, there was no evaluation of learning that took place in the group due to collaboration. Laurillau and Nigay [10] demonstrated how multiple users could navigate the web in a collaborative environment with their *CoVitesse* system. They presented evaluations for the user interface as well as various network-related parameters. However, no clear understanding of the effects on the retrieval performance was reported. Aneiros and Estivill-Castro [1] presented a questionnaire to the participants of their user study to evaluate the usability of their Group Unified History (GUH) tool. Typical questions on their questionnaire were "How difficult was it to interpret the user identity symbols used in the tool?" and "Did you visit any websites found by your team/peers using the group history?"

Some of the application designers also let *real* users use their systems and evaluated the effectiveness of their system from these users' feedback and/or their success in solving their *real* problems with it. For instance, Twidale et al. [25] invited volunteers to bring a problem that they already have to solve. Students from a wide range of academic backgrounds (including Psychology, Computing, Women's Studies, Chemistry, Religious studies and Environmental Science) used their Ariadne system. The typical case was that they were about to write an extended essay, dissertation or group project and needed to do a literature search. The testing informed the iterative development of the system.

7.2.2 System-Based Training-Testing

Smyth et al. [23] tested their I-Spy system with leave-one-out evaluation methodology. From 20 users, they left one user as a *testing user* and used the other 19 users as the *training users*. The relevancy results of the training users were used to populate I-Spy's hit matrix and the results of each query were re-ranked using I-Spy's relevancy metric. Then they counted the number of those results listed as relevant by the test user for various result-list sizes and finally, they made the equivalent relevancy measurements by analyzing the results produced by the untrained version of I-Spy to serve as a baseline.

Not surprisingly, this line of evaluation is more popular with system or algorithmically mediated collaboration. For instance, Pickens et al. [16] used search query suggestions provided by individuals and showed how their algorithm could achieve an effective collaboration by way of simulation. Shah et al. [21], similarly, used the notions of relevance and novelty to demonstrate how search processes that were virtually combined could result in achieving results that are both relevant and diverse.

7.2.3 Qualitative Evaluation

Prekop [17] presented a qualitative way of evaluating collaborative information seeking studies. He proposed this by measuring *information seeking patterns*. These patterns describe prototypical actions, interactions, and behaviors performed by participants in a collaborative endeavor. The three patterns that the author described were *information seeking by recommendation*, *direct questioning*, and *advertising information paths*. On a similar line of studying the participants by analyzing their behavior and patterns, Olson et al. [15] studied 10 design meetings from four projects in two organizations. The meetings were videotaped, transcribed, and then analyzed using a coding scheme that looked at participants' problem solving and the activities they used to coordinate and manage themselves. The authors also analyzed the structure of their design arguments. The authors claimed that the coding schemes developed might be useful for a wide range of problem-solving meetings other than design.

7.2.4 Task or Application Based Evaluation

Wilson and schraefel [29] analyzed an evaluation framework for information seeking interfaces in terms of its applicability to collaborative search software. Extending Bates' tactics model [3] and Belkin's model of users [4], they showed that the framework can be just as easily applied to collaborative search interactions as individual information seeking software, but pointed out that there are additional considerations about the individual's involvement within a group that must be maintained as the assessment is carried out.

These efforts of evaluating various factors in CIS can be summarized as measuring (1) retrieval performance of the system, (2) effectiveness of the interface in facilitating collaboration, and (3) user satisfaction and involvement. Despite these efforts, there is still a lack of clarity and methods in evaluating CIS environments that can measure factors such as learning, user engagement, and group performance. In the following two sections, we will describe a number of measures that one could employ for overcoming this gap.

7.3 System Measures

We will first look at measures that evaluate different aspects related to the system used for CIS. Many of these measures are taken from traditional and non-traditional IR evaluation metrics. The data for running these evaluations are typically obtained by capturing various objects and processes during the CIS processes. For a grounded discussion on these measures, let us consider a web-based application, where the collaborators in their CIS project are searching, viewing, and collecting information from the web. The unit of information here, therefore, will be a webpage, but one could easily substitute any other reasonable objects (e.g., documents, pictures, videos) without affecting these measures. The reader may find it helpful to have Fig. 7.1 as a reference while following the discussion in this section.

7.3.1 Precision, Recall, and F-measure

First, we will talk about traditional information retrieval measures—precision, recall, and F-measure. To compute these quantities, we need a universal set of webpages. Assuming that the search domain is open web, we need a more confined set that we could use to compare with. For this, we can take the union of all the webpages visited by all the participants involved. Thus, the universe of webpages is defined by combining the visited webpages of each participant/team in every condition. This can be expressed as

$$U = \bigcup_t Coverage(t). \qquad (7.1)$$

Here, $Coverage(t)$ is the coverage (webpages visited) by team t.

We also need to calculate how much of this coverage is relevant. We can map the relevant coverage to the webpages that participants save or collect. Bookmarking,

Fig. 7.1 A framework for
IR-focused system-based
evaluation measures

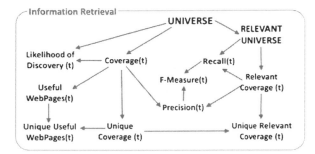

saving, or printing actions may correspond to this. Once again, we can take the union of all such webpages by each team to form a universe of relevant webpages.

$$U_r = \bigcup_t RelevantCoverage(t). \qquad (7.2)$$

Here, $RelevantCoverage(t)$ is the set of webpages that team t visited and found as relevant.

Using these two quantities, we can now define precision, recall, and F-measure, which are listed below.

$$Precision(t) = \frac{RelevantCoverage(t)}{Coverage(t)}, \qquad (7.3)$$

$$Recall(t) = \frac{RelevantCoverage(t)}{U_r}, \qquad (7.4)$$

$$F = \frac{2 \cdot Precision \cdot Recall}{Precision + Recall}. \qquad (7.5)$$

7.3.2 Coverage

To expand our analysis beyond the most common measures used in information retrieval, we can look at the coverage of information by each team. Let us define coverage of a given team as the total number of distinct webpages visited within the universe of webpages:

$$Coverage(t) = \{wp_i : wp_i \text{ was visited by } t \wedge t \in U\}. \qquad (7.6)$$

We could also consider a particular region of the coverage of teams that was unique within the universe. Let's call such region unique coverage, which consists of all webpages within the coverage of a given team t that were visited only by t:

$$UniqueCoverage(t) = Coverage(t) \backslash \bigcup_{t_i \in (T\{t\})} Coverage(t_i). \qquad (7.7)$$

In addition, we can define relevant coverage as the region of coverage of a given team that intersects with the universe of relevant webpages:

$$RelevantCoverage(t) = Coverage(t) \cap U_r. \tag{7.8}$$

In a similar way, we can call unique relevant coverage to the set of webpages within the unique coverage of a given team that intersect with the universe of all relevant webpages:

$$UniqueRelevantCoverage(t) = UniqueCoverage(t) \cap U_r. \tag{7.9}$$

7.3.3 Effectiveness

To go deeper into understanding each team's accomplishment and effectiveness, let's look at two factors: usefulness of webpages, and diversity of their search queries.

To derive usefulness of webpages visited, we can use an implicit measure based on the dwell time on a webpage as described in [28], which is supported by previous findings [6]. As reported in these prior works, we can consider a webpage to be useful if a participant spent at least 30 seconds on it. Using the log data, we can compute dwell time on a given webpage by a participant/team, and if it was greater than or equal to 30 seconds, marked it as useful for that participant/team. Note that we should only consider content pages, discounting any search engine homepage or search engine results pages (SERPs).

7.3.4 Likelihood of Discovery

To evaluate effectiveness of a team/participant in discovering hard to find information, we can use a measure called likelihood of discovery proposed in Shah and Gonzalez-Ibanez [20]. Here, we assume that webpages with a high likelihood are easier to find and are common among the majority of the users. On the other hand, those webpages with a low likelihood are difficult to reach and probably beyond the first results page of search engines. A participant/team finding these webpages are being more effective in discovering information that is not just relevant, but also diverse.

In order to operationalize this idea, we can use a formulation similar to that of inverse document frequency (IDF). Using the frequency of each webpage in our log data, we can compute its likelihood to be visited; in addition, we can multiply each webpage's likelihood by -1 in order to denote the IDF. As a result, each webpage is assigned with a normalized value between -1 and 0. In this sense, those webpages with a value close to 0 are rare (and even unique) to be reached by teams/participants, while those close to -1 are more likely to be visited.

$$\text{Likelihood of discovery}(w) = -1 \cdot \frac{|t_w|}{|t|}. \tag{7.10}$$

Here, $|t_w|$ is the number of teams that discovered webpage w, and $|t|$ is the total number of teams being studied. As we can see, the value of this measure ranges from -1 to 0, providing a quantitative sense of how difficult it is to find a webpage/resource. Note that this does not help with assessing likelihood of discovery for the webpages that no team/participant found.

7.3.5 Diversity

In addition to the sources that teams visited during the tasks, we could also study how they approach the task in terms of the queries they issued to find information. We can study how similar or different were the queries formulated by participants in a given team. In order to evaluate query diversity, Lavenshtein distance [26] is a good choice for computing the distance between pairs of queries for each team. Based on the results of this computation, for a given pair of queries; the closer the distance to 0, the higher the similarity between them. On the other hand, the higher the distance between queries, more different (therefore diverse) were the queries formulated within a team.

7.4 User Measures

Now we will look at a number of measures that are user-focused. Common ways of collecting data for these measures are through questionnaires, interviews, and focus groups.

7.4.1 Collaborative Aptitude

Based on the principles of collaboration developed by Johnson et al. [9], Olivares [14] developed a set of questions to obtain information about a person's collaborative background. These questions are focused on five dimensions of collaboration as presented below. The original questionnaire was designed to be responded in a 7-points Likert scale, but one could change it to 5-points scale.

1. When I work in a group, it is important that all the work is done by me.
2. If I work in a group, I do everything.
3. When I participate in a group works, it is important that everybody cooperate in order to finish them.
4. When I participate in a team, I cooperate in the work for finishing it.
5. When I work in a group, it is important that everybody make sure to do the tasks they were given.
6. When I work in a group, I make sure to do the tasks that were given to me.

7. When a member of the group make their tasks, it is good for the whole group.
8. When I do my part in a group work, it is good only for me.
9. When group members make sure of performing their tasks, it is good only for them.

---

10. When I do my part in a group work it is good for the rest of the team.
11. When I work in a group, if something goes wrong I am the only responsible.
12. When I work in a group, if something goes wrong the others are responsible of everything.
13. When I work in a group, if something goes wrong all of us are responsible of that.
14. When I work in a group, if the work ends well, I am the only responsible of that.
15. When I work in a group, if the work ends well, all of us are responsible of that.
16. When I work in a group, it is important knowing what tasks have to be performed by each of us.
17. When I work in a group, I am aware of the tasks that my mates have to perform.

---

18. When I work in a group, it is important congratulate to others for what they do well.
19. When I work in a group, I congratulate to others when they do their tasks well.
20. When I participate in a group and others congratulate me for my work, I feel more confident in what I do.
21. When I work in a group, I care that others tell me that I am doing well.
22. When I work in a group, I tell to my mates when they do something well.
23. When I work in a group, it is important to provide help to my mates when they make mistakes or when they do not know what to do.
24. When I work in a group, I provide help to my mates if they make mistakes or if they do not know what to do.
25. When I work in a group, it is important to receive help from others if I have problems in solving something.
26. When I work in a group, I am capable of receiving help from my mates for solving some problem.

---

27. When I work in a group, it is important to agree and coordinate.
28. When I work in a group, I agree with my mates of dividing the work and coordinating.

29. When I work in a group, it is important that each member has a defined task assigned.
30. When I work in a group, we define tasks for each group member.
31. When I work in a group, it is important to feel like doing the task.
32. I like to work in a group.

33. When I work in a group, it is important talk about the things we were done and also about the things that remain for finishing the work.
34. When I work in a group, we meet to talk about the things we have done and also about the things that remain for finishing our work.
35. When I work in a group, it is important to express my opinion about the things that my mates are doing.
36. When I work in a group, I provide ideas and also I comment about my mates' work.
37. When I work in a group, it is important review if we are doing well our work and redistributing tasks if necessary.
38. When I work in a group, we review how we are doing our work and if something goes wrong we exchange tasks.

7.4.2 Usability

Almost any interface-driven system is likely to employ usability measurements for evaluation that involves actual users. Evaluating usability typically involves measuring ease of learning, ease of use, and user satisfaction [13]. It is also common to measure things like effectiveness (typically of accomplishing the task), and efficiency (of the user doing a task). Here we will look at some of the popular instruments used in the literature for measuring various usability aspects during a user study.

Often questions about ease of learning, ease of use, and user satisfaction are combined in one questionnaire. For instance, the participants can be asked to rate (scale 1 to 5 or 1 to 7 is most common) several factors about the system at the end of each session as shown in the following set of questions. The questionnaire was derived from the original Computer System Usability Questionnaire [11],[1] removing those questions that were not relevant for CIS evaluation. Responses to these questions shed light on their perceived ease of use and satisfaction.

---

[1] Also available from http://oldwww.acm.org/perlman/question.cgi?form=CSUQ.

Q1. Overall, I am satisfied with how easy it is to use this system.
Q2. I can effectively complete my work using this system.
Q3. I am able to efficiently complete my work using this system.
Q4. I feel comfortable using this system.
Q5. It was easy to learn to use this system.
Q6. I believe I became productive quickly using this system.
Q7. It is easy to find the information I need.
Q8. The information provided for the system is easy to understand.
Q9. The organization of information on the system screens (toolbar, sidebar) is clear.
Q10. The interface of this system is pleasant.
Q11. I like using the interface of this system.
Q12. This system has all the functions and capabilities I expect it to have.
Q13. Overall, I am satisfied with this system.

7.4.3 Cognitive Load

The mental effort or cognitive load can be measured using a questionnaire derived from NASA's TLX instrument,[2] which can be presented to each participant at the end of every task. The participants can once again be asked to rate each of the following on the scale of 1 to 5/7.

Q1. How mentally demanding was this task? (Very low to Very high)
Q2. How physically demanding was this task? (Very low to Very high)
Q3. How hurried or rushed was the pace of the task? (Very low to Very high)
Q4. How successful were you in accomplishing what you were asked to do? (Perfect to Failure)
Q5. How hard did you have to work to accomplish your level of performance? (Very low to Very high)
Q6. How insecure, discouraged, irritated, stressed, and annoyed were you? (Very low to Very high)

7.4.4 Engagement

Since we are studying interactive collaborative activities, it is important to consider the level of users' engagement through these interactions. In order to measure this,

---

[2]Taken from http://www.cc.gatech.edu/classes/AY2005/cs7470_fall/papers/manual.pdf.

we can ask each participant to individually fill in a questionnaire at the end of the study. This questionnaire was taken from Ghani et al. [7], and consists of questions relating to perceived engagement with the system and the collaborative project. Note that the scale here is for 1–5, but one could make it 1–7.

Using the system was…
Q1. Uninteresting   1 2 3 4 5   Interesting
Q2. Not Enjoyable   1 2 3 4 5   Enjoyable
Q3. Dull   1 2 3 4 5   Exciting
Q4. Not Fun   1 2 3 4 5   Fun

How did you feel while collaborating with this system…
Q5. Not absorbed intensely   1 2 3 4 5   Absorbed intensely
Q6. Attention was not focused   1 2 3 4 5   Attention was focused
Q7. Did not concentrate fully   1 2 3 4 5   Concentrated fully
Q8. Not deeply engrossed   1 2 3 4 5   Deeply engrossed

7.4.5 Awareness

In addition to measuring their perceived awareness about the project, direct questions related to various aspects of situational self-awareness, derived from Govern and Marsch [8], can be asked as shown below for the participants to rate.

Q1. Right now, I am keenly aware of everything in my environment.
Q2. Right now, I am conscious of what is going on around me.
Q3. Right now, I am conscious of all objects around me.
Q4. Right now, I am concerned about what my teammate thinks of me.
Q5. Right now, I am aware of what my teammate just did.
Q6. Right now, I am conscious that my teammate is aware of my actions.
Q7. Right now, I am aware of how well we performed together in the team.

7.4.6 Affects/Emotions

As discussed earlier (Sect. 5.4.1), measuring emotions or affective dimension in a CIS process could be an important part of gaining a comprehensive understanding of the given CIS project and the collaborators involved. There are several methods that we could obtain from psychology and sociology fields. An example is Positive and Negative Affect Scale (PANAS) [27]. This instrument asks users to rate how they are feeling at the moment along 20 different emotional dimensions using 5-point scale. This scale and the list of emotions are given below.

1. Very slightly or not at all
2. A little
3. Moderately
4. Quite a bit
5. Extremely

1. Interested
2. Ashamed
3. Guilty
4. Jittery
5. Irritable
6. Upset
7. Determined
8. Enthusiastic
9. Distressed
10. Inspired
11. Scared
12. Active
13. Alert
14. Strong
15. Attentive
16. Proud
17. Excited
18. Nervous
19. Hostile
20. Afraid

7.5 Case Study

To understand how the measures—both system-based and user-based—could be used in research experiments, we will now look at a laboratory study involving a total of 70 participants—10 participants as single users, and 60 participants as collaborative teams. We will first describe the study procedure, the subjects, the system, the task, and the experimental conditions. Then, we will provide analysis and findings using the measures described in the above two sections. The details of this study

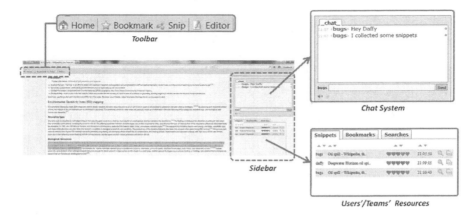

Fig. 7.2 A version of Coagmento used for the study

and the research questions it addressed using the evaluation measures provided here can be found in [20].

7.5.1 Subjects

Participants in this study were asked to sign up in pairs with someone with whom they had previous experience collaborating. In addition, they were informed of their compensation for participating in the study, which consisted of $10 per person and the possibility to obtain additional prizes if they were among the three best performing teams ($50, $25, and $15 per person additionally) at the end of the study. Overall, 60 participants in 30 pairs, all of them students from Rutgers University, were recruited and randomly assigned to different experimental scenarios (described later). In addition, 10 more participants were recruited to work individually in the same search task performed by teams.

7.5.2 System

We used a modified version of browser plugin-based Coagmento available at the time of doing this experiment, which provided appropriate tools and support for the participants working in various conditions. A screenshot of this plugin within Firefox is shown in Fig. 7.2. As shown, the plugin included a toolbar and a sidebar. The toolbar had the following buttons: (1) Home—for taking the participant to appropriate questionnaires, (2) Bookmark—for bookmarking a webpage, (3) Snip—for collecting a snippet using highlighted text from a webpage, and (4) Editor—for accessing a shared editor for writing the report.

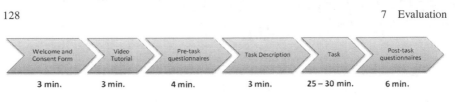

Fig. 7.3 Study session workflow

The sidebar had two major components: a chat-box and a resources panel. The chat-box allowed the collaborators in a given team to communicate with each other. The researcher conducting the study also used it to provide instructions to the participants. The resources panel included tabs for bookmarks, saved snippets, and executed queries.

7.5.3 Session Workflow

Each experimental session lasted less than an hour and was structured in six parts as depicted in Fig. 7.3 and described below.

1. Participants were introduced to the study and asked to sign a consent form.
2. Participants watched a brief tutorial in order to learn the basic functionalities required during the task.
3. Participants individually filled out a set of pre-task questionnaires. In the case of two participants working at the same computer (condition later explained), the participants were separated for this phase.
4. Participants read the task description (given later).
5. Each participant/team worked for approximately 25 minutes on the given task that included searching for relevant information, and using it to compose a report.
6. Participants filled out post-task questionnaires.

The researcher conducting the study communicated with the participants through the chat-box at different times during the study instructing them to start/stop the task or fill in a questionnaire.

7.5.4 Conditions

To study the difference between individual information seeking and CIS, as well as to understand how various CIS settings can affect a collaborative team's effectiveness in accomplishing an information-seeking task, we conducted experiments with four different conditions: single participants, two participants at the same computer, two participants in the same room but different computers, and two participants in different rooms with individual computers. In order to have a baseline to study the synergic effect of collaboration, we artificially created pairs of users from $C1_{SINGLE}$ (single users). We generated all possible combinations of pairs in groups

Table 7.1 Experimental conditions

Condition	Description
$C1_{SINGLE}$	Single participants
$C2_{ARTIFICIAL}$	Artificial team
$C3_{SAME\_COMPUTER}$	Co-located using the same computer
$C4_{SAME\_ROOM}$	Co-located using different computers
$C5_{REMOTE}$	Remotely located

Fig. 7.4 Experimental setup for four different conditions

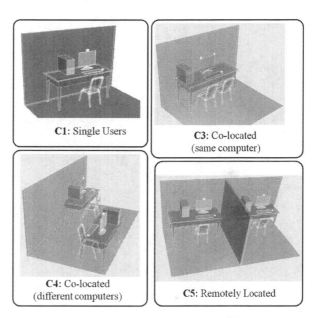

C1: Single Users

C3: Co-located (same computer)

C4: Co-located (different computers)

C5: Remotely Located

of 5, reaching a total of 49 groups and creating 245 artificial teams in total. This was done in order to cover all possible pairs of users while avoiding a given user appearing in more than one team within the same group of teams.

These five conditions are summarized in Table 7.1. Setups for four of these conditions are also depicted in Fig. 7.4. Note that in the real experiment, those in $C5_{REMOTE}$ condition were located in different rooms separated by walls, and not just a partition. They could not see or talk to each other directly, and the only communication channel they had was the text-box provided with the system.

7.5.5 Task

We chose "gulf oil spill" as the topic for this experimentation since it was quite popular and relevant at the time the study was being conducted. Our preliminary investigations, including a few pilot runs, indicated that there was a huge amount of

Table 7.2 Summary of various universes used in our analysis

	Total
Universe of all webpages (U)	562
Universe of unique webpages	377
Universe of all relevant webpages (U_r)	228
Universe of unique relevant webpages	159

material on this topic, and that the participants would find it interesting and challenging enough as an exploratory search task. Each participant was given the following task description.

> A leading newspaper has hired your team to create a comprehensive report on the causes, effects, and consequences of the recent gulf oil spill. As a part of your contract, you are required to collect all the relevant information from any available online sources that you can find. To prepare this report, search and visit any website that you want and look for specific aspects as given in the guideline below. As you find useful information, highlight and save relevant snippets. Make sure you also rate a snippet to help you in ranking them based on their quality and usefulness. Later, you can use these snippets to compile your report, no longer than 200 lines, as instructed. Your report on this topic should address the following issues: description of how the oil spill took place, reactions by BP as well as various government and other agencies, impact on economy and life (people and animals) in the gulf, attempts to fix the leaking well and to clean the waters, long-term implications and lessons learned.

The participants saw this description on the screen (phase 4 in the study), and were also given a printed copy to refer to during their session.

7.5.6　Results and Discussion

In this section, we present our results and their related discussions. To facilitate this, we first provide a summary of all the universal sets in Table 7.2. These sets were used to compute other constructs, such as precision, recall, and unique relevant coverage. Note that the numbers in this table represent the combined output of all the 70 participants.

The analyses reported here were done using one-way ANOVA. We tested for homogeneity of variance and performed appropriate post-hoc tests to measure the difference between the conditions. Note that we will only present the results and what they mean, but not the actual numbers derived from these tests. For that, the reader is recommended to look at Shah and Gonzalez-Ibanez [20].

To begin our analysis, we first looked at simple precision and recall for each condition as defined in the previous section. We found no difference between any of the conditions for precision. This is not surprising considering how it was computed and that it was relatively easy to find relevant results from the web, giving almost everyone a very high value for precision. This high precision was also due to the fact that the relevant set was constructed using the union of the relevance judgments provided by each participant.

We did, however, find differences among the conditions for recall. Not surprisingly, the single users ($C1_{SINGLE}$) had lower recall compared to every other condition except $C3_{SAME\_COMPUTER}$, where two collaborators used the same computer. Similarly, $C3_{SAME\_COMPUTER}$ had lower recall than $C2_{ARTIFICIAL}$, $C4_{SAME\_ROOM}$, or $C5_{REMOTE}$. In other words, teams with individual computers for their collaborators were able to achieve higher recall than those with a single or a shared computer. This was expected since the assigned task was recall-oriented and exploratory in nature, and given the limited amount of time, those with more resources achieved more results. If the task was non-dividable (e.g., brainstorming), we may not have found these differences.

Using F-measure, once again, we found that in real collaboration, those with individual computers ($C4_{SAME\_ROOM}$ and $C5_{REMOTE}$) outperformed those with shared computers ($C3_{SAME\_COMPUTER}$).

While precision and recall correspond to relevance in the traditional IR sense, they are not very appropriate in the present CIS setting given that the participants were searching the web, where a huge amount of information on the given topic existed, and that each participant/team was given the same amount of limited time, in which they could easily find a good amount of relevant information. Given this, a more important and interesting aspect to investigate here is coverage—a measure of the amount of information explored. Just as in recall, we found those with two people and two computers were able to cover more information than those with only one person and/or one workstation.

To extend our investigation for coverage, we looked at unique coverage for each individual/team, which is defined as the set of unique webpages that one covered and others did not. We found that $C4_{SAME\_ROOM}$ and $C5_{REMOTE}$ came out on the top with this measure, indicating their effectiveness in covering information that others could not. In fact, $C5_{REMOTE}$ outperformed not only $C1_{SINGLE}$ and $C3_{SAME\_COMPUTER}$, but also $C2_{ARTIFICIAL}$. In other words, when two real collaborators worked in remote CIS, they were able to cover more unique information than artificially created pairs of collaborators. Given that $C2_{ARTIFICIAL}$ and $C4_{SAME\_ROOM}$ had no difference, we can say that there is a value in remote collaboration when the task has clear independent components, and at the same time, having interactions that one finds in a real collaboration helps over completely working independently as $C2_{ARTIFICIAL}$ participants did.

We also looked at how much of the unique coverage was actually relevant, and found that $C5_{REMOTE}$ did better than $C1_{SINGLE}$ and $C3_{SAME\_COMPUTER}$. While we found no difference between $C2_{ARTIFICIAL}$ and $C4_{SAME\_ROOM}$ or $C5_{REMOTE}$, we can clearly see that those in $C5_{REMOTE}$ were able to get to the information

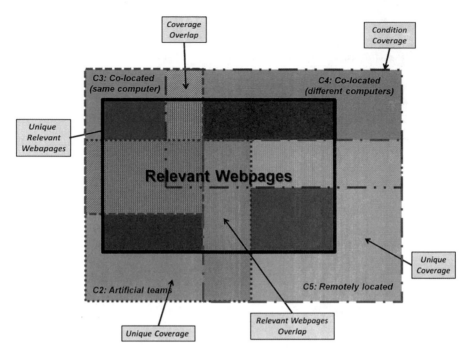

Fig. 7.5 Depiction of coverage by various conditions (drawn to scale)

that is not discovered by single users ($C1_{SINGLE}$), collaborators at the same computer ($C3_{SAME\_COMPUTER}$), or artificially created collaboration ($C2_{ARTIFICIAL}$). At the same time, the amount of unique relevant information that they discovered was found to be significantly more than what was found by $C1_{SINGLE}$ or $C3_{SAME\_COMPUTER}$. In other words, remotely located teams were able to leverage real interactions (as opposed to no interactions in artificial teams), and at the same time carry on independent exploration to achieve the synergic effect through collaboration.

Figure 7.5 provides a depiction of various forms of coverage for $C2_{ARTIFICIAL}$, $C3_{SAME\_COMPUTER}$, $C4_{SAME\_ROOM}$, and $C5_{REMOTE}$. The figure is drawn to scale, with the area of a coverage region, proportional to the value of that kind of coverage for a given condition. Visually also, we could see that $C5_{REMOTE}$ has more coverage (total and unique), as well as more unique relevant coverage.

Moving beyond information exploration and relevancy, we looked at the usefulness of viewed information. As defined in the previous section, this referred to visiting webpages that one spends considerable amount of time (30 seconds or more).

We found that $C1_{SINGLE}$ and $C3_{SAME\_COMPUTER}$ visited significantly fewer useful webpages than those by $C4_{SAME\_ROOM}$ and $C5_{REMOTE}$ participants. More importantly, real teams with individual computers ($C4_{SAME\_ROOM}$ and $C5_{REMOTE}$) outperformed artificial teams ($C2_{ARTIFICIAL}$) when it came to visiting useful webpages, including the webpages that were unique to a given team. In other words,

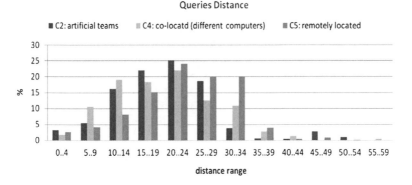

Fig. 7.6 Query distance for $C2_{\text{ARTIFICIAL}}$, $C4_{\text{SAME\_ROOM}}$, and $C5_{\text{REMOTE}}$ using Lavenshtein algorithm

with real collaboration, the teams were able to avoid overlapping their exploration and reach out to more sources of information. This is important for exploratory and recall-oriented search task like the one used for our study.

In addition, we found that $C4_{\text{SAME\_ROOM}}$ and $C5_{\text{REMOTE}}$ participants visited many more difficult to reach (less likely visited) webpages than those in $C1_{\text{SINGLE}}$. This shows that collaboration, in this case, allowed a unit (a pair or users) get to the information that was otherwise ignored by those who worked alone. In fact, even when we combined two independent participants' explorations ($C2_{\text{ARTIFICIAL}}$), those who collaborated while remotely located ($C5_{\text{REMOTE}}$) could discover more information. Once again, $C5_{\text{REMOTE}}$ participants leveraged on the interactions through real collaboration while exercising their independence and exploring individual information trails.

To understand searching behavior of various individuals and teams, we looked at their querying effectiveness. Given that the assigned task was exploratory in nature, that there was plethora of useful information on the web, and that the time was limited, it was important that the participants construct a variety of queries and cover as large a ground as they could. To measure this, we computed query diversity for each participant/team as defined previously. A general overview of query distances for each condition is given in Fig. 7.6. Those in $C4_{\text{SAME\_ROOM}}$ had more queries with higher distances among them. In other words, those in $C5_{\text{REMOTE}}$ tried more diverse queries.

Using ANOVA, we found that those in real collaborations with individual computers and remotely located ($C5_{\text{REMOTE}}$) had higher diversity in their queries than those co-located using different computers ($C4_{\text{SAME\_ROOM}}$). $C5_{\text{REMOTE}}$ participants also exhibited a larger variety in their queries than those by artificially created teams ($C2_{\text{ARTIFICIAL}}$). Combining these two facts indicates that (1) participants remotely located were able to successfully divide the task up and explore unique information through different queries, and (2) these participants had a chance to work more independently than those in the same space.

We believe that query similarity for teams in $C4_{SAME\_ROOM}$ is due to space sharing, which may influence the way in which users formulated their queries. Even though most teams split up the task, the physical closeness of users could enable them to hear what their peers think aloud; or even have brief conversations (facilitated by face-to-face interaction). This may have influenced implicitly common queries between those participants. On the other hand, we think that users working remotely located and using only text chat for communicating with each other ($C5_{REMOTE}$) were more able to generate different queries because they were less directly influenced by their peers during the task.

Fidel et al. [5] showed that collaboration induces additional cognitive load, what they referred to as the *collaborative load*. Often, this is the price to pay for gaining the advantages of collaborating. We used NASA's TLX instrument to measure user perceived cognitive load during the task (see the previous section). For analysis, we combined the responses obtained from six different questions and created an index, since these responses were found to be statistically reliable for this instrument.

Using this index, we performed the ANOVA and found no difference between the four conditions. This indicates that the participants who worked in collaboration ($C3_{SAME\_COMPUTER}$, $C4_{SAME\_ROOM}$, and $C5_{REMOTE}$) experienced no more cognitive load than what was reported by those in $C1_{SINGLE}$. In other words, the collaborators in our experiment (at least $C4_{SAME\_ROOM}$ and $C5_{REMOTE}$) were able to gain the advantages of creating synergy without additional mental load.

7.5.7 Conclusion

Using a user study with 70 participants working on an information-seeking task in different setups, we showed how various evaluation measures could be defined and operationalized. Here, we summarize our findings and their implications.

It is argued that the traditional measures of evaluating relevance are not appropriate for such situations, and proposed either modified or new kinds of evaluations. These included coverage, usefulness, likelihood of discovery, and query diversity. We believe this itself is an important contribution to the community, helping the researchers evaluate and design CIS systems and interfaces. The results of the experiments reported here indicated that in a recall-oriented exploratory search task, two collaborators working at the same computer achieve similar results to the individual users. It also became clear that those in remote collaboration were able to work more independently than those that were co-located. Independence is considered an important characteristic of a successful collaboration [18, 24]. Our results also provided a strong support for synergic effect in remotely located collaborators. In particular, we showed that two people working in collaboration ($C4_{SAME\_ROOM}$ and $C5_{REMOTE}$) is not the same as having the outcomes of two completely independent individuals combined ($C2_{ARTIFICIAL}$); they do better in terms of discovering more and diverse information for an information-seeking task. Not only that, but the cognitive load in a real collaborative situation was found to be no more than what was perceived by those working individually. Thus, the synergic effect of the whole being greater than the sum of all was demonstrated and evaluated.

We also want to point out a few of the limitations of these experiments. The study reported here was conducted with synchronous CIS task. The findings may be impacted if the collaborators were working asynchronously. Due to the nature of the laboratory study, we also gave a limited amount of time to the participants. It has been shown that collaborations lasting longer and done over multiple sessions may produce significantly different results and user experiences [18, 19]. Having more than two participants per team could also lead to different group dynamics, influencing the results. Despite these limitations, we believe the methodology and the evaluation measures proposed and demonstrated here could help us further investigations of CIS with different setups, including asynchronous, non-time bound, multi-session, and non-dividable tasks, as well as collaborations that involve more than two participants. These contributions could be helpful for not just CIS, but IR in general.

7.6 Summary

Evaluation is always one of the core and often challenging issues of any information seeking/retrieval problem. Collaboration adds another level of complexity on top of it. It is not just the act of collaboration during information seeking process that increases the complexity of evaluation for CIS, but also everything else that collaboration causes or requires. For example, it is probably not very helpful to collaborate over simple fact-finding tasks, and so when we see collaboration in information seeking, we invariably deal with complex information needs, with seeking/searching processes spanning over multiple sessions. Thus, one needs to look at various elements of interactive IR, user and system efficiency and effectiveness, user engagement, learning and satisfaction, as well as social and even cultural dimensions of information seeking.

The current chapter introduced several methodologies from the literature for evaluating CIR/CIS systems and environments before providing a more detailed list of numerous system and user-based measurements. A case study was presented to show how these measures can be used and what we can learn from them. Let us end this discussion by noting that one needs to employ several measures for evaluating any useful CIS system to be able to explain and compare the effectiveness of that system/technique/approach.

References

1. Maria Aneiros and Vladimir Estivill-Castro. Usability of real-time unconstrained WWW-co-browsing for educational settings. In *Proceedings of the IEEE/WIC International Conference on Web Intelligence*, pages 105–111, Compiègne University of Technology, France, September 2005.

2. Ricardo Baeza-Yates and Jose A. Pino. A first step to formally evaluate collaborative work. In *Proceedings of GROUP*, pages 56–60, 1997.
3. Marcia J. Bates. Information search tactics. *Journal of the American Society for Information Science*, 30(4):205–214, 1979.
4. N.J. Belkin, P.G. Marchetti and C. Cool. BRAQUE: design of an interface to support user interaction in information retrieval. *Information Processing and Management*, 29(3):325–344, 1993.
5. Raya Fidel, Annelise Mark Pejtersen, Bryan Cleal and Harry Bruce. A multidimensional approach to the study of human-information interaction: A case study of collaborative information retrieval. *Journal of the American Society for Information Science and Technology*, 55(11):939–953, 2004.
6. S. Fox, K. Karnawat, M. Mydland, S. Dumais and T. White. Evaluating implicit measures to improve web search. *ACM Transactions on Information Systems*, 23(2):147–168, 2005.
7. Jawaid A. Ghani, Roberta Supnick and Pamela Rooney. The experience of flow in computer-mediated and in face-to-face groups. In *Proceedings of International Conference on Information Systems*, pages 229–237, University of Minnesota, Minneapolis, MN, USA, 1991.
8. John M. Govern and Lisa A. Marsch. Development and validation of the situational self-awareness scale. *Consciousness and Cognition*, 10(3):366–378, 2001.
9. D. Johnson, R. Johnson, E. Holubec and P. Roy. *Circles of Learning. Cooperation in the Classroom*. Association for Supervision and Curriculum Development, Alexandria, 1984.
10. Yann Laurillau and Laurence Nigay. CoVitesse: a groupware interface for collaborative navigation on the WWW. In *Proceedings of the ACM Conference on Computer Supported Cooperative Work (CSCW)*, pages 236–240, New Orleans, Louisiana, USA, November 2002.
11. J.R. Lewis. IBM computer usability satisfaction questionnaires: psychometric evaluation and instructions for use. *International Journal of Human-Computer Interaction*, 7(1):57–58, 1995.
12. Meredith Ringel Morris and Eric Horvitz. SearchTogether: an interface for collaborative web search. In *ACM Symposium on User Interface Software and Technology (UIST)*, pages 3–12, Newport, RI, October 2007.
13. Jakob Nielsen. Usability inspection methods. In *Conference Companion on Human Factors in Computing Systems—CHI '94*, pages 413–414, New York, USA, April 1994. ACM, New York.
14. R. Olivares. *Evaluación del Impacto de un Juego Colaborativo Basado en Computador en el Apoyo al Aprendizaje de la Colaboración en Escolares de Enseñanza Básica*. Master's thesis, Universidad de Santiago de Chile, Santiago, Chile, 2006.
15. Gary M. Olson, Judith S. Olson, Mark R. Carter and Marianne Storrosten. Small Group Design Meetings: An Analysis of Collaboration. *Human-Computer Interaction*, 7(4):347–374, 1992.
16. Jeremy Pickens, Gene Golovchinsky, Chirag Shah, Pernilla Qvarfordt and Maribeth Back. Algorithmic mediation for collaborative exploratory search. In *Proceedings of the Annual ACM Conference on Research and Development in Information Retrieval (SIGIR)*, Singapore, July 2008.
17. Paul Prekop. A qualitative study of collaborative information seeking. *Journal of Documentation*, 58(5):538–547, 2002.
18. Chirag Shah. Working in collaboration—what, why, and how. In *Proceedings of Collaborative Information Retrieval workshop at CSCW 2010*, Savannah, GA, 2010.
19. Chirag Shah and Roberto Gonzalez-Ibanez. Exploring information seeking processes in collaborative search tasks. In *Annual Meeting of the American Society for Information Science*, Pittsburgh, PA, 2010.
20. Chirag Shah and Roberto Gonzalez-Ibanez. Evaluating the synergic effect of collaboration in information seeking. In *Proceedings of the Annual ACM Conference on Research and Development in Information Retrieval (SIGIR)*, pages 913–922, Beijing, China, 2011.
21. Chirag Shah, Jeremy Pickens and Gene Golovchinsky. Role-based results redistribution for collaborative information retrieval. *Information Processing & Management*, 46(6):773–781, 2010.

22. Barry Smyth, Evelyn Balfe, Oisin Boydell, Keith Bradley, Peter Briggs, Maurice Coyle and Jill Freyne. A live-user evaluation of collaborative web search. In *Proceedings of the International Joint Conference on Artificial Intelligence (IJCAI)*, Edinburgh, Scotland, July 2005.
23. Barry Smyth, Evelyn Balfe, Peter Briggs, Maurice Coyle and Jill Freyne. Collaborative web search. In *Proceedings of the International Joint Conference on Artificial Intelligence (IJCAI)*, pages 1417–1419, Acapulco, Mexico, August 2003. Morgan Kaufmann, San Mateo.
24. James Surowiecki. *Wisdom of Crowds: Why the Many Are Smarter Than the Few and How Collective Wisdom Shapes Business, Economies, Societies and Nations*. Doubleday, New York, 2004.
25. Michael B. Twidale, David M. Nichols and Chris D. Paice. Supporting collaborative learning during information searching. In *Proceedings of Computer Supported Collaborative Learning (CSCL)*, pages 367–374, Bloomington, Indiana, 1995.
26. Robert A. Wagner and Michael J. Fischer. The string-to-string correction problem. *Journal of the ACM*, 21(1):168–173, 1974.
27. David Watson, Lee A. Clark and Auke Tellegen. Development and validation of brief measures of positive and negative affect: The PANAS scales. *Journal of Personality and Social Psychology*, 54(6):1063–1070, 1988.
28. Ryen W. White and Jeff Huang. Assessing the scenic route: measuring the value of search trails in web logs. In *Proceedings of the 33rd International ACM SIGIR Conference on Research and Development in Information Retrieval (SIGIR 2010)*, pages 587–594, 2010.
29. Max L. Wilson and m.c. schraefel. Evaluating collaborative search interfaces with information seeking theory. In *Workshop on Collaborative Information Retrieval*, Pittsburgh, PA, June 2008.

Chapter 8
Conclusion

Abstract Collaborative information seeking (CIS) sits at a very interesting intersection of information seeking/retrieval, computer-supported cooperative work (CSCW), human–computer interaction (HCI), and social media/networking. Through an extensive review of a number of works, which included theories, models, and systems, we saw how one could understand, study, and develop for CIS. In this final chapter, we wrap up our discussion on this topic with a look to the future. There are several interesting questions remaining to be addressed in the field of CIS. This chapter highlights some of these questions, along with suggestions to extend the work reported here.

8.1 CIS—Looking Back, Looking Forward

Collaborative information seeking (CIS) stands at a very interesting intersection. It is a relatively young field that has been shaped by several veteran domains such as IR, CSCW/groupware, and HCI. While CIS today retains the traces of these domains due to its interdisciplinary nature, it is also constantly evolving and creating its own identity through carving out a unique space of research problems. Figure 8.1 depicts CIS as an interdisciplinary field that is at the intersection of Information seeking, collaboration, CSCW, HCI, and social media/networking. Also shown in the figure are some of the issues that emerge from different aspects of CIS field. For instance, one interested in the HCI aspect of CIS may need to think about issues such as interface design for CIS systems, reducing collaborative load to the participants, and providing appropriate amounts and kinds of awareness.

The following two sections will take a detailed look at many of these issues in CIS that are divided into theoretical and experimental categories.

8.2 Theoretical Issues

Despite the importance of studying CIS and providing solutions that support it, there is a lack of comparable CIS theories and models similar to those that exist for individuals information seeking, such as Belkin [2], Marchionini [7], and Wilson [13].

C. Shah, *Collaborative Information Seeking*, The Information Retrieval Series 34,
DOI 10.1007/978-3-642-28813-5_8, © Springer-Verlag Berlin Heidelberg 2012

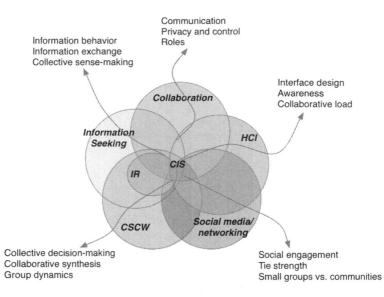

Fig. 8.1 CIS as an interdisciplinary field, along with some of the issues stemming from different parts of it

Development of sustainable CIS models will depend on addressing some of the fundamental issues in the field, including user motivations and methods for collaboration, social aspects of working in collaboration, individual and group benefits, user roles, CIS system design challenges, as well as evaluating a number of aspects about the user and the system in a CIS environment.

Similarly, there is a need to identify and understand information synthesis and sense-making processes that take place when people work in collaboration. We have models for information search processes (ISP), such as the one by Kuhlthau [5, 6], and a mapping of this model to CIS [3, 4, 12]. Similar extensions need to be explored that look at not only ISP, but also other processes in collaboration context, as well as extending such mappings beyond office environments.

A few works, such as Reddy and Jansen [10], have looked at collaborative information behavior (CIB) in specific setups such as healthcare. Such efforts need to be extended further encompassing more situations and domains.

Following is a list of specific issues and questions on the theoretical front of CIS that we need to address next.

1. We have a fairly good understanding of why people collaborate. However, these motivations are often not identified in the context of situations in which collaboration occurs. Often, even if collaboration can be useful, people do not see the value in collaborating. We need to identify such situations and learn to promote collaboration to people. Similarly, the literature points us to a list of tools and methods that people use for collaborating. However, the relative merits of these tools and methods are not very clear. Often people collaborate using tools that were not specifically designed for collaboration. One could argue that we need

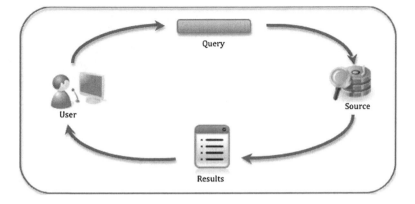

Fig. 3.2 A typical scenario of information seeking in an IR environment

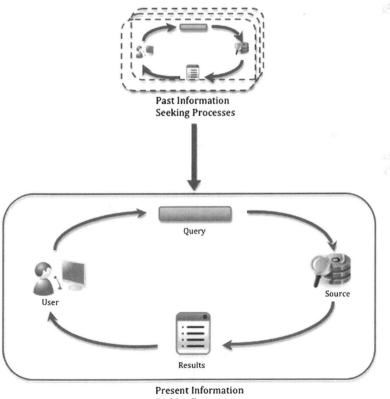

Fig. 3.3 Content-based information filtering

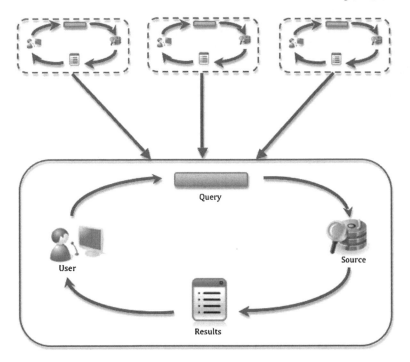

Fig. 3.4 Collaborative information filtering

seeking behavior of other users to aid the given user in his process of information seeking. Typically, these mappings are done based on like-interests among the users. For instance, if users A and B both liked x, and if A liked y, there are good chances that B will also like y. Thus, the system will recommend y to B. In the literature, such kinds of recommendation are called collaborative recommendation [1].

It is also possible to combine the two kinds of approaches described above combined to create a hybrid approach.

As we saw earlier, collaboration among users based on common information need and asynchronous communication flow results in collaborative filtering. In other words, collaborative filtering refers to a process in which a user benefits from other users' past actions on the same/similar information seeking tasks. In practice, this concept is realized as recommender systems. Examples of such applications include Amazon.com [38], movies recommendations by MovieLens [41], and news filtering by VERSIFI Technologies [7].

Often the systems that are built for supporting collaborative filtering are promoted as CIS systems. A typical characteristic of such systems is a way to combine information requests and/or results in some way. However, due to asynchronous and unidirectional interactive nature of these systems, they do not fulfill the requirements for CIS that is of interest here. An example of this can be found in the work by Klink [33], where a method for improving the original query by an automatic reformulation method is proposed. This method uses the term-concept correspondence learned from the documents given by the feedback of the actual or of the other users. Here, there is no direct interaction among the users of the system to carry out a common goal. Thus, even though the users are benefiting from their own or other users' past behavior (content-based or collaborative filtering), they are not collaborating in a strict sense.

Furnas [19] demonstrated the power of community knowledge and collaborative filtering with his adaptive indexing scheme, which helps re-weight indexing terms by the past usage of more experienced users. Along the line of reformulating the queries, Hust et al. [27] showed how to use previously learned queries and their relevant documents for improving overall retrieval quality of an issued query. They do so by expanding the new query by extracting terms from documents which have been judged as relevant to previously learned queries. This approach is further formalized in Hust et al. [26], and [25]. Once again, we see that objects and actions from the past are used to improve retrieval effectiveness, but the "interactions" among the users were asynchronous and unidirectional.

Similarly, Romano Jr. et al. [49] presented *Collaborative Information Retrieval Environment* (CIRE), a system architecture constructed using the user experiences with IR and Group Support Systems (GSS). Their prototype system employed a client-server architecture, where the server was responsible for connecting the client requests to the AltaVista search engine and recording all the interactions as well as annotations by the participants. The executed queries, stored search results, annotations, and relevance judgments are shared among the group members to facilitate collaborative IR. This is similar to Smyth's I-Spy system,[2] in which the participants of a workgroup can benefit from others' searches on the same/similar topics. Once again, such systems or environments facilitate collaborative filtering rather than an active and interactive collaboration among the information seeking participants.

How Information Filtering Relates to CIS   It is important to note here that in many of these applications, a user receiving the recommendations may not know the other users in the network personally. Thus, a user is not *intentionally* and *interactively engaged* in a true collaboration with other users; he is merely getting filtered content based on other users' actions on the similar information. There have been some applications that go beyond such a constraint and exploit more tightly connected social networks of a user instead of the entire network to filter and recommend information. For instance, Kautz et al. [31] presented *ReferralWeb*, which was based on providing recommendations via chains of named entities instead of anonymous users in the network.

In addition to this difference, the goal of collaborative filtering systems is to use the opinions of a community of users to help individuals identify content of interest with ease from a potentially overwhelming set of choices [48]. Looking carefully, we can see that the flow of information and the direction of filtering at a given time is only one way (shown in Fig. 3.4). Collaboratively seeking information, on the

---

[2]This has been transposed to HeyStaks (http://www.heystaks.com/).

other hand, involves both the agents actively engaging in an information sharing situation; thus making the flow of information and filtering in both the directions at any given moment.

Another characteristic of a typical information filtering system is the asynchronous nature of user interaction. A user of an information filtering system is provided with the filtered information based on the actions that other users took in the past. In contrast, the focus of the work related to CIS is on active user interaction among the users of a system who are working in the *same time frame*.[3]

References

1. Gediminas Adomavicius and Alexander Tuzhilin. Toward the next generation of recommender systems: a survey of the state-of-the-art and possible extensions. *IEEE Transactions on Knowledge and Data Engineering*, 17(6):734–749, 2005.
2. Saleema Amershi and Meredith Ringel Morris. CoSearch: a system for co-located collaborative Web search. In *Proceedings of ACM SIGCHI Conference on Human Factors in Computing Systems*, pages 1647–1656, Florence, Italy, April 2008..
3. Maria Aneiros and Vladimir Estivill-Castro. Foundations of unconstrained collaborative web browsing with awareness. In *Proceedings of the IEEE/WIC International Conference on Web Intelligence*, pages 18–25, Beijing, China, October 2003.
4. R.M. Baecker. *Readings in Human–Computer Interaction: Towards the Year 2000*. Morgan Kaufmann, San Mateo, 1995.
5. Nicholas J. Belkin and W. Bruce Croft. Information filtering and information retrieval: two sides of the same coin? *Communications of the ACM*, 35(12):29–38, 1992.
6. Berelson, Lazarsfeld and McPhee. *Voting*. University of Chicago Press, Chicago, 1954.
7. Daniel Billsus, Clifford A. Brunk, Craig Evans, Brian Gladish and Michael Pazzani. Adaptive interfaces for ubiquitous web access. *Communications of the ACM*, 45(5):34–38, 2002.
8. Alan F. Blackwell, Mark Stringer, Eleanor F. Toye and Jennifer A. Rode. Tangible interface for collaborative information retrieval. In *Proceedings of ACM SIGCHI Conference on Human Factors in Computing Systems*, pages 1473–1476. Vienna, Austria, April 2004. ACM, New York.
9. C. Blake and W. Pratt. Collaborative information synthesis {I}: a model of information behaviors of scientists in medicine and public health. *Journal of the American Society for Information Science and Technology*, 57(13):1740–1749, 2006.
10. Harry Bruce, Raya Fidel, Annelise Mark Pejtersen, Susan T. Dumais, Jonathan Grudin and Steven Poltrock. A comparison of the collaborative information retrieval behaviour of two design teams. *The New Review of Information Behaviour Research*, 4(1):139–153, 2003.
11. Giacomo Cabri, Letizia Leonardi and Franco Zambonelli. Supporting cooperative WWW browsing: a proxy-based approach. Technical report, University of Modena, Italy, 1999.
12. Judith S. Donath and Niel Robertson. The sociable web. In *Proceedings of the World Wide Web (WWW) Conference*, CERN, Geneva, Switzerland, 1994.
13. Alan W. Esenther. Instant co-browsing: lightweight real-time collaborative web browsing. In *Proceedings of the World Wide Web (WWW) Conference*, pages 107–114, Honolulu, Hawaii, USA, May 2002.
14. Brynn M. Evans and Ed H. Chi. Towards a model of understanding social search. In *Proceedings of JCDL 2008 Workshop on Collaborative Exploratory Search*, Pittsburgh, PA, June 2008.

---

[3]It is not implied here that the interactions should be strictly synchronous; they simply need to be in the *same time frame*, letting the users work synchronously or asynchronously as needed.

15. Raya Fidel, Harry Bruce, Susan T. Dumais, Jonathan Grudin, Steven Poltrock and Annelise Mark Pejtersen. Collaborative Information Retrieval. Technical report, University of Washington, March 1999.
16. Raya Fidel, Harry Bruce, Annelise Mark Pejtersen, Susan T. Dumais, Jonathan Grudin and Steven Poltrock. Collaborative Information Retrieval (CIR). *The New Review of Information Behaviour Research*, 1(1):235–247, 2000.
17. J. Foster. Collaborative information seeking and retrieval. *Annual Review of Information Science and Technology (ARIST)*, 40:329–356, 2006.
18. Jill Freyne, Barry Smyth, Maurice Coyle, Evelyn Balfe and Peter Briggs. Further experiments on collaborative ranking in community-based web search. *Artificial Intelligence Review*, 21:229–252, 2004.
19. George W. Furnas. Experience with an adaptive indexing scheme. In *Proceedings of ACM SIGCHI Conference on Human Factors in Computing Systems*, pages 131–135, 1985.
20. Luca Gerosa, Alessandra Giordani, Marco Ronchetti, Amy Soller and Ron Stevens. Symmetric synchronous collaborative navigation. In *Proceedings of the 2004 IADIS International WWW/Internet Conference*, pages 1–7, Madrid, Spain, October 2004.
21. T.C. Nicholas Graham. GroupScape: integrating synchronous groupware and the World Wide Web. In *Proceedings of INTERACT*, Sydney, Australia, July 1997. Chapman and Hall, London.
22. Saul Greenberg and Mark Roseman. GroupWeb: A WWW browser as real time groupware. In *Proceedings of ACM SIGCHI Conference on Human Factors in Computing Systems*, pages 271–272, Boston, MA, November 1996. ACM Press, New York.
23. Richard Han, Veronique Perret and Mahmoud Naghshineh. WebSplitter: a unified XML framework for multi-device collaborative web browsing. In *Proceedings of Computer Supported Cooperative Work (CSCW)*, pages 221–230. ACM Press, New York, 2000.
24. Morten Hertzum. Collaborative information seeking: the combined activity of information seeking and collaborative grounding. *Information Processing and Management*, 44:957–962, 2008.
25. Armin Hust. Query expansion methods for collaborative information retrieval. *Informatik*, 19(4):224–238, 2005.
26. Armin Hust, Markus Junker and Andreas Dengel. A mathematical model for improving retrieval performance in collaborative information retrieval. *Kluwer Information Retrieval Special Issue: Advances in Mathematical/Formal Methods in Information Retrieval*, pages 1–28, 2004.
27. Armin Hust, Stefan Klink, Markus Junker and Andreas Dengel. Query reformulation in collaborative information retrieval. In *Information and Knowledge Sharing*, 2002.
28. Jette Hyldegard. Collaborative information behaviour—exploring Kuhlthau's Information Search Process model in a group-based educational setting. *Information Processing and Management*, 42:276–298, 2006.
29. Jette Hyldegard. Beyond the search process—exploring group members' information behavior in context. *Information Processing and Management*, 45:142–158, 2009.
30. Murat Karamuftuoglu. Collaborative information retrieval: toward a social informatics view of IR interaction. *Journal of the American Society for Information Science*, 49(12):1070–1080, 1998.
31. Henry Kautz, Bart Selman and Mehul Shah. Referral Web: combining social networks and collaborative filtering. *Communications of the ACM*, 40(3):63–65, 1997.
32. Richard M. Keller, Shawn R. Wolfe, James R. Chen, Joshua L. Rabinowitz and Nathalie Mathe. A bookmarking service for organizing and sharing URLs. *Computer Networks and ISDN Systems*, 29:1103–1114, 1997.
33. Stefan Klink. Query reformulation with collaborative concept-based expansion. In *First International Workshop on Web Document Analysis*, pages 19–22, 2001.
34. R. Krishnappa. Multi-user search engine: supporting collaborative information seeking and retrieval. Master's thesis, University of Missouri-Rolla, 2005.

35. Carol C. Kuhlthau. Towards collaboration between information seeking and information retrieval. *Information Research*, 10(2), 2005.
36. Yann Laurillau. Synchronous collaborative navigation on the WWW. In *Proceedings of ACM SIGCHI Conference on Human Factors in Computing Systems*, pages 308–309, 1999.
37. Yann Laurillau and Laurence Nigay. CoVitesse: a groupware interface for collaborative navigation on the WWW. In *Proceedings of the ACM Conference on Computer Supported Cooperative Work (CSCW)* pages 236–240, New Orleans, Louisiana, USA, November 2002.
38. G. Linden, B. Smith and J. York. Amazon.com recommendations: item-to-item collaborative filtering. *IEEE Internet Computing*, 7(1):76–80, 2003.
39. George Lucas. American Graffitti. Movie, 1973.
40. Vladimir Menkov, David J. Neu and Qin Shi. AntWorld: a collaborative web search tool. In *Workshop on Distributed Communities on the Web (DCW)*, Quebec City, Quebec, Canada, June 2000.
41. S.M. Miller and C.E. Mangan. Interesting effects of information and coping style in adapting to gynaecological stress: should a doctor tell all? *Journal of Personality and Social Psychology*, 45:223–226, 1983.
42. Meredith Ringel Morris and Eric Horvitz. SearchTogether: an interface for collaborative web search. In *ACM Symposium on User Interface Software and Technology (UIST)*, pages 3–12, Newport, RI, October 2007.
43. Gary M. Olson, Judith S. Olson, Mark R. Carter and Marianne Storrosten. Small group design meetings: an analysis of collaboration. *Human–Computer Interaction*, 7(4):347–374, 1992.
44. Jeremy Pickens and Gene Golovchinsky. Collaborative exploratory search. In *Proceedings of Workshop on Human–Computer Interaction and Information Retrieval*, pages 21–22, MIT CSAIL, Cambridge, Massachusetts, USA, October 2007.
45. Jeremy Pickens, Gene Golovchinsky, Chirag Shah, Pernilla Qvarfordt and Maribeth Back. Algorithmic mediation for collaborative exploratory search. In *Proceedings of the Annual ACM Conference on Research and Development in Information Retrieval (SIGIR)* Singapore, July 2008.
46. Steven Poltrock, Jonathan Grudin, Susan T. Dumais, Raya Fidel, Harry Bruce and Annelise Mark Pejtersen. Information seeking and sharing in design teams. In *GROUP*, pages 239–247, 2003.
47. M.C. Reddy and B.J. Jansen. A model for understanding collaborative information behavior in context: a study of two healthcare teams. *Information Processing and Management*, 44(1):256–273, 2008.
48. Paul Resnick and Hal R. Varian. Recommender systems. *Communications of the ACM*, 40(3):56–58, 1997.
49. Nicholas C. Romano Jr., Dmitri Roussinov, Jay F. Nunamaker Jr. and Chen Hsinshun. Collaborative information retrieval environment: integration of information retrieval with group support systems. In *Proceedings of the 32nd Hawaii International Conference on System Sciences*, pages 1–10, 1999.
50. Robert W. Root. Design of a multi-media vehicle for social browsing. In *Proceedings of the Conference on Computer-Supported Cooperative Work (CSCW)*, pages 25–38, 1988.
51. Chirag Shah. A framework to support user-centric collaborative information seeking, 2010.
52. Barry Smyth, Evelyn Balfe, Peter Briggs, Maurice Coyle and Jill Freyne. Collaborative web search. In *Proceedings of the International Joint Conference on Artificial Intelligence (IJCAI)*, pages 1417–1419, Acapulco, Mexico, August 2003. Morgan Kaufmann, San Mateo.
53. Michael B. Twidale and David M. Nichols. Collaborative browsing and visualisation of the search process. *Aslib Proceedings*, 48(7–8):177–182, 1996.

Part II
Conceptual Understanding of CIS

This part is focused on CIS as a stand-alone domain. A series of frameworks, theories, and models will be introduced to provide a conceptual ground for CIS.

"Teamwork is the ability to work together toward a common vision; the ability to direct individual accomplishment toward organizational objectives. It is the fuel that allows common people to attain uncommon results."

Andrew Carnegie

Chapter 4
Frameworks for CIS Research and Development

Abstract Before one could start investigating various aspects and issues of CIS, or developing solutions to address them, it is important to have ways to think about them. Several frameworks are found in the relevant literature, which form the basis for the current chapter. It starts with the most common and probably the longest established framework with time and space as the primary dimensions, and moves to more complex and comprehensive frameworks of group activities. Next, it extends space–time framework with the additional dimension of users. Then it discusses the issues of control, communication, and awareness in CIS environments. Finally, the chapter introduces a more comprehensive model of group activities with twelve different dimensions.

4.1 Introduction

The previous section of the book introduced the readers to general concepts of collaboration, information seeking, and CIS. Now the question is—how does one study CIS? What mental models and frameworks are available? What aspects should be considered while developing or evaluating CIS systems? All of these questions ask for ways to think about and investigate CIS-related concepts, issues, and applications. This element of work on CIS, viz., identifying appropriate frameworks is extremely important for researchers and developers alike. It provides researchers ways to compartmentalize various aspects or issues related to CIS for conducting better scientific studies, and it allows developers to create and test CIS solutions with well-balanced trade-offs for a given situation.

Of course, as one may imagine, there is no perfect framework for CIS despite several recent attempts to provide one (e.g., [14, 34]). Therefore, we will start with the most common and longest-established framework of space–time dimensions, and then more toward other variations as well as more complex frameworks. Which of these works or helps one will depend on context and applications.

4.2 Space and Time Aspects of CIS

The classical way of organizing collaborative activities is based on two factors: location and time [30]. Recently, Hansen and Jarvelin [16] and Golovchinsky et al. [14]

C. Shah, *Collaborative Information Seeking*, The Information Retrieval Series 34,
DOI 10.1007/978-3-642-28813-5_4, © Springer-Verlag Berlin Heidelberg 2012

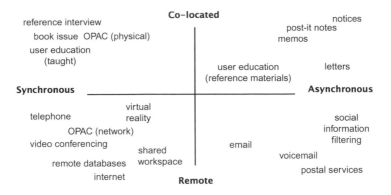

Fig. 4.1 Space–time dimensions for library activities [43]. Permit pending

also classified approaches to collaborative IR using these two dimensions of space and time. Figure 4.1 shows various library activities on these two dimensions as proposed by Twidale and Nichols [43].

As we can see from this figure, the majority of collaborative activities in conventional libraries are co-located and synchronous, whereas collaborative activities relating to digital libraries are more remote and synchronous. Social information filtering, or collaborative filtering, as we saw earlier, is a process benefitting from other users' actions in the past; thus, it falls under asynchronous and mostly remote domain. These days email also serves as a tool for doing asynchronous collaboration among users who are not co-located. Chat or IM (represented as 'internet' in the figure) helps to carry out synchronous and remote collaboration.

The placement of a CIS environment on this figure has implications for its implementation, functionalities, and evaluation. For instance, Adobe Connect[1] facilitates online meetings where the participants can share and discuss information. Such an environment will fall under Synchronous–Remote collaboration in Fig. 4.1. Thus, this environment needs to have (1) a way to connect remote participants, (2) a shared space for exchanging information, and (3) a communication channel to provide real-time message passing among the participants.

A similar depiction as Twidale and Nicholas [43] is provided in Fig. 4.1 to present various collaborative methods and systems on space–time dimensions. This arrangement is shown in Fig. 4.2.

4.3 User–Source–Time Configuration for CIS

While space–time configurations offer a neat way of conceptualizing collaborative systems at macro level, one could look at them with a different lens at micro level.

---

[1] http://www.adobe.com/products/acrobatconnect/.

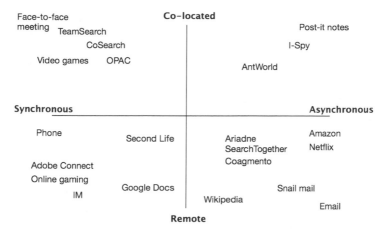

Fig. 4.2 Various collaborative activities and systems along space and time dimensions

Table 4.1 CIS in the context of user–source–time dimensions

User	Source	Time	Examples
Single	Single	–	Typical search
Single	Multiple	Asynchronous	Multi-source search
Single	Multiple	Synchronous	Meta-search
Multiple	Single	Asynchronous	Collaborative filtering, Collaborative navigation, CIR/CIS
Multiple	Single	Synchronous	Collaborative navigation, CIR/CIS
Multiple	Multiple	Asynchronous	Collaborative filtering, CIR/CIS
Multiple	Multiple	Synchronous	Collaborative navigation, CIR/CIS

One such lens uses three important aspects: user(s), source(s), and time. These aspects and their corresponding examples are consolidated in Table 4.1, followed by brief descriptions of them.

- *Single user mode search*
  This is a typical search scenario. A user issues a query to a search engine and receives a ranked list. Relevance is found by considering various factors about individual documents, the whole collection, and links [3, 21]. Relevance feedback [4] and personalization [42] are common ways to improve search in this mode.
- *Multi-source search*
  No search engine has full coverage of the web [41]. Issuing the same query to different search engines typically yields different sets of results. Here, it is still the same user who is responsible for running searches on different sources or search engines, and combining the results somehow. No real collaboration is tak-

ing place; the user is simply synthesizing a solution derived from multiple sources
of information.

- *Meta-searching*
  Instead of a user issuing a query to different search engines, a system can do so si-
  multaneously. It then combines the results obtained from a set of search engines,
  re-ranks them and presents a single rank list to the user [1]. Examples include
  Dogpile[2] and Clusty.[3] Does this seem like collaboration? Only if by collaboration you mean a system combining results from multiple sources without human
  intervention.
- *Collaborative filtering or recommender systems*
  If there are multiple users using the same source for their information need, the
  source can keep track of what the users are looking for and what they are finding.
  Based on the tracking statistics, it can then make recommendations to other users
  who are also looking for the same or similar things. Amazon.com is an example
  of such a system, and there are plenty of other applications in use.

  Several systems designed to provide co-browsing experience tend to facilitate
  collaborative filtering than browsing due to their asynchronous nature and lack of
  two-way interaction among the participants. For instance, Wittenburg et al. [46]
  came up with the notion of *Group Asynchronous Browsing* (GAB) to provide
  tools for people to leverage the information hunting and gathering activities of
  other people or group of people on the web. The authors created a server that collected and merged bookmark files of participating users and then served subsets
  of those merged bookmark files to either standard HTML client browsers or to a
  client built with the multiscale visualization tool Pad++. For the latter, they built
  a tool called WebWatch that could monitor URLs of interest and alert users when
  significant updates appear.
- *Collaborative IR*
  This refers to multiple users working synchronously or asynchronously on single
  or multiple sources for the same information need. More details on this topic can
  be found in Sect. 3.2.
- *Collaborative navigation*
  This refers to multiple users browsing single or multiple sources together (co-
  located or remote, but synchronous). More details on this topic can be found in
  Sect. 3.3.

4.4 Control, Communication, and Awareness in a CIS Environment

Three components specific to group-work or collaboration that are highly predominant in the CIS or CSCW literature are control, communication, and awareness. In

---

[2]http://www.dogpile.com/.

[3]http://www.clusty.com/.

this section, key definitions and related works for these components will be high-lighted. Understanding their roles can also help us address various design issues with CIS systems.

4.4.1 Control

Rodden [30] identified the value of control in CSCW systems and listed a number of projects with their corresponding schemes for implementing control. For instance, the COSMOS project [45] had a formal structure to represent control in the system. They used roles to represent people or automatons, and rules to represent the flow and processes. Roles of the people could be supervisor, processor, or analyst. Rules could be a condition that a process needs to satisfy in order to start or finish. Due to such a structure seen in projects like COSMOS, Rodden classified these control systems as procedural based systems.

Most of these systems were studied in office environments, where the subjects interacted with one another through personal conversations, group meetings, and phone calls. Several of the recommendations and findings of these studies were primarily based on observations.

To express control in a collaborative environment, early CSCW systems used var-ious mechanisms to pass the messages around. These messages were often referred to as Structured Definition Language (SDL) messages. In the most basic sense, these were email messages that were sent back and forth among the participants of a col-laborative project. However, for a collaborative project, an organization often needs more support than simply passing the information in messages. SDL provides this support by imposing a structure to these messages, and incorporating additional fields of information that can be used to filter and distribute messages appropriately.

For instance, Malone et al. [24] proposed the InformationLens framework, in which the messages carried additional information (some of which was automati-cally generated) that can later be used to filter and classify the messages to suit an individual's need in a group.

Let us see an example. Sam sends a message to circulate in the group, that he belongs to, asking for an opinion. At the time of sending this, Sam was not clear about who might be the right person in the group to inquire about that question, but since the system has additional information, such as user profiles and preferences, it can use it to redirect and distribute the message to appropriate individuals. This way, Sam does not have to worry about looking for the right people, and the receivers do not have to worry about getting the messages that are not right for them, even though they are useful for the group as a whole.

Looking at the above scheme with a different perspective, we are distributing the control between humans and automatons involved in the whole group process. Instead of explicitly deciding by himself who should receive the message, Sam is letting the system take charge of this process, thus relinquishing the control to the system. The system is driven by the rules that guide its decision-making. It is impor-tant to note that such a system is different than a traditional collaborative filtering system, where the system filters information based on similarities among the users. Here, the messages are filtered based on sender's intention (Sam chose to distribute his message this way), and receivers' intention to receive such messages that are relevant to them. Malone referred to such kind of filtering as *cognitive filtering*.

Later Malone extended the above framework to ObjectLens [25], in which the participants could create not only the messages to pass the information around, but any kind of objects. Each of these objects would have similar structure imposed on them that could guide further control and distribution processes. ObjectLens also let people create links among those objects formed. Malone pointed out that this was similar to hypertexts on the World Wide Web.

4.4.2 Communication

This is one of the most critical components of any collaboration. In fact, Rodden [30] identified message or communication systems as the class of systems in CSCW that is most mature and most widely used.

Since the focus here is on CIS systems that allow its participants to engage in an intentional and interactive collaboration, there must be a way for the participants to communicate with each other. What is interesting to note is that often, collaboration could begin by letting a group of users communicate with each other. For instance, Donath and Robertson [6] presented a system that allows a user to know that others were currently viewing the same webpage and communicate with those people to initiate a possible collaboration or at least a co-browsing experience. Providing communication capabilities even in an environment that was not originally designed for carrying out collaboration is an interesting way of encouraging collaboration.

Using four multidisciplinary design situations in the USA and Europe, Sonnenwald [40] came up with 13 communication roles. The author showed how these roles can support collaboration, among other aspects of information seeking process, such as knowledge exploration and integration, and task and project completion, by filtering and providing information and negotiating differences across organizational, task, discipline and personal boundaries.

More discussion on computer-mediated communication (CMC) will be covered in Appendix D.

4.4.3 Awareness

Awareness is one of the most important issues that is identified and addressed in the CSCW literature. A clear definition and a methodology for providing awareness, though, are lacking. One of the often-asked questions about awareness in CSCW is "awareness of what?" Schmidt [33] argued that we should talk about awareness not as a separate entity, but as somebody's being aware of some particular occurrence.

In other words, the term 'awareness' is only meaningful if it refers to a person's awareness *of* something. Heath et al. [19] suggested that awareness is not simply a 'state of mind' or a 'cognitive ability', but rather a feature of practical action which is systematically accomplished within developing course of everyday activities.

Several related terms and definitions are used in the CSCW literature to refer to awareness in collaborative projects. For instance, Dourish and Bellotti [7] defined awareness as "an understanding of the activities of others, which provides a context for your own activity" (p. 107). Dourish and Bly [8] suggested the following definition for awareness: "Awareness involves knowing who is "around", what activities are occurring, who is talking with whom; it provides a view of one another in the daily work environments. Awareness may lead to informal interactions, spontaneous connections, and the development of shared cultures—all important aspects of maintaining working relationships which are denied to groups distributed across multiple sites" (p. 541).

A set of theories and models for understanding and providing awareness emerged in the early works reported in the CSCW literature. Gaver [10] argued that an intense sharing of awareness characterizes *focused collaboration* in which people work closely together on a shared goal. He further claimed that less awareness is needed for division of labor, and that more casual awareness can lead to serendipitous communication, which can turn into collaboration. He proposed a *general awareness* model that incorporates and supports all of such activities.

Bly et al. [2] also identified the importance of such general awareness by saying, "When groups are geographically distributed, it is particularly important not to neglect the need for informal interactions, spontaneous conversations, and even general awareness of people and events at other sites" (p. 29).

Some of the early works reported using ethnographic field studies in CSCW (e.g., [17, 18, 20]) identified the need to seamlessly align and integrate the activities of the participants of a collaborative project. While they did not refer to it as 'awareness', soon, the term 'awareness' was adopted to address such practices that support connecting collaborators without the activities of asking, suggesting, requesting, ordering, or reminding.

Several works argued that providing audio-video communication channel could suffice for awareness [12, 26]. However, the use of communication as a substitute for awareness turned out to be very limited in its applicability [11]. Another line of research focused on providing awareness using *computational environments* based on 'event propagation mechanisms' for collecting, disseminating, and integrating information concerning collaborative activities. Some of the notable works in this stream of research include awareness models based on a spatial metaphor by Rodden [31], and Sandor et al. [32].

As we saw above, there are several ways of defining and implementing awareness. Various research projects have used their own taxonomy and interpretation of awareness for creating frameworks and systems. For instance, Gutwin and Greenberg [15] classified awareness in two types: *situational*, and *workspace*, and suggested that situational awareness underlies the idea of workspace awareness in groupware systems. Their definition of workspace awareness included how people interact with the workspace, rather than just awareness of the workspace itself.

Simone and Bandini [37] identified two kinds of awareness: *by-product awareness* that is generated in the course of the activities people must do in order to accomplish their collaborative tasks; and *add-on awareness* that is the outcome of an additional activity, which is a cost for the collaborators to what they must do and is discretional in that it depends on collaborators' evaluation of the contingent situation. Chalmers [5], likewise, divided the awareness in two kinds: awareness of *people*, and of *information artifacts*. He suggested implementing an activity-centered awareness tool, in that it focuses on presenting the ongoing appearance and activity of people.

For the purpose of this book, a more comprehensive and well-accepted taxonomy of awareness, which addresses four kinds of awareness [22] as listed below, will be used.

1. *Group awareness.* This kind of awareness includes providing information to each group member about the status and activities of the other collaborators at a given time.
2. *Workspace awareness.* This refers to a common workspace that the group members share and where they can bring and discuss their findings, and create a common product.
3. *Contextual awareness.* This type of awareness relates to the application domain, rather than the users. Here, we want to identify what content is useful for the group, and what the goals are for the current project.
4. *Peripheral awareness.* This relates to the kind of information that has resulted from personal and the group's collective history, and should be kept separate from what a participant is currently viewing or doing.

Different CIS systems have different ways of providing awareness to the collaborators depending on the domain and the kind of application. Take, for example, Ariadne [44], who developed to support the collaborative learning of database browsing skills. To facilitate complex browsing processes in collaboration, Ariadne presents a visualization of the search process. This visualization consists of thumbnails of screens, looking like playing cards, which represented command-output pairs. Any such card can be expanded to reveal its details. The support for awareness, in this case, is driven by the specific domain (library) and application (catalogue search).

SearchTogether [28], on the other hand, was based on information seeking (application) on the web (domain). It instantiates awareness in several ways, one of which is per-user query histories. This is done by showing each group member's screen name, and his/her photo and queries in the "Query Awareness" region. The access to the query histories is immediate and interactive, as clicking on a query brings back the results of that query from when it was executed. The authors identified query awareness as a very important feature in collaborative searching, which allows group members to not only share their query terms, but also learn better query formulation techniques from one another. Another component of SearchTogether that facilitates awareness is the display of page-specific metadata. This region includes several pieces of information about the displayed page, including group members who viewed the given page, and their comments and ratings. The authors claim that such visitation information can help one either to choose to avoid a page already visited by someone in the group to reduce the duplication of efforts, or perhaps choose to visit such pages, since they provide a sign of promising leads as indicated by the presence of comments and/or ratings.

4.4.4 Importance of Control, Communication, and Awareness in CIS Systems

The findings from empirical observations and other studies of usability testing relating to control, communication, and awareness inform us that an effective CIS system should have the following attributes.

1. A flexible mechanism to incorporate structured message passing.
2. A way of facilitating control among the participants as well as with automaton components.
3. Facilities to present awareness of various objects, processes, and people at any given time to everyone in the group.

While these attributes are derived from general collaborative systems, they apply to CIS systems too. Let us explore how such attributes can fit in a CIS system.

Several CIS systems, such as SearchTogether [28] incorporate support for chat or IM. Such a support is crucial as the group members need a way to communicate with each other. Some works have also tried to provide other sorts of communication channel in a collaborative workspace, such as audio chat, video conferencing, and bulletin board support.

While chat is an obvious choice for synchronous communication, email still prevails when it comes to providing asynchronous communication. In fact, Krutz claimed (in the 80s) that the most successful CSCW application was email. Recently, Morris [27] found from a survey of knowledge workers that email is still one of the most used methods of communicating while working on a collaborative project. Given the importance of email, and the level of familiarity and comfort that most people have with it, an effective CIS system should provide support for passing such messages among the participants during collaboration.

In addition to this, we need to have some kind of structure imposed on the messages passed to incorporate additional information, such as time stamps, tags, and associated processes. Such structure and information can be helpful in distributing the messages with some sort of filtering and/or following rules and roles of a system. For instance, Pickens et al. [29] demonstrated a collaborative video search system where one of the participants was responsible for issuing queries (prospector), and the other participant was responsible for going through the results looking for relevant information (miner). In its most basic version, this system had predefined roles and these roles followed a fixed set of rules. However, with the ability to have structured messages with appropriate information, we can have more flexible roles with dynamic distribution of control among the participants and the system.

Finally, providing awareness is highly important for a CIS system. Since the users of a CIS system will be working with different sources, documents, queries, snippets, and annotations of varying kind, we need to keep everyone in the group aware of all such objects as they are collected and modified. In addition to this, it is important to show various attributes associated with an object. For instance, it is useful to indicate on the interface that a document has already been viewed.

Several systems supporting collaboration have identified the above issues (control, communication, and awareness) as critical to their design. For instance, Farooq et al. [9] presented a collaborative design for CiteSeer, a search engine and digital library of research literature in the computer and information science disciplines. Based on a survey and follow-up interviews with CiteSeer users, the authors presented four novel implications for designing the CiteSeer collaboratory: (1) visualize query-based social networks to identify scholarly communities of interest, (2) provide online collaborative tool support for upstream stages of scientific collaboration, (3) support activity awareness for staying cognizant of online scientific activities, and (4) use notification systems to convey scientific activity awareness.

4.5 Nature and Level of Mediation

Yet another way to study CIS (or in general, collaborative) systems is by looking at how collaboration is mediated. Pickens et al. [29] saw two extremes: system or algorithmically mediated, and user or interface mediated.

4.5.1 System/Algorithmically Mediated Collaboration

Here, the system (more specifically, the behind the scenes part of the system) acts as an active component for collaboration, and helps the collaborators get the most out of their collaborative projects by doing one or more of the following.

- Combine various inputs from the users (e.g., queries, annotations) to produce better versions of them.
- Join multiple streams of results—produced by the same action (e.g., search) but different people—into a better set of results.
- Redistribute the results keeping in mind every participant's abilities, roles, and responsibilities.
- Optimize workload for each individual involved in collaboration.

Pickens et al. [29] showed how algorithmic mediation could be provided in a time-bound, recall-oriented task to let the collaborators get to the results that otherwise they would have missed had they been working individually. Their algorithm was based on catering to different (predefined) roles played by the collaborators. Later, Shah et al. [36] showed how a system-mediated collaboration that takes into account the asymmetric roles collaborators play to enhance both relevance and novelty in retrieval.

Often system-mediated CIS systems come close to being collaborative filtering tools, but what sets them apart is the notion of intention. Those working with system-mediated collaboration are assumed to have intention to collaborate, with their explicit involvement in the process. Collaborative filtering, on the other hand, may not have explicit consent or intention of those being involved or affected.

4.5.2 *User/Interface Mediated Collaboration*

This method of collaboration implies that either the participants doing collaboration are in full control of how the collaborative processes and/or such control are being exercised through the user interface of the system. In other words, the collaboration in question is very transparent to the involved parties, and the control vests with the users. The system, here, is serving as a passive element that helps with aspects such as communication and awareness, keeping the control with the users.

An example is Ariadne system [43], where the collaborators (a reference librarian and an information seeker) work through their information seeking process using the co-browsing interface provided by the system, but the system is not doing anything more than responding to user actions. Recent systems such as SearchTogether [28] and Coagmento [35] could also be seen as interface-mediated CIS tools where the control lies within the users, through such systems often employ a few system-mediatory components. For instance, SearchTogether has a split search feature, whereby a team could ask the system to *intelligently* split the search results among the collaborators. The authors, however, found this feature to be under-used [28]. More discussions on these systems and their features will be covered in Chap. 6.

4.6 Dimensions of Collaborative Systems

Having seen several frameworks for understanding CIS, it is easy to realize that the usefulness or validity of any of these depends on the context. Therefore, instead of trying to provide a comprehensive framework that fits all needs, we will enumerate various elements or dimensions of groupwork/collaborative systems. One could, hopefully, pick and choose the elements needed to study or explain a given context for collaborative systems from the list presented here and depicted in Figs. 4.3 and 4.4.

1. *Intent*

   This dimension describes the level of intention one has in a collaborative process, or in other words, how explicitly collaboration is defined. This dimension

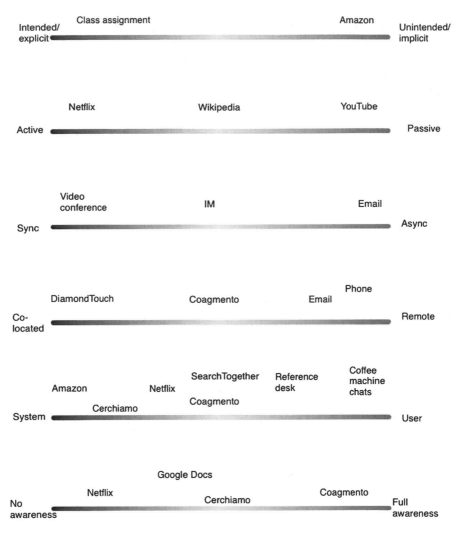

Fig. 4.3 A framework for CIS environments (part 1 of 2)

is introduced to differentiate systems that are truly collaborative to those that are merely collaborative filtering systems.

An intentional or explicitly defined collaboration is when various aspects of collaboration are clearly stated and understood. For instance, a group of students working on a science project together know that (1) they are collaborating, and (2) who is responsible for doing what. When collaboration happens without explicit specifications, it can be considered unintentional or implicitly defined. For instance, visitors to Amazon.com receive recommendations based on other people's searching and buying behavior without knowing those people.

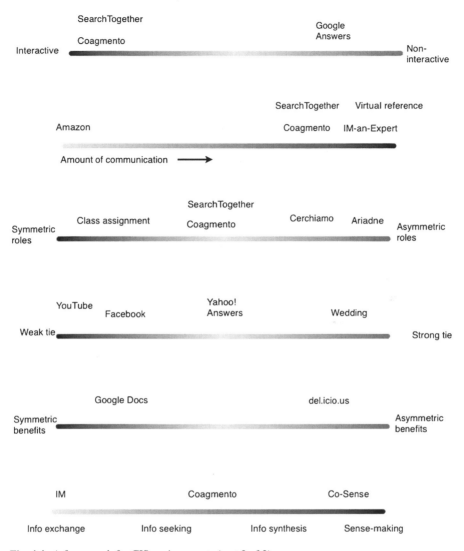

Fig. 4.4 A framework for CIS environments (part 2 of 2)

2. *Activeness*

The level of activeness is another important dimension in understanding the nature of a collaborative endeavor. This dimension is useful to talk about the involvement of a user in a group activity.

An active collaboration is similar to explicit collaboration with the key difference being the willingness and awareness of the user. For instance, when a user of Netflix rates a movie, he is actively playing a part in collaborating with other users. However, since he did not explicitly agree to collaborate with others; he may not even know those users. A passive collaboration is simi-

Table 4.2 Differentiating
between intent and activeness

	Intended	Unintended
Active	Amazon wedding registry	Amazon book purchase
Passive	YouTube video viewing	Auto-subscribing

lar to implicit collaboration with the key difference being the willingness and awareness of the user. For instance, when a user visits a video on YouTube, he passively contributes to the popularity of that video, affecting the ranking and social relevance of that video for other users.

The key difference between active and passive collaboration is the user's willingness and control over the actions. In the case of active collaboration, the user agrees to do it (rating, comments), whereas in the case of passive collaboration, the user has very little control (click-through, browsing patterns). To demonstrate this difference further, Table 4.2 lists a few examples for these two dimensions.

3. *Concurrency*
   One of the traditional ways of classifying a collaborative process is by its concurrency. A video conference or a meeting typically requires the participants to be present in the same time (synchronous), whereas email could help a team work asynchronously. A chat program can support both synchronous and asynchronous collaborations, even though it is intended as a synchronous communication channel.

4. *Location*
   This is another traditional dimension that is often used to place different collaborative systems in context. DiamondTouch [38, 39] requires the participants to be physically present around the system for a collaborative session. SearchTogether [28] and Coagmento, on the other hand, facilitate collaboration among remotely located participants.

5. *Role/mediation of system and user*
   Collaboration can be entirely done by a group of people, and it could also incorporate support of systems, such as computers or phones. However, this dimension says a bit more than that. In a collaborative project, the collaboration could be mediated by the system, in which case some underlying algorithm would drive the collaboration. Or the people or the users of the system could do mediation themselves, making the system (if it is used) a passive component. Cerchiamo [13] is an example of the former, and Coagmento is an example of the latter.

6. *Level of awareness*
   Gaver [10] used awareness as a factor to identify different situations for collaboration. He claimed that less awareness is needed for division of labor, and that more casual awareness can lead to serendipitous communication, which can turn into collaboration. Awareness, therefore, is an important dimension to consider.

   The amount and the kind of awareness provided in an environment with a group of people depends on several factors, including the cost and benefit of such awareness, available technology, and privacy. On one hand, services like Netflix and Amazon connect multiple users without making them aware of one another. On Google Docs, one has workspace awareness, whereby one can work with the group's artifact in collaboration, but does not see his collaborators' individual contributions. Cerchiamo provides a system-driven collaboration, where the users have limited and filtered access to their collaborators' actions and results. Coagmento, on the other extreme, provides a very transparent interface, in which a user can be aware of the task at hand, the shared workspace, as well as the group's history and products.

7. *Level of interaction*
   Once again, to differentiate systems with very little or no user interaction to those that are highly interactive, a dimension that considers level of user interaction is needed. This dimension defines how interactive collaboration is. Systems such as SearchTogether and Coagmento are designed to support interactive collaboration. Google Answers, on the other hand, was a non-interactive service, where the information seeker could pose their questions to experts and receive answers without going back-and-forth.

8. *Amount of communication*
   Similar to the level of interaction, collaborative systems also vary in terms of the amount of communication that takes place among the participants. In fact, dimensions such as intention and communication could help us even determine if a given system is truly a collaborative system. For instance, on Amazon, the users do not necessarily talk to each other directly for accomplishing a common goal. Systems such as Coagmento, on the other hand, provide explicit support for communication since the participants are expected to have a high level of communication while working on their collaborative project.

9. *User roles*
   While an effective collaboration must be *democratic* and *inclusive*, that is, it must be free of hierarchies of any kind and it must include all parties who have a stake in the problem [23], to include several scenarios of people working together, we should consider their roles in collaboration.
   Division of labor and combining diverse sets of skills are two of the most attractive appeals for collaborative projects. Invariably, the former assumes symmetric roles, and the latter assumes asymmetric roles of the participants. For example, a group project for a class typically involves students who all have more or less the same background and skills. Ariadne [43], on the other hand, was designed to connect a patron to a reference librarian—each with a different background.

10. *Strength of the connection*
    As realized during the literature review on social networking, a big difference between a social group and a collaborative group is the strength of the ties that connect them. Often, one group could be transformed to the other one based on these ties. A collaborative endeavor could involve more or less of the social element.

Facebook is a social networking utility, where the users may not have stronger ties or common goals. Co-authoring a research article, on the other hand, involves multiple parties being connected with a stronger bond.

11. *Balance of benefits*
    This dimension follows the dimension of user roles. A typical collaboration is mutually beneficial for those participating. However, there can be a gradation of these benefits. Co-authoring a research article benefits all the involving authors, whereas one's collection of useful bookmarks on del.icio.us may benefit the author and the subscribers differently.

12. *Usage of information*
    Finally, this dimension allows us to see how the information flows in the system. Often, information exchange is the focus of collaboration. An example is an on-line help service using chat. The other possible segments on this dimension are information seeking, information synthesis, and sense-making. A collaborative system could support one or several of these elements.

It is important to note here that all of these 12 dimensions are not independent. They have an interaction effect; that is, fixing or altering of one dimension changes the rest appropriately. For instance, if we fix the 'Location' dimension to co-located, our options for 'Concurrency' dimension are reduced to synchronous, as the collaborators are likely to be meeting with each other at the same place and time. If, on the other hand, the collaborators could not meet face-to-face (remotely located), they may use synchronous (e.g., chat), or asynchronous (e.g., email) communication. On the other hands, several of the dimensions exhibit an apparent correlation. For instance, there is a high level of match between 'Communication' and 'System-user' dimensions.

4.7 Summary

In this chapter, we saw a number of ways researchers have tried to understand and present ideas on CIS, and in general, collaborative systems. These frameworks, while not perfect, provide a mechanism for exploring various issues relating research and development of CIS methods and tools. Following are a few possible uses of such framework to aid one in studying, creating, and evaluating CIS systems.

- For a given organizational structure or a set of scenarios, one could find all the possible methods for collaboration and place them on a space–time configuration as shown in Fig. 4.2. This may allow one to identify gaps where support for collaboration along an area of space–time is missing.
- Using the control-communication-awareness framework, one could evaluate the cost-benefit ratio of various levels of support that a CIS system should provide since often inclusion or exclusion of these elements pose design questions relating to trade-offs of features. For instance, if the system has appropriate and adequate support for awareness, it could reduce the need for communication.

- The dimensions presented in Sect. 4.6 also provide similar opportunities for understanding various trade-offs in designing and evaluating CIS systems. For example, if a CIS system's primary goal is to encourage students to explore new avenues of information on a given topic and make sense out of their discoveries together, the system needs to be as high as possible along the interactive, user-focused, and communication dimensions as possible in terms of providing features or support.

References

1. Javed A. Aslam and Mark Montague. Models for metasearch. In *Proceedings of the Annual ACM Conference on Research and Development in Information Retrieval (SIGIR)*, pages 276–284, 2001.
2. Sara A. Bly, Steve R. Harrison and Susan Irwin. Media spaces: bringing people together in a video, audio, and computing environment. *Communications of the ACM*, 36(1):28–46, 1993.
3. Sergey Brin and Lawrence Page. The anatomy of a large-scale hypertextual web search engine. In *Proceedings of the Seventh World Wide Web Conference*, 1998.
4. Chris Buckley, Gerald Salton and James Allen. The effect of adding relevance information in a relevance feedback environment. In *Proceedings of the Annual ACM Conference on Research and Development in Information Retrieval (SIGIR)*, pages 292–300, Dept. of Computer Science, Cornell University, 1994. Springer, New York.
5. Matthew Chalmers. Awareness, representation and interpretation. *Computer Supported Cooperative Work (CSCW)*, 11(3–4):389–409, 2002.
6. Judith S. Donath and Niel Robertson. The sociable web. In *Proceedings of the World Wide Web (WWW) Conference*, CERN, Geneva, Switzerland, 1994.
7. P. Dourish and V. Bellotti. Awareness and coordination in shared workspaces. In *Proceedings of the Conference on Computer-Supported Cooperative Work (CSCW)*, pages 107–114, Toronto, Ontario, 1992.
8. Paul Dourish and Sara A. Bly. Portholes: supporting awareness in a distributed work group. In *Proceedings of ACM SIGCHI Conference on Human Factors in Computing Systems*, pages 541–547, Toronto, Canada, 1992. ACM, New York.
9. Umer Farooq, Craig H. Ganoe, John M. Carroll and C. Lee Giles. Designing for e-science: requirements gathering for collaboration in CiteSeer. *International Journal of Human Computer Studies*, 67:297–312, 2009.
10. William W. Gaver. Sound support for collaboration. In L.J. Bannon, M. Robinson and K. Schmidt, editors, *Proceedings of European Conference on Computer Supported Cooperative Work (ECSCW)*, Amsterdam, The Netherlands, 1991. Kluwer Academic, Dordrecht.
11. William W. Gaver. The affordances of media spaces for collaboration. In J. Turner and R.E. Kraut, editors, *Proceedings of the Conference on Computer-Supported Cooperative Work (CSCW)*, pages 17–24, Toronto, Canada, 1992.
12. William W. Gaver, Thomas P. Moran, Allan MacLean, Lennart Lövstrand, Paul Dourish, Kathleen Carter and William A.S. Buxton. Realizing a video environment: EuroPARC's RAVE system. In P. Bauersfeld, J. Bennett and G. Lynch, editors, *Proceedings of ACM SIGCHI Conference on Human Factors in Computing Systems*, pages 27–35, Monterey, California, 1992. ACM, New York.
13. Gene Golovchinsky, John Adcock, Jeremy Pickens, Pernilla Qvarfordt and Maribeth Back. Cerchiamo: a collaborative exploratory search tool. In *Proceedings of Computer Supported Cooperative Work (CSCW)*, 2008.
14. Gene Golovchinsky, Jeremy Pickens and Maribeth Back. A taxonomy of collaboration in online information seeking. In *Proceedings of JCDL 2008 Workshop on Collaborative Exploratory Search*, Pittsburgh, PA, June 2008.

15. Carl Gutwin and Saul Greenberg. A descriptive framework of workspace awareness for real-time groupware. *Computer Supported Cooperative Work (CSCW)*, 11(3–4):411–446, 2002.
16. Preben Hansen and Kalervo Jarvelin. Collaborative information retrieval in an information-intensive domain. *Information Processing and Management*, 41:1101–1119, 2005.
17. Richard H.R. Harper, John A. Hughes and Dan Z. Shapiro. The functionality of flight strips in ATC work. Technical report, Lancaster Sociotechnics Group, Department of Sociology, Lancaster University, January 1989.
18. Richard H.R. Harper, John A. Hughes and Dan Z. Shapiro. Working in harmony: an examination of computer technology in air traffic control. In *Proceedings of European Conference on Computer Supported Cooperative Work (ECSCW)*, pages 72–86, Gatwick, London, 1989.
19. Christian Heath, Marcus Sanchez Svensson, Jon Hindmarsh, Paul Luff and Dirk vom Lehn. Configuring awareness. *Computer Supported Cooperative Work (CSCW)*, 11(3–4):317–347, 2002.
20. Christian C. Heath and Paul Luff. Collaborative activity and technological design: task coordination in London Underground control rooms. In, L.J. Bannon, M. Robinson and K. Schmidt, editors, *Proceedings of European Conference on Computer Supported Cooperative Work (ECSCW)*, pages 65–80, Amsterdam, The Netherlands, 1991. Kluwer Academic, Dordrecht.
21. Jon M. Kleinberg. Authoritative sources in a hyperlinked environment. *Journal of the ACM (JACM)*, 46(5):604–632, 1999.
22. O. Liechti and Y. Sumi. Editorial: Awareness and the WWW. *International Journal of Human Computer Studies*, 56(1):1–5, 2002.
23. Scott London. Collaboration and community. http://scottlondon.com/reports/ppcc.html, November 1995.
24. Thomas W. Malone, K.R. Grant, F.A. Turbak, S.S. Brobst and M.D. Cohen. Intelligent information sharing systems. *Communications of the ACM*, 30(5):390–402, 1987.
25. Thomas W. Malone and K. Lai. Object Lens: a spreadsheet for cooperative work. In *Proceedings of the Conference on Computer-Supported Cooperative Work (CSCW)*, Portland, OR, September 1988.
26. Marilyn M. Mantei, Ronald M. Baecker, Abigail J. Sellen, William A.S. Buxton and Thomas Milligan. Experiences in the use of a media space. In S.P. Robertson, G.M. Olson and J.S. Olson, editors, *Proceedings of ACM SIGCHI Conference on Human Factors in Computing Systems*, pages 203–208, New Orleans, Lousiana, 1991. ACM, New York.
27. Meredith Ringel Morris. A survey of collaborative web search practices. In *Proceedings of ACM SIGCHI Conference on Human Factors in Computing Systems*, pages 1657–1660, Florence, Italy, 2008.
28. Meredith Ringel Morris and Eric Horvitz. SearchTogether: an interface for collaborative web search. In *ACM Symposium on User Interface Software and Technology (UIST)*, pages 3–12, Newport, RI, October 2007.
29. Jeremy Pickens, Gene Golovchinsky, Chirag Shah, Pernilla Qvarfordt and Maribeth Back. Algorithmic mediation for collaborative exploratory search. In *Proceedings of the Annual ACM Conference on Research and Development in Information Retrieval (SIGIR)*, Singapore, July 2008.
30. Tom Rodden. A survey of CSCW systems. *Interacting with Computers*, 3(3):319–353, 1991.
31. Tom Rodden. Populating the application: a model of awareness for cooperative applications. In *Proceedings of Computer Supported Cooperative Work (CSCW)*, pages 87–96, Boston, MA, November 1996. ACM, New York.
32. Ovidiu Sandor, Cristian Bogdan and John Bowers. Aether: an awareness engine for CSCW. In J.A. Hughes, W. Prinz, T.A. Rodden and K. Schmidt, editors, *Proceedings of European Conference on Computer Supported Cooperative Work (ECSCW)*, pages 221–236, Lancaster, U.K., 1997. Kluwer Academic, Dordrecht.
33. Kjeld Schmidt. The problem with 'Awareness': introductory remarks on 'Awareness in CSCW'. *Computer Supported Cooperative Work (CSCW)*, 11(3):285–298, 2002.
34. Chirag Shah. A framework to support user-centric collaborative information seeking, 2010.

35. Chirag Shah. Coagmento—a collaborative information seeking, synthesis and sense-making framework (an integrated demo). In *Proceedings of Computer Supported Cooperative Work (CSCW)*, Savannah, GA, 2010.
36. Chirag Shah, Jeremy Pickens and Gene Golovchinsky. Role-based results redistribution for collaborative information retrieval. *Information Processing & Management*, 46(6):773–781, 2010.
37. Carla Simone and Stefania Bandini. Integrating awareness in cooperative applications through the reaction-diffusion metaphor. *Computer Supported Cooperative Work (CSCW)*, 11(3–4):495–530, 2002.
38. Alan F. Smeaton, Hyowon Lee, Colum Foley and Sinead Mc Givney. Collaborative video searching on a tabletop. *Multimedia Systems Journal*, 12(4):375–391, 2006.
39. Alan F. Smeaton, Hyowon Lee, Colum Foley, Sinead Mc Givney and Cathal Gurrin. Físchlár-DiamondTouch: collaborative video searching on a table. In *SPIE Electronic Imaging— Multimedia Content Analysis, Management, and Retrieval*, volume 6073, SPIE, San Jose, 2006.
40. Diane H. Sonnenwald. Communication roles that support collaboration during the design process. *Design Studies*, 17(3):277–301, 1996.
41. Danny Sullivan. Search engine sizes. http://searchenginewatch.com/showPage.html?page=2156481, January 2005.
42. Jaime Teevan, Susan T. Dumais and Eric Horvitz. Personalizing search via automated analysis of interests and activities. In *Proceedings of the Annual ACM Conference on Research and Development in Information Retrieval (SIGIR)*, pages 449–456, 2005.
43. Michael B. Twidale and David M. Nichols. Collaborative browsing and visualisation of the search process. *Aslib Proceedings*, 48(7–8):177–182, 1996.
44. Michael B. Twidale, David M. Nichols and Chris D. Paice. Supporting collaborative learning during information searching. In *Proceedings of Computer Supported Collaborative Learning (CSCL)*, pages 367–374, Bloomington, Indiana, 1995.
45. S.B. Wilbur and R.E. Young. The COSMOS project: a multi-disciplinary approach to design of computer supported group working. In R. Speth, editor, *EUTECO 88: Research into Networks and Distributed Applications*, Vienna, Austria, April 1988.
46. Kent Wittenburg, Duco Das, Will Hill and Larry Stead. Group asynchronous browsing on the World Wide Web. In *Proceedings of the World Wide Web (WWW) Conference*, Boston, MA, December 1995.

Chapter 5
Toward a Model for CIS

Abstract Being a new and emerging area, CIS lacks a sophisticated and comprehensive set of theories and models that other fields such as IR and information seeking have enjoyed. Therefore, this chapter is not about definitive theories and models
relating to CIS; rather, it shows how traditional information seeking models could
help us create similar models for CIS. To situate the discussion on theories and
models pertaining to CIS, this chapter provides a brief overview on various models
developed for collaboration as well as information seeking. An attempt is then made
to show how a model for CIS can be developed using Kuhlthau's information search
process (ISP) model. The success and shortcomings of this approach are shown using data from a user study. Further discussion is provided on understanding and
incorporating an affective dimension to create a comprehensive model of CIS.

5.1 Models for Collaboration

A discussion on various definitions, theories, and models was presented in Sect. 2.1.
Instead of repeating those details, we will simply summarize a couple of important
points here, focusing on the relevant models of collaboration from the literature.

Denning and Yaholkovsky [13] suggested that coordination and cooperation are
weaker forms of working together, and that all of these activities require sharing
some information with each other. Taylor-Powell et al. [57] added another component to this—contribution, as they realized that in order to have an effective collaboration, each member of the group should make an individual contribution to the
collaboration. Using communication, contribution, coordination, and cooperation as
essential steps toward collaboration, they showed how a true collaboration requires
a tighter form of integration (Fig. 5.1).

Based on these two works, a model of collaboration is synthesized and presented
in Fig. 5.2. This model has five sets: *communication* (information exchange), *contribution*, *coordination*, *cooperation*, and *collaboration*. Considering the notion of
sets, the model shows which activity is supporting the other. For instance, coordination is a subset of collaboration, which indicates that, for a meaningful collaboration,
we need to have some way of coordinating people and events (see [55]). Collaboration is a superset of cooperation, which means in order to have a true collaboration,

C. Shah, *Collaborative Information Seeking*, The Information Retrieval Series 34,   61
DOI 10.1007/978-3-642-28813-5_5, © Springer-Verlag Berlin Heidelberg 2012

Fig. 5.1 Steps to
collaboration
(http://www.empowerment.
state.ia.us/files/annual_
reports/2001/Collaboration.
pdf)

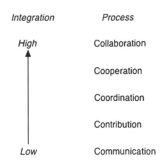

we need something more than cooperation. These five sets are described below in
more detail.

- *Communication*. This is the process of sending or exchanging information, which
  is one of the core requirements for carrying out collaboration, or maintaining any
  kind of productive relationship.
- *Contribution*. This is an informal relationship by which individuals help each
  other in achieving their personal goals.

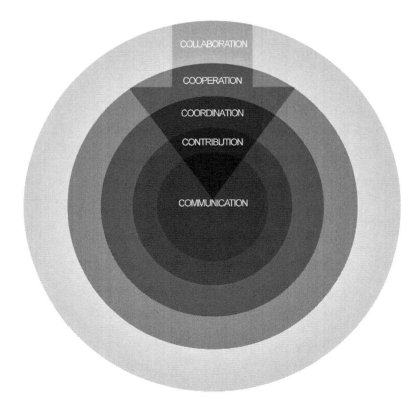

Fig. 5.2 A set-based model of collaboration. An inner set is essential to or supports the outer set

- *Coordination.* This is a process of connecting different agents together for a harmonious action. This often involves bringing people or systems under an umbrella at the same time and place. During this process, the involved agents may share resources, responsibilities, and goals.
- *Cooperation.* This is a relationship in which different agents with similar interests take part in planning activities, negotiating roles, and sharing resources to achieve joint goals. In addition to coordination, cooperation involves all the agents following some rules of interaction.
- *Collaboration.* This is a process involving various agents that may see different aspects of a problem. They engage in a process through which they can go beyond their own individual expertise and vision by constructively exploring their differences and searching for common solutions. In contrast to cooperation, collaboration involves creating a solution that is more than merely the sum of each party's contribution. The authority in such a process is vested in the collaboration rather than in an individual entity.

5.2 Models for Information Seeking

We begin our discussion on information seeking models by first looking at how researchers view information seeking. Marchionini [38] defines information seeking as a process in which humans purposefully engage in an activity to change their state of knowledge. This process of information seeking goes beyond simply retrieving information; it is usually associated with higher level cognitive processes such as learning and problem solving [37]. Dervin and Nilan [15] presented a view of information seeking that emphasized communication and the needs, characteristics, and actions of the information seeker rather than mere representation, storage, and retrieval of information.

Several models have been proposed to understand and explain the information seeking process and information seeking behavior. Dervin [14] presented a model with three phases of users facing and solving their information problems.

1. *Situation.* This phase establishes the context for the information need, called the situation.
2. *Gap.* People often find that given the situation, there is a gap between what they understand and what they need to make sense of the current situation.
3. *Use.* Once this gap is realized, it is manifested by questions. The answers to these questions are put to use and then the user moves on to the next situation.

Belkin [5] proposed a model of information seeking that focuses on information seekers' anomalous states of knowledge (ASK). In this model, the information seekers do not have a clear understanding of the problem they are trying to solve or the information needed to do so. Information seekers have to go through the stage of articulating their search request, and the search system helps to refine that request. Thus, the ASK model serves as a theoretical basis for the design of interactive information systems.

Wilson [62] presented a model of information seeking process showing how the work by Ellis [18] can be incorporated into the original model. The stages of information seeking behavior shown in this figure were reported in Ellis et al. [19] as *Starting, Chaining* (following citation linkages), *Browsing, Differentiating, Monitoring, Extracting, Verifying,* and *Ending.* Ellis' model is based on empirical research and has been tested in various domains, most recently in the context of an engineering company [20]. Kuhlthau, in her work [33] and [34], supplemented Ellis' work by attaching to the stages what she called *information seeking process,* the associated feelings, thoughts and actions, and the appropriate information tasks. Her model's stages were: *Initiation, Selection, Exploration, Formulation, Collection* and *Presentation.* Wilson [63] presented a comparison of Ellis' and Kuhlthau's models: "*... the two models are fundamentally opposed in the minds of the authors: Kuhlthau posits stages on the basis of her analysis of behavior, while Ellis suggests that the sequences of behavioral characteristics may vary.*"

Wilson's 1997 model [62] incorporated information behavior, with a proposal to fill the *gap* that Dervin labeled in her model by inserting the concept of activating mechanism. Wilson proposed to do this using the stress/coping model proposed by Miller and Mangan [39].

The models described above assume individual information seekers. In this section, extensions to CIS are outlined. As we can see, all of these models of information seeking incorporate various stages of an information seeker's behavior. For the purpose of this book, the focus is on how an information seeker can use various methods and tools to seek information that is mediated by computer(s), and what he does when/if information that he is looking for is found. Of course, the information that he is looking for may not exist and the seeker may not have a clear idea about the kind of information that may be useful for his task. Marchionini's model [38] incorporating eight subprocesses of information seeking can be useful for the purpose of defining such a process-based model for CIS. In order to map various processes in a CIS environment to Marchionini's model, the focus will be on how two participants can seek and process information in collaboration.

A four layer model of information seeking, centered around information access and organization is presented in Fig. 5.3 to facilitate the discussion. On the left side, four layers are labeled; on the right side, examples are given for these layers; and in the middle, a typical scenario is presented. These four layers are described below in detail.

Layer-1: Sources   This layer contains information in various sources and formats (structured, semi-structured, and unstructured). The sources include digital libraries, wikis, blogs, databases, and webpages; formats include text, images, and videos. In fact, a person or a group of people could also act as a source.

Layer-2: Tools   This layer consists of tools and techniques a user can use to interface with the sources and access the information of layer-1. They include search services, relevance feedback mechanisms [9], and query term suggestions [2]. In addition, since this layer also acts as a mediating layer between information sources

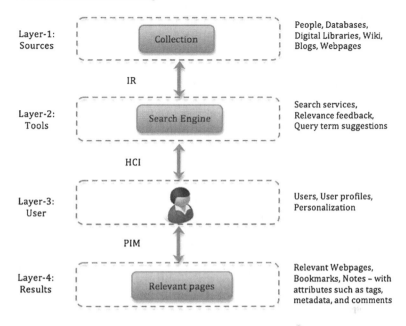

Fig. 5.3 Four layer model of information seeking centered around information access and organization

and users, it includes a variety of user interfaces, starting from results as rank-lists to touch panels with mechanisms to visualize results. We can see that a large amount of research in IR is focused on the link between layer-1 and layer-2; that is, developing tools and services appropriate for retrieving information of various forms.

Layer-3: User   This layer consists of a user, who uses the tools in layer-2 to access the information in layer-1 and accumulate the knowledge in layer-4. We can see that the focus of Human–Computer Interaction (HCI) research has been on the link between layer-2 and layer-3; that is, presenting the information and the information access tools in effective ways to the user. This layer-3 also includes elements relating to a user, such as user profiles, which can be used for personalization [58].

Layer-4: Results   The user of layer-3 accumulates the information relevant to him in layer-4. In the most basic sense, this could be a set of webpages that the user found relevant from his searches on the web. Extending this further, we can have bookmarks, notes, and other kinds of results, sometimes stored with attributes such as tags, metadata, and comments. At a more conceptual level, this layer consists of the knowledge that the user gained by his information seeking process. The focus of research in personal information management (PIM) [16] has been on the link between layers 3 and 4, addressing the issues of information storage and organization by users.

Fig. 5.4 Extension of the
four layer model of
information access and
organization

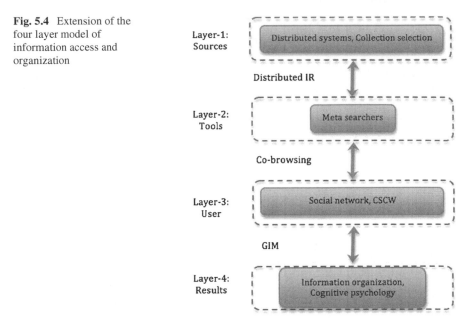

Let us now see how each of these layers can be extended by allowing various
entities at those layers collaborate, and how other fields play out in this extension
(see Fig. 5.4).

Layer-1. Combining various information sources is covered under shared resources
and distributed systems. From the IR perspective, collection selection also becomes
an important issue to address here.

Layer-2. Combining two or more search engines for search process creates meta-
search process [3]. Clusty[1] and Dogpile[2] are good examples of such meta-search
engines.

Layer-3. Putting more than two users together can create a workgroup. Users in a
workgroup who access and explore some information together are studied as co-
browsing or social navigation [24]. Extending the workgroup further with connections among users that exhibit some social characteristics, creates a social network.
When multiple user profiles are considered as one entity to optimize the services
for that group, personalization is transformed into *groupization* [42].

Layer-4. Combining relevant information of various sorts falls under information
organization and cognitive psychology. Customizing information for a group of
users is the topic of research named Group Information Management (GIM) [21].

Based on various combinations at individual layers and various kinds of interconnections among these layers, we can imagine a large array of possible scenarios.

---

[1]http://www.clusty.com.

[2]http://www.dogpile.com.

Discussion of these scenarios is beyond the scope of this work. Instead, possible combinations at the user layer will be explored. There are several ways and reasons the users can connect with each other in an information seeking process. The kind of collaboration considered here is *intentional*, and *interactive* among users with the *same information goal*. In order to create and study such an environment, the general model of information access and organization given in Fig. 5.3 will be used and stripped down to suit the needs.

To be specific, the situations in which a group of users collaborate using traditional or collaborative tools to achieve personal or common information goals will be investigated. A model with such a configuration is given in Fig. 5.5. This is obtained by extending the original model of information access and organization for two users.[3] These users can access and organize information individually, or decide to collaborate with each other. In the case of collaboration, they will have a way to communicate with one another. They may have a common or shared interface. They may also have a shared space where they can store and organize their results. In other words, collaboration between these two users can occur at various levels: (1) while formulating an information request, (2) while obtaining the results, and (3) while organizing and using the results.

The model described above should help in clarifying the presented approach to CIS with the kind of information seeking process, centered around information access and organization. Later while discussing specific approaches to address various issues in CIS, we can revisit this model and see how those other works fit in here.

Looking back to the three phases of collaboration proposed by Gray [29] (pp. 57–94), and the eight subprocesses of information seeking proposed by Marchionini [38], we can identify corresponding phases, adding a phase for aggregation, for a collaborative information seeking endeavor as given below.

1. *Pre-negotiation or problem-setting phase*
     (i) Recognize and accept an information problem: this stage presumably brings a set of people together for a possible collaboration as they identify their common goals.
     (ii) Define and understand the problem: the group can discuss the problem and if required, negotiate for a common understanding of the problem (Fig. 5.5, layer-3).
     (iii) Choose a search system: the group can choose source(s) to use and if possible or desired, divide them up among themselves (Fig. 5.5, layer-1).
2. *Direction-setting phase*
     This is an important phase that is more specific to the collaboration. In this phase, the participants need to identify the interests which brought them together, deter-

---

[3]Considering only two users is merely for the simplicity; theoretically, the model can incorporate more than two users. However, in practice, beyond a certain number of users we may start seeing a point of diminishing return. Worse yet, having too many users for a collaborative project may decrease the productivity of the group. Morris [40] found from her survey of knowledge workers that the typical size of a collaborative group was 4 to 6 participants.

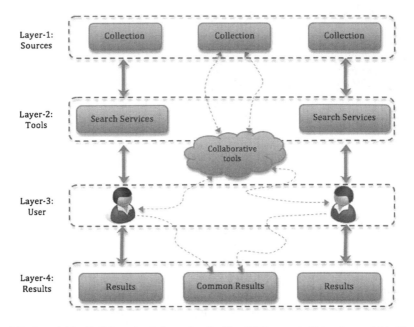

Fig. 5.5   A model for Collaborative Information Seeking (CIS) extended from the model in Fig. 5.3

mine how they differ from the interests of the others, set directions, and establish shared goals (Fig. 5.5, layer-3).

3. *Implementation phase*
   (iv) Formulate a query: given the participants are allowed to work independently, each one formulates his/her search request. At this time, it is beneficial to be aware of the search requests formulated by other participants in the group [41] (Fig. 5.5, layer-3).
   (v) Execute search: everyone executes his/her request on the source(s) being used (Fig. 5.5, layer-2).
   (vi) Examine results: participants can now examine their own results, and if required, results of the other participants (Fig. 5.5, layer-4).
   (vii) Extract information: required information is extracted (Fig. 5.5, layer-4).
   (viii) Reflect/interate/stop: participants can repeat steps (iv)–(vii) or stop. They may also choose to annotate the results.
   (ix) Aggregate: this phase is more specific to the collaboration, in which the acquired information, processes, and *knowledge* are aggregated to create a shared information and understanding (Fig. 5.5, layer-4).

5.3   Models for User and System Interaction

Interactions between users and systems in an information seeking environment are crucial and sometimes inevitable for effective information retrieval. To put the interactions in a single-user or collaborative environment into perspective, several possible scenarios are presented below.

1. *Person to person.* This is a simple case of person to person communication. Almost any dialog between two people can be considered as an example of such an interaction.
2. *System to system.* This is a simple case of two systems interacting with each other without any human intervention. Consider the following communication between a client and a Network Time Server (NTS).

> *Client*: Hello, I need to know the time.
> *Server*: OK. What's your time-zone?
> *Client*: It's EST.
> *Server*: Then it's 10:43:56 where you are. And it took 0.16 seconds for your message to arrive, so don't forget to account for that time-lag.
> *Client*: Got it. Thanks.

Of course, the actual communication between the client and server is different than this, but the essence of this description is that two autonomous entities are interacting without any feedback from a human.
3. *Person to system.* We encounter this scenario quite often in day-to-day life when we have an interactive session with a system. Consider using any interactive search engine. You type in a query and it reports that you have a typo in your query. You correct that and try your search again. You are not satisfied with your search results, and so you try a different query. Thus, the process of accomplishing some task may take several cycles of interactions.
4. *Person to person mediated by a system.* This is a scenario when two users have a system between them, mediating the interactions. IM or online chatting is a good example of such an interaction. This is also the scenario that is studied very frequently in IR, more specifically for relevance feedback.
5. *System to system mediated by a person.* It is not clear if the scenario where a user is mediating two systems is practically useful or not, while it is certainly possible.
6. *Group of people.* This scenario covers our traditional social and economical bonds where a group of people interact with each other as they belong to a social, economical, political, or ethnic class.
7. *Group of systems.* Similar to the previous scenario, where a group of people created a network, a group of systems can be connected to form a computer network. We see such networks everywhere around us—as the Internet, for Cloud Computing, or to facilitate parallel and distributed processing and storage.
8. *Group of people mediated by a system.* Combining scenarios 3 and 6, we can have a situation where a group of people are interacting with each other mediated by a system. Most of the online social networking sites can fall under this scenario.

Since the focus here is on studying computer-supported collaboration, the process of CIS, by the given definition, involves at least two users and one intermediary system. As shown earlier in Fig. 5.5, the users of a CIS environment could communicate with each other through the system or interface provided to them, but we can

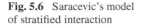

Fig. 5.6 Saracevic's model
of stratified interaction

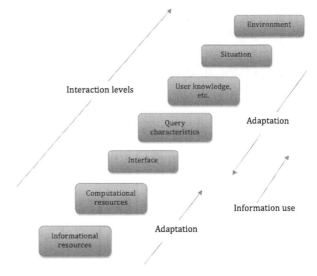

also imagine having interactions that do not require such an intermediary if the users
are co-located. For instance, Root [46] showed how exchange of ideas around the
coffee machine is a popular way of collaborating with other people, often without
using any system. This suggests that while designing a CIS system, we should be
open to the possibility of different forms of interactions: human to human, human
to system, and human to human mediated by a system.

Consider the user interactions with IR systems. Saracevic [47] provided a good
review of various models of such interactions. To be specific, he identified three
models.

1. *Traditional model.* This model, as he said, "... represents IR as a two prong
   set (system and user) of elements and processes converging on comparison or
   matching ..."
2. *Ingwersen's cognitive model.* This model [32] "... concentrates on identifying
   processes of cognition which may occur in all the information processing elements involved."
3. *Belkin's episode model.* This model [6] "... considers user interaction with an
   IR system as a sequence of differing interactions in an episode of information
   seeking ..."

Saracevic himself then provided a model, which he called the *stratified interaction model* (Fig. 5.6). This model was developed within an overall framework of an
'acquisition-cognition-application' model of information use. The levels or strata
posited by Saracevic are simplified to three: *surface*, or the level of interaction between the user and the system interface; *cognition*, or the level of interaction with
the texts or their representation; and the *situation*, or the context that provides the
initial problem at hand.

With such a stratified model with multiple interaction and processing strata for
the user and for the system, Saracevic [49] suggested that the user and the system

Table 5.1 Information seeking strategies (Belkin et al., 1995)

ISS	Method	Goal	Mode	Resources
1	Scan	Learn	Recognize	Information
2	Scan	Learn	Recognize	Meta-Information
3	Scan	Learn	Specify	Information
4	Scan	Learn	Specify	Meta-Information
5	Scan	Select	Recognize	Information
6	Scan	Select	Recognize	Meta-Information
7	Scan	Select	Specify	Information
8	Scan	Select	Specify	Meta-Information
9	Search	Learn	Recognize	Information
10	Search	Learn	Recognize	Meta-Information
11	Search	Learn	Specify	Information
12	Search	Learn	Specify	Meta-Information
13	Search	Select	Recognize	Information
14	Search	Select	Recognize	Meta-Information
15	Search	Select	Specify	Information
16	Search	Select	Specify	Meta-Information

have equal constraints on the search. The system side of this model was later extended by Spink et al. [56], who added a graduated relevance dimension, and Bates [4], who identified additional levels that interact and affect each other. The key idea of these stratified models of interaction is that even if all other components but one are executed effectively on either the user or system side, the component that was done poorly can hinder the value of the entire system. For instance, a user's interpretation of results may seriously affect their success in achieving their goals with the system. This allows us to evaluate every layer of the model to check for the bottlenecks in the performance. However, stratified models themselves do not provide a way to evaluate the layers. This and some of the other shortcomings of the stratified models were addressed by episodic models proposed by Belkin et al. [6]. These kind of models define the flow of scenarios in human-system interactions. The flow definitions are called "scripts", which define the typical steps of interaction between a user and a system. To do this, Belkin et al. proposed the use of four binary dimensions—*Method, Goal, Mode*, and *Resources*. Possible combinations of these four dimensions produce what they called Information Seeking Strategies (ISS), presented in Table 5.1. They calculate separate scripts for each of these 16 ISS conditions, which allow for switching between them.

Let us see how these ISS conditions inform user interactions in various information seeking situations. A typical information seeking situation is a user searching on the web with a search engine. This interaction can be fit in ISS15, where the user is searching (Method) to select (Goal) by specifying (Mode) attributes of a spe-

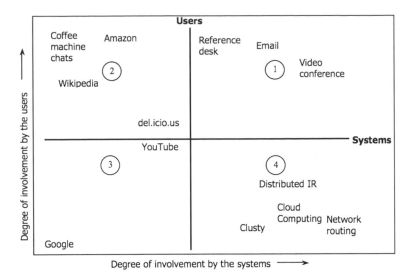

Fig. 5.7 Looking at collaboration with the amount of user and system involvement

cific information object (Resource). For collaborative information seeking, we can imagine the users going through various forms of such interactions, the knowledge of which could provide us with enough information to evaluate the quality of the whole information seeking experience.

How User and System Interaction Relates to CIS   The models that are listed above give us a plethora of information for observing and evaluating various forms of user and system interactions. However, they do not tell us enough about the degree to which a user or a system is involved. While it is also assumed that the interactions are intentional or explicitly specified, we can imagine a gradation of involvement for both the user and the system in an interactive environment. Such understanding is important to extend interactions among users and systems to collaboration. To address these issues, two different ways of looking at the interplay of the user and the system in collaboration are presented below.

5.3.1 Degree of Involvement

Figure 5.7 presents collaborative systems in the context of the degree of involvement that a user or system component has. The four quadrants, starting top-right and going in the counter-clockwise direction are explained below.

- The first quadrant shows the applications where a high degree of interactions among users and systems produce collaboration. In the case of email or a video conference, there is an end-to-end collaboration between users and it is facilitated by certain protocols and communications between systems of those ends.

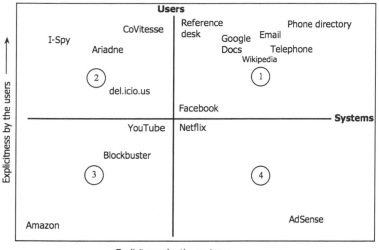

Fig. 5.8 Looking at collaboration with the amount of explicitness or intention from user and system

- The second quadrant shows the situations in which the users have a high degree of interaction to facilitate the collaboration, but the systems do not play much of a role. For instance, an exchange of ideas around the coffee machine is a popular way of collaborating with people, often without using any system [46].
- The third quadrant represents most of the IR systems that are designed for a single user.
- The fourth quadrant shows the applications where there is a higher degree of interactions among systems than among users. For instance, meta-search engines, such as Clusty, allow a single user to search different systems and combine the results. In the far right corner of this quadrant, we can also see applications such as Cloud Computing and distributed IR (see [10] for a thorough treatment on this topic).

5.3.2 Explicitness of Collaboration

Figure 5.8 presents various collaborative systems in the light of how explicit or intentional a user or system component is. The four quadrants, starting top-right and going in the counter-clockwise direction are explained below.

- The first quadrant shows applications where both the system and the user explicitly collaborate. For instance, in case of a patron walking up to the reference desk in a library for an information need, there is an explicit collaboration between users and some degree of explicit collaboration with the system (e.g., using OPAC). In case of a phone directory, a user agrees to put his information in the public; he and others receive the directory that has everybody's public information.

- The second quadrant has applications where there is more explicitness for collaboration from the user side and less from the system side. For instance, the *Ariadne* system [60, 61] allows two users to explicitly collaborate while handling a lot of aspects of collaboration implicitly. Another example in this quadrant is a social bookmarking service such as del.icio.us, where the users store bookmarks, not only for their own reference, but also to share with others. The system handles this aspect of collaboration internally.
- The third quadrant shows applications where the users' collaboration as well as the system's implementation of this collaboration is more implicit. For instance, users of Amazon.com receive certain information that is influenced by other users, but not formally defined or intended.
- The fourth quadrant shows applications where implicit collaboration among the users is done explicitly by the systems.[4] For instance, users of Google implicitly agree to receive ads based on their searching; Google puts targeted ads (AdSense[5]) on search pages.

It is implied that a *true* collaboration occurs among humans, and that there has to be intentionality for doing so. For the purpose of this book, it is useful to think of collaboration as *only* those activities where a group of people have explicitly agreed to work together. This immediately discards any of the collaborative filtering systems that we saw earlier as they do not support *true* collaboration. Thus, a need to differentiate between implicit and explicit collaboration is eliminated, inferring that a *true* collaboration is among humans, and it is intentional or explicit, and interactive.

5.4 Toward a Cognitive Model for CIS

While there are many theories relating to CIS, and no comprehensive model, it is important for the fair treatment of this book's subject to at least look at one way of creating a CIS model. For that, we will start with Kuhlthau's information search processes (ISP) model [33], and see how this could help us create a cognitive model for CIS, with similar stages of search process as well as considering the affective dimension of information seeking.

5.4.1 Capturing Affective Dimension of CIS

It has been recognized by many that emotions play an important role in human life. To this effect, emotions, moods, or feelings may alter our decisions, behaviors,

---

[4]See glossary section of this book for the definitions of implicit and explicit collaborations.

[5]https://www.google.com/adsense/.

thoughts, memories, interactions, and so on [12]. For many years researchers have been studying emotions and trying to explain their participation in various contexts. Information science has not been the exception; indeed, it has been argued that emotions have an active participation in information-related activities.

In the particular case of CIS, some have attempted to explain how affective processes of individuals working in collaboration with others relate to the way they perform when searching information. Studies from communication and CSCW have provided an important theoretical and empirical framework to generate research questions and hypothesize about possible explanations of the relation between emotions and CIS.

Emotions were considered a secondary area of studies for several centuries, in part due to initial claims that placed them as an irrational and negative component of human behavior. Only during the past century, a paradigm shift regarding emotions placed them on top of various research domains. Primary fields of research about emotions such as philosophy, neurophysiology, and psychology, generated a great deal of concepts, definitions, and theories. At the same time, the participation in this process of different currents of thoughts led to several controversies that have not reached consensus yet. To date it is possible to find hundreds of definitions for the word "Emotion", which makes it almost impossible to define this concept in a way that matches with all other authors' definitions [43]. In information science, this problem has been recognized in a recent work by Lopatovska and Arapakis [35].

This situation has not stopped the progress of other areas in the study of emotions; however, not having a clear definition has led information scientists to refer to emotions and related concepts in a broad sense. As a result, it is not uncommon to find in the literature of these fields the interchangeable use of concepts such as emotion, affect, feeling, and mood. The problem is that such concepts may refer to different psychological and physiological processes.

As described in Palmero et al. [43], when compared to emotion and mood, affect is the most general of all three. It is linked directly to physiological processes and normally described under a dimensional approach, which involves valence (positive or negative) and intensity (high or low). Affects usually are addressed toward external or internal aspects such as situations, people, or objects, which result in approximation to pleasant conditions and estrangement from unpleasant ones.

In a similar way, Palmero et al. [43] describes mood as a particular form of affective process also characterized by valence and intensity. Unlike affects, mood lasts less time and includes implicit components such as beliefs that indicate how likely an individual will experience certain affects in the future. Other authors such as Echeverría [17] have added that mood may determine our actions as human beings.

Emotions on the other hand have been defined as primitive responses of individuals to external or internal stimuli. Unlike affect and mood, emotions are shorter in duration, but intense and spontaneous. Emotions are usually classified into basic and secondary [8] categories (discrete approach). While the former are inherent and universal (e.g., happiness, sadness, and surprise) for human beings, the latter are socially developed (e.g., gratitude and ambition) and are expressed in terms of the basic ones.

Finally, feelings as presented by Palmero et al. [43] are the subjective dimension of emotions. Compared to emotions, affects, and moods, feelings are conceived to be at a higher order. Feelings appear when individuals become aware that they are experiencing a particular emotion.

Regardless these conceptual problems, there is an important corpus of literature covering emotions in information science. Since Kuhlthau's [33] information search process (ISP), several other authors have been exploring the affective dimension of individuals when engaging in information-related activities. Even though similar models were proposed during that time, the main distinction of Kuhlthau's was the incorporation of affective and cognitive components linked to each stage.

During the last twenty years, some authors have explored the participation of emotions in various information domains, from daily life activities to very specific settings. Both qualitative and quantitative studies have revealed how emotions, in a broad sense, are influenced by or influence the way individuals search information [7, 27, 43, 48, 59].

One major distinction between the ISP of groups and individuals is the social interaction among group members as a result of the workgroup. Either they work synchronously or asynchronously, co-located or remotely located; people need to interact in order to accomplish their goals. Such interactions are driven by communication among group members (face-to-face or mediated).

With regard to the affective dimension, unlike the ISP of individuals, in collaborative scenarios emotions are derived not only from specific episodes as a result of searching information but also from interactions with people. In this sense the dynamics of emotions, feelings, or moods are much more complex to explain than in individual settings.

Few researchers have explored, implicitly or explicitly the affective dimension in CIS. For example, Hyldegard [30, 31] studied the applicability of Kuhlthau's model in educational and collaborative settings, this includes the participation of emotions/feelings. Similarly, Shah and Gonzalez-Ibanez [54] attempted to map Kuhlthau's ISP stages to collaborative search tasks. One particular aspect of this study was the identification of polarity-based affects (positive and negative) from conversation analyses. As a result, authors found particular affective patterns linked to each stage. Based on the same study, González-Ibáez and Shah [54] identified that affective relevance in CIS is affected not only by the interaction with information objects, but also by the interaction with people. Elements like reinforcement, support, opposition, agreement, or disagreement (which does not appear in individual information seeking situations) play a fundamental role in the way people perceive and determine what information is relevant and what is not. In a more recent study, Gonzalez-Ibanez et al. [28] described that the expression of emotions such as happiness derives primarily from the interaction among group members. In contrast, emotions in individual settings are barely expressed by information seekers.

In a natural overlap with areas such as computer supported cooperative work (CSCW) and communication, studies about the affective dimension in CIS could be benefited by a great deal of research corpus in these fields. For example, studies about collaboration from a positive psychology standpoint have argued that emotions have such important participation in a workgroup that could even predict how teams will perform [22, 36].

In order to achieve a better understanding about the affective dimension in CIS, it is necessary to properly define the underlying theoretical framework to formulate research questions and hypothesize in accordance. In addition to that, it is necessary to find adequate tools that allow researchers to measure emotions accurately. The existence of particular research frameworks and resource in fields such as communication and CSCW could facilitate this process; however, the challenge of determining what theoretical frameworks, concepts, findings, as well as resources are more appropriated for the particular domain of CIS, is still a highly complex goal.

5.4.2 Extending Information Seeking Processes (ISP) Model for Collaboration

As one of the most representative models in information seeking, Kuhlthau's information search process (ISP) model [33] formally described from user's perspective the flow of activities that he/she goes through while seeking information. Unlike other models, this model includes the cognitive and affective dimension as distinctive elements of each stage. More specifically, this model has six stages, which include feelings, thoughts, and actions that were identified through empirical studies.

A key aspect of this model is the idea of uncertainty, defined by the author as a negative feeling; however, as pointed out by other authors, such as Anderson [1], uncertainty can also be considered positive. Note that the identification of this particular affective state as well as the others was achieved subjectively through self-reports and interviews. To date, few studies have explored the affective dimension from a physiological, linguistic, and expressive perspective.

As mentioned before, the area of information seeking as social and collaborative phenomenon has been under-studied. Only in recent years some researchers have embarked on the development of particular models of CIS, which include the evaluation and applicability of traditional information seeking models, like the one proposed by Kuhlthau's. Some examples in this regard are the works of Hyldegard [30, 31], Reddy and Jansen [44], Reddy, Jansen, and Krishnappa [45], and Yue and He (2010). In particular, Hyldegard [31] studied Kuhlthau's ISP in the context of teams in educational settings, and found that although there were similarities at the general stages between individual and collaborative behaviors in information seeking, there were also important differences with regard to contextual aspects associated to social factors. As a result, the author concluded that Kuhlthau's ISP did not completely meet the social dimension of CIS and also that affective states (negative and positive) of participants did not necessarily coincide with those specified in the original model.

Our interest in exploring Kuhlthau's model in collaborative context is not limited to the study of the stages and the affective dimension, but also extends to some of the actions associated to ISP, in particular those related to the identification of relevant information. When people seek information collaboratively, they also share and evaluate the collected information. In this regard, as pointed out by Kuhlthau [33] (p. 363), people's affective state may influence the relevance judgments, which are directly related to the concept of affective relevance [50, 51]. According to Saracevic [50], affective relevance corresponds to the "relation between the intents, goals, emotions, and motivations of a user, and information (retrieved or in the systems file, or even in existence)" (p. 1931). In addition, our particular interest in studying affective relevance in the context of CIS and ISP is due to works such as Carasik and Grantham [11] who argue that in collaborative environments emotions play a role that should be studied in detail to understand the behaviors of teams. Indeed, it has been shown that both positive and negative feelings are necessary for improving the performance of teams [36]. Several other works have also showed that by improving the emotional resources of the communication media used for collaborating, teams may achieve better results (e.g., [23, 26]).

We conducted a laboratory study with 84 participants in 42 pairs, who came to the lab for two separate sessions, each time working on two tasks (the same two tasks from the first session were continued in the second session). We collected log data as well as the messages the participants exchanged during the study. We showed how various actions and the kinds of messages exchanged in such a CIS project could be mapped to different stages of Kuhlthau's ISP model. A summary of our analyses is reported below. The details can be found in [54].

Since we did not measure a participant's mental state, nor observe them directly for their behavior during various phases of their tasks, we will depend on the log and other forms of data collected during the study for mapping six different ISP stages for our analysis. These mappings, pertaining to the presented study, are described below.

1. *Initiation*: This is the part when the participants read the task and greet each other. It is measured by the number of chat messages exchanged between the participants during this phase. Due to the interactive nature of our study, we decided to expand this stage to also include the messages that were exchanged in- between stages for checking on each other's status.
2. *Selection*: This is when the participants discuss how they want to divide up the task and proceed. It is measured by the number of messages exchanged discussing the strategy for a given task.
3. *Exploration*: This is mapped to the number of search queries used by a given team.
4. *Formulation*: This is measured by the number of webpages looked at by a given team.
5. *Collection*: This is measured by the number of webpages or snippets collected by a given team.
6. *Presentation*: This occurs only during the second session when the participants are asked to organize their collected snippets. It is measured by the number of moving actions performed by each team on their collected snippets.

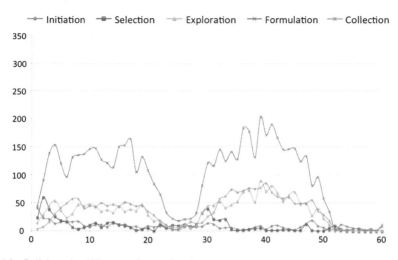

Fig. 5.9 Collaborative ISP stages for session-1

To study ISP stages and participants' feelings, as well as affective relevance within a team, we analyzed the coded messages per session (see [54] about how the coding was done). Since each of the two sessions lasted for about 60 minute, discounting the preparation and the ending phases (from login to filling in end-session questionnaire), we divided up each team's session into 60 segments, roughly reflecting one minute each, and looked at six ISP stages as well as polarity of their feelings and the corresponding affective relevance expressed in each of those segments. The combined plots for all the 42 teams for their two sessions are presented in Figs. 5.9, 5.10, 5.11 and 5.12. Let us analyze these plots by studying the most prominent parts.

We can see that during the first session (Fig. 5.9), the participants exchanged a few messages in the beginning (task-1) as well as somewhere in the middle (task-2), around the time they were reading a given task (Initiation). Right after these parts, the participants engaged in discussing the task and devising a strategy (Selection). For the rest of the session, we see the participants working through three stages: querying (Exploration), looking through webpages (Formulation), and saving relevant webpages and snippets (Collection).

During the second session (Fig. 5.11), in addition to the above five stages, we also see two distinctive peaks occurring at the end of each task. These peaks represent the parts when the participants were organizing their collected snippets (Presentation).

In addition to the analysis above, the affective dimension of the CIS process was explored through the presence of positive and negative messages in the chat logs, discarding the neutral ones. Here, positive messages were associated with pleasant feelings such as clarity, satisfaction, and relief; while negative messages were related with unpleasant feelings such as uncertainty, confusion, and disappointment. Based on this dichotomy, we can observe abundance of positive messages in comparison to the negative ones during the initial segments of the first session (Fig. 5.10). These messages were typically related to greetings between the participants and their positive attitude prior performing the tasks. After this short period, while both Initiation

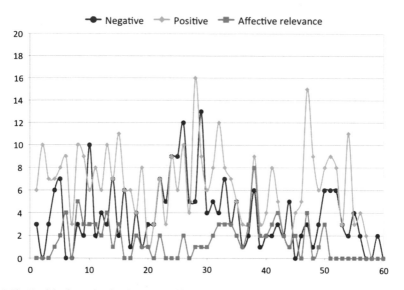

Fig. 5.10 Positive/negative feelings, and affective relevance for session-1

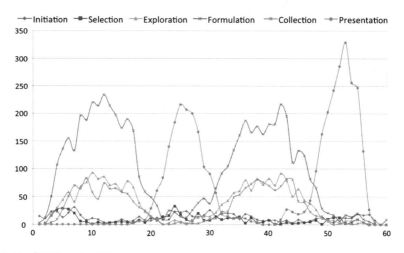

Fig. 5.11 Collaborative ISP stages for session-2

and Selection stages begin to converge and Exploration increases; negative messages grow and they start varying similarly to positive messages. This may be due to frustration and confusion experienced by users in the exploration stage as well as some problems with the system.

Overall, positive messages are greater (63 %) than negative ones (37 %); however, in certain segments the latter exceed the former, specially when stages intersect and also in the inflection points of the Collection stage. Moreover, as the participants make a transition from the first task to the second, negative message show a surge.

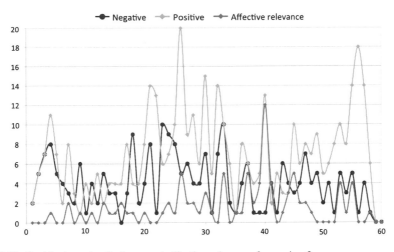

Fig. 5.12   Positive/negative feelings, and affective relevance for session-2

As the second task continues, negative messages decrease and variations occur in a similar way as the first task. It is only in the last segments of the second task that we can once again see an important difference between positive and negative messages.

The second session exhibits similar behaviors as the first one in terms of the categories of the messages; however, a visible distinction can be observed at the end of each task, which coincides with the emergence of the Presentation stage. As presented in Fig. 5.12, abundance of positive feelings and low levels of negative ones appear at the segments associated to this stage. This may be related to the experience of relief and satisfaction of the participants as they finish each task.

The constant variations of the polarity of messages can be linked to the discussion between the participants with regard to the information sources explored and shared. Indeed, it is in these periods where users exposed their individual and affective judgments about the information they collected, in addition to receiving affective (positive or negative) feedback from their collaborator. For each session, approximately 14 % of the messages were coded as related to affective relevance.

Although the identification of specific affects within the ISP is limited when done by analyzing sentiments at the linguistic level, the use of the polarity approach allows us to cover the diversity of feelings at the macro level. Hence, in contrast to Kuhlthau's ISP, individuals in CIS tasks may experience pleasant and unpleasant feelings in each stage, with the predominance of one over the other in certain points.

In relation to the affective relevance explained above, users expressed their feelings regarding the information they found and shared during the ISP, especially within the segments associated to high levels of Exploration, Formulation, and Collection. In the transitions from one task to another, as well as in the Presentation phase the affective relevance practically vanishes. It was also observed that the selection of relevant information was first done by an individual participant and then subjected to the group's judgment and reflection. Table 5.2 summarizes the predom-

Table 5.2 Summary of participants' feelings and affective relevance through ISP stages

ISP Stage	Predominant Feelings	Level of Affective Relevance
Initiation	Positive and Negative	No
Selection	Positive and Negative	Low
Exploration	Positive	High
Formulation	Positive	High
Collection	Positive	High
Presentation	Positive	Low
Transitions	*Positive and Negative*	*Low*

inant feelings and levels of affective relevance for the ISP stages and also for the transitions among them.

We found that for both the sessions, Initiation was highly correlated with Selection ($p < 0.001$), whereas Exploration, Formulation, and Collection were strongly correlated ($p < 0.001$). Not surprisingly, Presentation was negatively correlated with Exploration, Formulation, and Collection ($p < 0.001$).

5.5 Summary

Mining the cumulative data of all the groups over two sessions, we clearly identified the stages of Initiation, Selection, Exploration, Formulation, Collection, and Presentation. In addition, we also analyzed all the chat messages for expressed feelings (positive or negative), and relevance by the participants. Our analysis revealed some interesting insights into ISP stages as well as affective relevance in CIS. We discovered that Exploration, Formulation, and Collection were not distinct stages. In fact, they were found to be highly correlated indicating quick switches between them by the participants. In other words, we discovered that the participants went back and forth between trying search queries, exploring various sources, and collecting relevant information as they worked through the task while interacting with their collaborators.

In a larger picture, we realized that ISP is a reasonable model to begin exploring various information seeking processes that take place during collaborative search tasks, and could provide us interesting insights into individual and group dynamics during a CIS project. In addition to Hyldegard's finding that ISP model lacks social element in a collaborative setting, the work reported in the previous section indicates that various ISP stages in CIS setting also need to be considered in the light of affective dimension for the collaborators, as well as group's affective relevance.

References

1. T.D. Anderson. Uncertainty in action: observing information seeking within the creative processes of scholarly research. *Information Research*, 12(1):283, 2006.
2. Peter Anick. Using terminological feedback for web search refinement—a log-based study. In *Proceedings of the Annual ACM Conference on Research and Development in Information Retrieval (SIGIR)*, pages 88–95, 2003.
3. Javed A. Aslam and Mark Montague. Models for metasearch. In *Proceedings of the Annual ACM Conference on Research and Development in Information Retrieval (SIGIR)*, pages 276–284, 2001.
4. Marcia J. Bates. The cascade of interactions in the digital library interface. *Information Processing and Management*, 38(3):381–400, 2002.
5. Nicholas J. Belkin. Anomalous states of knowledge as a basis for information retrieval. *Canadian Journal of Information Science*, 5:133–143, 1980.
6. Nicholas J. Belkin, Colleen Cool, Adelheit Stein and Ulrich Thiel. Cases, scripts, and information-seeking strategies: on the design of interactive information retrieval systems. *Expert Systems with Applications*, 9:379–395, 1995.
7. Dania Bilal. Children's use of the Yahooligans! Web search engine: I. Cognitive, physical, and affective behaviors on fact-based search tasks. *Journal of the American Society for Information Science*, 51(7):646–665, 2000.
8. Susana Bloch. ALBA emoting: a psychophysiological technique to help actors create and control real emotions. *Theatre Topics*, 3(2):121–138, 1993.
9. Chris Buckley, Gerald Salton and James Allen. The effect of adding relevance information in a relevance feedback environment. In *Proceedings of the Annual ACM Conference on Research and Development in Information Retrieval (SIGIR)*, pages 292–300, Dept. of Computer Science, Cornell University, 1994. Springer, New York.
10. Jamie Callan. *Distributed Information Retrieval*, volume 7 of The Information Retrieval Series, pages 127–150. Springer, Dordrecht, 2002.
11. R.P. Carasik and C.E. Grantham. A case study of CSCW in a dispersed organization. In *Proceedings of the SIGCHI Conference on Human Factors in Computing Systems*, pages 61–66, 1988. ACM, Washington.
12. Antonio R. Damasio. *Descartes' Error: Emotion, Reason, and the Human Brain*. 1st edn. Harper Perennial, New York, 1995.
13. Peter J. Denning and Peter Yaholkovsky. Getting to "We". *Communications of the ACM*, 51(4):19–24, 2008.
14. Brenda Dervin. Useful theory for librarianship: communication, not information. *Drexel Library Quarterly*, 13(3):16–32, 1977.
15. Brenda Dervin and Michael S. Nilan. Information needs and uses. *Annual Review of Information Science and Technology (ARIST)*, 21:3–33, 1986.
16. Susan T. Dumais, Edward Cutrell, J.J. Cadiz, Gavin Jancke, Raman Sarin and Daniel C. Robbins. Stuff I've seen: a system for personal information retrieval and re-use. In *Proceedings of the Annual ACM Conference on Research and Development in Information Retrieval (SIGIR)*. ACM, New York, 2003.
17. Rafael Echeverría. *La ontología del lenguaje*. Dolmen Ediciones, Caracas, 1994.
18. D. Ellis. A behavioral approach to information retrieval design. *Journal of Documentation*, 46:318–338, 1989.
19. D. Ellis, D. Cox and K. Hall. A comparison of the information seeking patterns of researchers in the physical and social sciences. *Journal of Documentation*, 49:356–369, 1993.
20. D. Ellis and M. Haugan. Modelling the information seeking patterns of engineers and research scientists in an industrial environment. *Journal of Documentation*, 53(4):384–403, 1997.
21. Tom Erickson. From PIM to GIM: personal information management in group contexts. *Communications of the ACM*, 49(1):40–43, 2006.

22. B.L. Fredrickson and M.F. Losada. Positive affect and the complex dynamics of human flourishing. *The American Psychologist*, 60(7):678–686, 2005.
23. O. García, J. Favela and R. Machorro. Emotional awareness in collaborative systems. In *Proceedings of String Processing and Information Retrieval Symposium, 1999 and International Workshop on Groupware*, pages 296–303, 1999.
24. Luca Gerosa, Alessandra Giordani, Marco Ronchetti, Amy Soller and Ron Stevens. Symmetric synchronous collaborative navigation. In *Proceedings of the 2004 IADIS International WWW/Internet Conference*, pages 1–7, Madrid, Spain, October 2004.
25. Gene Golovchinsky, Jeremy Pickens and Maribeth Back. A taxonomy of collaboration in online information seeking. In *Proceedings of JCDL 2008 Workshop on Collaborative Exploratory Search*, Pittsburgh, PA, June 2008.
26. Roberto González. *Evaluación de la Integración del Darse-Cuenta Emocional en una Aplicación Colaborativa*. Master's thesis, Universidad de Santiago de Chile, 2006.
27. Roberto I. González-Ibáñez and Chirag Shah. Group's affective relevance: a proposal for studying affective relevance in collaborative information seeking. In *Proceedings of the 16th ACM International Conference on Supporting Group Work, GROUP '10*, pages 317–318, 2010. ACM, New York.
28. Roberto Gonzalez-Ibanez, Chirag Shah and N.R. Cardova. Smile! Studying expressivity of happiness as a synergic factor in collaborative information seeking. In *Proceedings of American Society of Information Science & Technology (ASIST) Annual Meeting*, 2011.
29. Barbara Gray. *Collaborating: Finding Common Ground for Multiparty Problems*. Jossey-Bass, San Francisco, 1989.
30. Jette Hyldegard. Collaborative information behavior—exploring Kuhlthau's Information Search Process model in a group-based educational setting. *Information Processing and Management*, 42:276–298, 2006.
31. Jette Hyldegard. Beyond the search process—exploring group members' information behavior in context. *Information Processing and Management*, 45:142–158, 2009.
32. P. Ingwersen. Cognitive perspectives of information retrieval interaction: elements of a cognitive IR theory. *Journal of Documentation*, 52:3–50, 1996.
33. Carol C. Kuhlthau. Inside the search process: information seeking from the user's perspective. *Journal of the American Society for Information Science and Technology*, 42(5):361–371, 1991.
34. Carol C. Kuhlthau. *Seeking Meaning: A Process Approach to Library and Information Services*. Ablex Publishing, Norwood, 1994.
35. Irene Lopatovska and Ioannis Arapakis. Theories, methods and current research on emotions in library and information science, information retrieval and human–computer interaction. *Information Processing and Management*, 47(4):575–592, 2011.
36. M. Losada and E. Heaphy. The role of positivity and connectivity in the performance of business teams: a nonlinear dynamics model. *American Behavioral Scientist*, 47(6):740–765, 2004.
37. Gary Marchionini. Information-seeking strategies of novices using a full-text electronic encyclopedia. *Journal of the American Society for Information Science*, 40(1):54–66, 1989.
38. Gary Marchionini. *Information Seeking in Electronic Environments*. Cambridge University Press, Cambridge, 1995.
39. S.M. Miller and C.E. Mangan. Interesting effects of information and coping style in adapting to gynaecological stress: should a doctor tell all? *Journal of Personality and Social Psychology*, 45:223–226, 1983.
40. Meredith Ringel Morris. A survey of collaborative web search practices. In *Proceedings of ACM SIGCHI Conference on Human Factors in Computing Systems*, pages 1657–1660, Florence, Italy, 2008.
41. Meredith Ringel Morris and Eric Horvitz. SearchTogether: an interface for collaborative web search. In *ACM Symposium on User Interface Software and Technology (UIST)*, pages 3–12, Newport, RI, October 2007.

42. Meredith Ringel Morris, Jaime Teevan and Steve Bush. Enhancing collaborative web search with personalization: groupization, smart splitting, and group hit-highlighting. In *Proceedings of Computer Supported Cooperative Work (CSCW)*, San Diego, CA, November 2008.
43. Diane Nahl and Carol Tenopir. Affective and cognitive searching behavior of novice end-users of a full-text database. *Journal of the American Society for Information Science*, 47(4):276–286, 1996.
44. M.C. Reddy and B.J. Jansen. A model for understanding collaborative information behavior in context: a study of two healthcare teams. *Information Processing and Management*, 44(1):256–273, 2008.
45. Madhu C. Reddy, Bernard J. Jansen and R. Krishnappa. The role of communication in collaborative information searching. In *Proceedings of American Society of Information Science & Technology (ASIST) Annual Meeting*, Columbus, OH, 2008.
46. Robert W. Root. Design of a multi-media vehicle for social browsing. In *Proceedings of the Conference on Computer-Supported Cooperative Work (CSCW)*, pages 25–38, 1988.
47. Tefko Saracevic. Modeling interaction in information retrieval (IR): a review and proposal. In *Annual Meeting of the American Society for Information Science*, pages 3–9, Silver Spring, MD, 1996.
48. Tefko Saracevic. Relevance reconsidered. Information science: Integration in perspectives. In *Proceedings of the Second Conference on Conceptions of Library and Information Science*, Copenhagen, Denmark, pages 201–218, 1996.
49. Tefko Saracevic. The stratified model of information retrieval interaction: extension and applications. In *Proceedings of American Society of Information Science*, pages 313–327, 1997.
50. Tefko Saracevic. Relevance: a review of the literature and a framework for thinking on the notion in information science. Part II: Nature and manifestations of relevance. *Journal of the American Society for Information Science and Technology*, 58(13):1915–1933, 2007.
51. Tefko Saracevic. Relevance: a review of the literature and a framework for thinking on the notion in information science. Part III: Behavior and effects of relevance. *Journal of the American Society for Information Science and Technology*, 58(13):2126–2144, 2007.
52. Chirag Shah. Toward Collaborative Information Seeking (CIS). In *Proceedings of JCDL 2008 Workshop on Collaborative Exploratory Search*, Pittsburgh, PA, 2008.
53. Chirag Shah. Working in collaboration—what, why, and how? In *Proceedings of Collaborative Information Retrieval Workshop at CSCW 2010*, Savannah, GA, 2010.
54. Chirag Shah and Roberto Gonzalez-Ibanez. Exploring information seeking processes in collaborative search tasks. In *Annual Meeting of the American Society for Information Science*, Pittsburgh, PA, 2010.
55. Chirag Shah, Gary Marchionini and Diane Kelly. Learning design principles for a collaborative information seeking system. In *Extended Proceedings of ACM SIGCHI Conference on Human Factors in Computing Systems*, Boston, MA, April 2009.
56. Amanda Spink, Howard Greisdorf and Judy Bateman. From highly relevant to not relevant: examining different regions of relevance. *Information Processing and Management*, 34(5):599–621, 1998.
57. Ellen Taylor-Powell, Boyd Rossing and Jean Geran. Evaluating collaboratives: reaching the potential. Technical report, University of Wisconsin-Extension, Madison, Wisconsin, July 1998.
58. Jaime Teevan, Susan T. Dumais and Eric Horvitz. Personalizing search via automated analysis of interests and activities. In *Proceedings of the Annual ACM Conference on Research and Development in Information Retrieval (SIGIR)*, pages 449–456, 2005.
59. Carol Tenopir, Peiling Wang, Yan Zhang, Beverly Simmons and Richard Pollard. Academic users' interactions with ScienceDirect in search tasks: Affective and cognitive behaviors. *Information Processing and Management*, 44(1):105–121, 2008.
60. Michael B. Twidale and David M. Nichols. Collaborative browsing and visualisation of the search process. *Aslib Proceedings*, 48(7–8):177–182, 1996.

61. Michael B. Twidale, David M. Nichols and Chris D. Paice. Browsing is a collaborative process. *Information Processing and Management*, 33(6):761–783, 1997.
62. T.D. Wilson. Information behavior: an interdisciplinary perspective. *Information Processing and Management*, 33(4):551–572, 1997.
63. T.D. Wilson. Models in information behavior research. *Journal of Documentation*, 55(3):249–270, 1999.

specialized tools to support CIS, but we do not know what such tools may look like and how we could promote them to people without causing additional burden to them.

2. We have seen a number of works done to understand people working with collaborative systems such as SearchTogether, and people's behavior in online communities and social networking sites. A link that connects these two is missing. In other words, we do not know how we can leverage people's engagement in social networking sites to promote collaborations, or support various social activities with collaborative systems.

3. How to measure the costs and benefits of collaboration? We saw that providing awareness induces additional cost, but if we are careful designing our CIS system, we can harvest many benefits of this awareness without causing any significant burden on the user. Similar investigations for other important issues for CIS, such as control and communication, are needed for developing a comprehensive understanding of various design issues in CIS.

4. What are the information seeking situations in which collaboration is beneficial? When does it not pay off? This book started with an acknowledgement that collaboration is not always useful or desired, and then focused on only those situations where it is intentional and beneficial. Further investigations are needed to also study the situations where collaboration is potentially harmful. This understanding can help us do a better cost-benefit analysis of doing collaboration in a given situation.

5. How to extend individual information seeking, synthesis, and sense-making models to incorporate collaboration? This book was focused on people working on information seeking process in collaboration. It is possible that certain form of information synthesis and sense-making are also taking place during such information seeking process. For the sake of simplifying the studies, such possibilities were ignored here, and needs further investigation in the future studies. Chapter 4 outlined several traditional and new frameworks for CIS. Similar frameworks for collaborative information synthesis and sense-making are needed.

6. How can we convert a social tie to a collaborative tie and vice versa? Through relevant literature review, this book suggested that there might be ways to facilitate collaborative processes in social environments. Given the ubiquitous nature of online social networks, this issue merits further investigation.

8.3 Experimental and Practical Issues

1. Several of the research studies reported in the literature are targeted toward a specific population—college students, professionals in social sciences, and knowledge workers. Further investigations are needed to study other specialized populations, such as families with health issues, and intelligent analysts working in teams. This may require employing different methods of studying collaboration, including cognitive walkthroughs, and empirical observations.

2. The laboratory studies, which many of the research works employ, can be extended to field studies, allowing the participants to work without several limitations the controlled lab study had. The participants in a field study could work with the system as they please, creating their own projects of interest, and initiating collaborators with their colleagues and friends as they see fit. Running a field study over a long period of time (at least a few weeks) will also allow one to study long-term adoption effects, appropriation factor, and specialization with various features of the system.

3. What kind of visualization methods can be useful for CIS interfaces? Systems such as SearchTogether [8] and Coagmento [11] provide a very basic interface for viewing personal and shared information. However, the issue of having new kinds of dynamic and interactive interfaces appeared highly important during the participatory design sessions reported here. This issue deserves more advance treatment with interface designs and experimentations.

4. What additional tools are required to enhance existing methods of collaboration, given a specific domain? Such domains may include office environments, educational settings, or even domestic projects. In this book, we saw that in order to extend an individual information seeking process to collaborative information seeking, we need to not only create a support system that connects the collaborators and makes it easy for them to communicate, but also provide appropriate and adequate awareness. Such requirements and specifications may vary from domain to domain.

5. One way to extend analyses done for many of the collaborative experiments is by considering a team, rather than an individual, as the unit of analysis. Allowing any size of group for a collaborative project, and studying the group dynamics can be a very complex procedure, but can also provide us with very insightful details into how people collaborate and what kind of support they need to make their collaborations more effective and engaging.

6. The CSCW literature identifies three major issues in a CIS environment: control, communication, and awareness. Control is domain specific; communication is system specific; but awareness may depend on several factors, including task, distribution of responsibilities among the collaborators, roles of the collaborators, nature of the final product, need for privacy and sharing among the collaborators, and the nature of their collaboration (synchronous vs. asynchronous, co-located vs. remote). The issue of awareness is highly understudied in the CIS literature and a good understanding of implementing support for awareness in a CIS system would add considerable value to CIS theory and practice. In general, there is a need to sketch out good design practices for building specialized CIS systems.

7. There are a few works in the literature with suggestions for evaluating a CIS system as well as users' performance while working with such a system (e.g., [1]). However, it still remains unclear what factors we should measure and how. This is likely to depend on the domain of the application. For instance, for a time-bound recall-oriented task such as the one reported in Pickens et al. [9], we can

use relevance and efficiency as measures. But such metrics may not be appropriate for an education setting, where learning is probably a more important factor to measure. A taxonomy of evaluation metrics for different CIS situations is needed.

8.4 Summary

In different fields and contexts, researchers have recognized the need to study and support people working in collaboration. In IR, this has been primarily achieved by extending single-user environments to accommodate multiple participants in information intensive situations. However, most of these approaches have been application-driven, and we still lack a set of models, specialized tools, and best practices that help us support collaborative information seeking (CIS) effectively. Such a need is identified in the present article in order to sketch out a research agenda. A set of key works, from different fields, was first recognized, putting both collaboration and CIS in perspective. It was discussed that the early works for supporting collaboration in information intensive domains were primarily focused on office environments or library settings, whereas recent projects for CIS have been targeted more specifically for online information seeking situations.

The advent of Web 2.0 and the fact that an increasing number of people have access to online information sources have driven new developments in CIS to focus more on building tools that leverage on these provisions. However, it is time we start paying more attention to some of the fundamental issues in CIS. They include understand user requirements and behavior in CIS environments, identifying motivations and best practices for people doing collaboration, and sketching good design guidelines for CIS systems. Above all, there is a dire need to devise new models, theories, and evaluation matrices for CIS. These issues are at the core of the CIS domain, and studying them could help us get closer to having a better understanding of people's behavior in CIS environments, designing better CIS systems, and achieving the synergic effect of collaboration—making the whole greater than the sum of all.

References

1. Ricardo Baeza-Yates and Jose A. Pino. A first step to formally evaluate collaborative work. In *Proceedings of GROUP*, pages 56–60, 1997.
2. Nicholas J. Belkin. Anomalous states of knowledge as a basis for information retrieval. *Canadian Journal of Information Science*, 5:133–143, 1980.
3. Jette Hyldegard. Collaborative information behaviour—exploring Kuhlthau's Information Search Process model in a group-based educational setting. *Information Processing and Management*, 42:276–298, 2006.
4. Jette Hyldegard. Beyond the search process—exploring group members' information behavior in context. *Information Processing and Management*, 45:142–158, 2009.

5. Carol C. Kuhlthau. *Seeking Meaning: A Process Approach to Library and Information Services*. Ablex, Norwood, 1994.
6. Carol C. Kuhlthau. Towards collaboration between information seeking and information retrieval. *Information Research*, 10(2), 2005.
7. Gary Marchionini. Information-seeking strategies of novices using a full-text electronic encyclopedia. *Journal of the American Society for Information Science*, 40(1):54–66, 1989.
8. Meredith Ringel Morris and Eric Horvitz. SearchTogether: an interface for collaborative web search. In *ACM Symposium on User Interface Software and Technology (UIST)*, pages 3–12, Newport, RI, October 2007.
9. Jeremy Pickens, Gene Golovchinsky, Chirag Shah, Pernilla Qvarfordt and Maribeth Back. Algorithmic mediation for collaborative exploratory search. In *Proceedings of the Annual ACM Conference on Research and Development in Information Retrieval (SIGIR)*, Singapore, July 2008.
10. M.C. Reddy and B.J. Jansen. A model for understanding collaborative information behavior in context: a study of two healthcare teams. *Information Processing and Management*, 44(1):256–273, 2008.
11. Chirag Shah. Coagmento—a collaborative information seeking, synthesis and sense-making framework (an integrated demo). In *Proceedings of Computer Supported Cooperative Work (CSCW)*, Savannah, GA, 2010.
12. Chirag Shah and Roberto Gonzalez-Ibanez. Exploring information seeking processes in collaborative search tasks. In *Annual Meeting of the American Society for Information Science*, Pittsburgh, PA, 2010.
13. T.D. Wilson. Models in information behaviour research. *Journal of Documentation*, 55(3):249–270, 1999.

Appendix A
Ten Stories of Five *C*s

A.1 Introduction

The purpose of this Appendix is to present the concept of collaboration in various contexts, mainly to distinguish it from similar concepts such as cooperation and coordination. This is done by proposing a five layer model of collaboration and then presenting ten different (fictional and real) scenarios showing the use of the model. The scenarios thus presented are by no means general situations; rather they show specific instances of particular environments that could help in distinguishing various concepts and emphasizing what it means to collaborate in different situations.

A.2 A Model of Collaboration

Based on the insights developed by Denning and Yahlkovsky [1], and Taylor-Powell et al. [2], we present a model of collaboration in Fig. A.1. This model consists of five layers, with collaboration encapsulating the others.

- *Communication*. This is a process of sending or exchanging information, which is one of the core requirements for carrying out a collaboration, or maintaining any kind of productive relationship for that matter.
- *Contribution*. This is an informal relationship by which individuals help each other in achieving their individual goals.
- *Coordination*. This is a process of connecting parties together for a harmonious action. This often involves bringing people under an umbrella at the same time and place. During this process, the involved parties may share resources, responsibilities, and goals.
- *Cooperation*. This is a relationship in which parties with similar interests take part in planning activities, negotiating roles, and sharing resources to achieve joint goals. In addition to coordination, cooperation involves all the parties following some rules of interaction.

C. Shah, *Collaborative Information Seeking*, The Information Retrieval Series 34,   145
DOI 10.1007/978-3-642-28813-5, © Springer-Verlag Berlin Heidelberg 2012

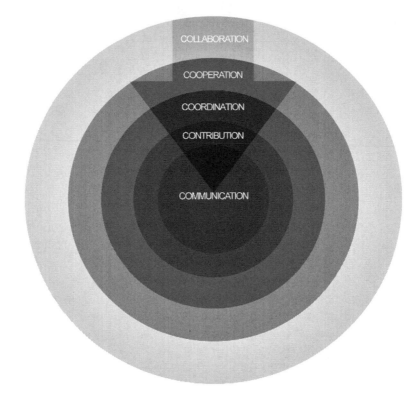

Fig. A.1   A model for collaboration

- *Collaboration*. This is a process of involving parties that may see different aspect of a problem. They engage in a process through which they can go beyond their own individual expertise and vision by constructively exploring their differences and searching for common solutions. In contrast to cooperation, collaboration involves creating a solution that is more than merely the sum of each party's contribution. The authority in such a process is vested in the collaboration rather than in an individual entity.

To summarize, we consider collaboration an explicitly established process among a group of people through which the participants work together in an interactive environment toward a common goal. We want to make it clear from this definition that

1. We do not regard autonomous processes between systems as collaboration.
2. A "collaboration", without the explicit agreement or awareness of every participant, is not a true collaboration. For us, by definition, collaboration is explicitly defined and an active process.
3. Our definition of collaboration is task-oriented. It assumes that a set of people are collaborating to solve a problem or create a product together. Once this is achieved, they may still have social interactions or start a new collaborative work, but their earlier collaboration is formally over.

A.3 Scenarios

A.3.1 Paying Taxes

Collaboration

Joe goes to his tax attorney Carol to work on his taxes this year. During their first meeting, Carol obtains a handful of information from Joe and starts filling out the forms. Later she gives a call to Joe to discuss the tax benefits and returns. Joe thinks he should be able to claim more. He returns to Carol with more documents that can be used to file more exemptions. Meanwhile, Carol finds a couple of spots where she can squeeze in more returns. Finally, they both are happy with the outcome and file the tax returns.

In this whole process, both Joe and Carol are working to solve the same problem. They both have the same interest about the outcome of the process, even though the rewards will be different for each one. At times, Joe cooperated with Carol giving her all the information she wanted, and at times Carol cooperated with Joe's higher expectations for tax returns. They both did certain tasks independently, but then they had to coordinate to put everything together. Joe contributed to the project by providing all the relevant information. Carol contributed by applying her expertise to handle such problems. Throughout the process, both parties had some way of communicating with each other for interactions.

Cooperation

Joe paying his taxes to the IRS is an act of cooperating with the government. Joe and the government are not exactly working together actively to solve a problem. Joe is simply complying with a set of rules set by the government.

The IRS communicates with Joe by the means of sending relevant tax documents and asking him to pay the taxes by certain day. Joe sends out his taxes (contribution) by that day, to a certain address, with all the required documents (coordination).

Coordination

The town council where Joe lives organizes free tax consultancy for the community every year. These consultancy sessions happen around certain dates, times, and places. This is an organizational effort, which could lead to collaboration, but by itself, it is a coordinated event only.

Contribution

Joe contributes to the economy by paying his taxes. Of course, this act is a part of his cooperation to the government in a coordinated fashion as we saw earlier.

Communication

State and federal revenue offices sending tax documents and notices to individuals, is a form of communication. If those individuals use these notices to cooperate with the IRS is up to them!

A.3.2 What's for Dinner?

Collaboration

Cary and Michelle got together to bake the new fudge cake recipe that Cary had found. They both worked toward creating one common product with the knowledge and resources they had. During this cooking session, they both cooperated with each other. For instance, Cary said she would take care of whisking the eggs and Michelle would be better at preparing the fudge. Michelle agreed to this.

To work on this project, they both had to get together at certain day, time, and place, and also pool together the resources that they needed (coordination). Both the parties contributed to the project in terms of their skills and efforts. Throughout the project, both Cary and Michelle had an active interaction, which started with Cary calling Michelle to discuss this recipe and make the plans to bake it, and continued throughout their project (communication).

Cooperation

There was a potluck party at Shelley's place last week. Everyone invited was expected to bring something to eat or drink. To keep things balanced, Shelley talked with everyone attending (communication) and instructed them to bring a main dish, a side, a dessert, or a drink.

Everyone complied with this (cooperation) and showed up at Shelley's place on a certain time (coordination). Almost everyone who showed up at this party, brought something (contribution), but they did not work together to create any of that. The success of Shelley's party was due to everyone's cooperation.

Coordination

Mike and Ryan have not seen each other since Mike moved to a different town. Now Ryan is visiting Mike's town and they decide to get together for lunch. To make this happen, they both talked on the phone (communication) and figured out a day and time. Since Ryan likes seafood, Mike does some research to find a good seafood restaurant (contribution). The essence of this event is being able to organize a meeting, and not solving a problem together.

Contribution

A website allrecipe.com allows its members to post and share their recipes online (contribution). This happens through their website or over email (communication). Any individual can thus contribute to the pool of recipes that are hosted on this website, without working with any other users of the site.

Communication

Robert's mom sent Robert a new easy pasta recipe that she thought Robert could cook easily and eat some healthy food. In this act, there was nothing more than sending a message (communication). Nothing was needed to be coordinated and there was no collaborative act. If Robert's mom contributed something or not will depend on further use of that message.

A.3.3 School Elections

Collaboration
Sarah is running for the student body president in her school. For her goal of presidency, she has taken the help of several organizations and individuals. Some of them are simply helping Sarah by giving their support (contribution/cooperation), whereas others are more actively involved, working with Sarah to run her campaign. These groups of people, who are primarily responsible for running the campaign, are collaborating with each other as they are working toward the same goal with their individual skills and connections (contribution), and bringing it all together (coordination). None of them are individually capable of running the whole campaign, but their collective efforts have the potential to achieve the goal.

Cooperation
During the campaign, another candidate, Michael, realizes that his and Sarah's campaigns are pretty much the same. So he decides to merge his campaign with that of Sarah. They negotiate their roles and responsibilities in this process with Sarah running for president and Michael for vice-president. They decide to cooperate, instead of compete.

Coordination
Assembling a group of students for Sarah's campaign address is an organizational effort (coordination). The gathered students are not expected to cooperate or collaborate with Sarah's campaign committee.

Contribution
Mark chipping in for Sarah's campaign fund is a contribution. Mark is not doing this act as a part of any cooperation or collaboration with Sarah.[1]

Communication
Sarah putting up flyers for her college student body president campaign is a form of communication that she is doing with the college community.

A.3.4 Group Project

Collaboration
Prof. Zimmerman teaches a class in HCI. As a part of his class he has assigned group projects. Each group is required to work on a project and present it at the end of the semester. In a given group, the students have the same goal (the project

---

[1]Compared to this example, paying taxes is cooperation since a tax-payer has an obligation to pay his taxes (contribution) according to the guidelines set by the IRS.

that they chose), and each one is working toward finishing it. Prof. Zimmerman left
the students to decide if they want to have a leader in their group or not. While
the groups may not have a designated leader, often one of the students in the group
suggests something that everyone else complies with (cooperation). Throughout the
semester the group members organize meetings (coordination), email each other
(communication), and share their individual works (contributions). All these efforts
are essential to the final product.

Cooperation

Prof. Zimmerman requires all the groups to turn in their final report before the last
day of the classes. Each group agrees (cooperation) to turn their reports in (contribution) by that day in the format given (coordination). In this case, the groups are
not collaborating with Prof. Zimmerman; they are simply cooperating.

Coordination

As a part of the group project, Prof. Zimmerman also wants each group to make
a presentation. He discusses in class the day that would be suitable for each group
to do this presentation (communication). After some discussion, Prof. Zimmerman
finalizes the schedule for each group for their presentations (contributions). Note
that if Prof. Zimmerman had fixed a date for these presentations that each group
would have to comply with, it would be cooperation, and not just coordination.

Contribution

Once the semester is over and all the projects submitted, Prof. Zimmerman plans to
host them all in the institute repository. This will be students' contributions to the
community, but it does not require to do any coordination, cooperation,[2] or collaboration.

Communication

Throughout the semester, Prof. Zimmerman sends out emails on the class listserv
with announcements and other forms of information (communication). Some of
these emails can be used for further purposes such as coordinating an event.

A.3.5 VidArch

Collaboration

VidArch is a group in SILS that involves a set of members with different roles
and backgrounds. While every member is aware of everything done under the umbrella of VidArch, each one has a different level of involvement depending on

---

[2]Yes, the students giving their consent for their work to be submitted to the repository would be
considered an act of cooperation.

the project. The majority of the projects are collaborative. For instance, the *ContextMiner* project involves many of the members of this group requiring all of them to contribute based on their roles and skills. Depending up on the aspect of the project, one member can take the lead and others cooperate. All these efforts are coordinated using meetings and emails. Some members contribute by designing an interface, whereas some others do user need analysis.

Cooperation
Laura, a member of the VidArch group, created a registry that incorporates entries of archival tools, documents, file formats etc. She asked other members of the team to input a few entries in the exchange to populate it (communication). Everyone complies with this (cooperation), by posting some entries on the VidArch Exchange site (contribution), where they are consolidated (coordination). Each individual's contributions are a part of their cooperation and that helps Laura directly, but the contributors are not working on this project beyond their individual contributions. In other words, they are not truly collaborating even though their cooperation helps to prepare a product that will have the group's name on it.

Coordination
The VidArch group meets once a week and/or exchanges email (communication) to share and discuss ideas (contribution). Some of these coordinated efforts could be part of cooperation or may result in collaborative work.

Contribution
In one of the projects, Rob asked a group of people to provide relevance judgments on a set of videos (communication). Some of these people ended up being more involved with the project and that resulted into collaboration; however, the rest of the folks did not go further than making this particular contribution.

Communication
Several emails are sent out every week on VidArch listserv, incorporating announcements, ideas, and discussions. Many of these emails are meant for no other purpose, but to share information.

A.3.6 Searching in a Library

Collaboration
Mark walks up to a reference librarian Susanne in a public library. He is studying 20th century American poets and trying to find all the material that could be relevant. Susanne helps him to locate the section of the library, where Mark can find the books on poetry. However, that would not be enough. Mark describes the scope of his study and that gives Susanne information to start suggesting specific books to Mark. After skimming through those books over a couple of day's time, Mark thinks he has a

lot more material than he needs. He returns to Susanne with this concern, and she suggests to him to look at a book on the Anthology of American Poets. This book not only helps Mark directly, but also lets Susanne refine her suggestions as she also flips through it. Finally, Mark has good material on this topic that is not too general and covers most of the information that he would like to have.

Working on this collaborative task required both Mark and Susanne to interact with each other (communication) person-to-person at a certain place and time (co-ordination). The starting point of this collaboration was Susanne agreeing to help Mark (cooperation). While Susanne seems to have done most of the work (contribution), she also learned a certain number of things in the process. Finally, while the rewards of this process were different for both the parties, it is important to note that they both worked together to solve the same problem.

Cooperation
If Susanne had simply pointed Mark to the relevant section for his query, she had cooperated, but they did not have collaboration. What extended a bunch of coopera-tive acts to collaboration is an active session of interaction in which both the parties worked together to solve a problem.

Coordination
Mark decides to study with his fellow student Richard in the library. They both get together at the library on a set day and study their own things. They both are in a way helping each other by keeping company (contribution), but they do not share a specific goal that they are working toward together.

Contribution
Mark has some old books that he no longer needs, but they could be of use to others. He, therefore, asks the library if they would take those books. Upon the library's approval (communication), Mark donates the books to the library (contribution).

Communication
There is a message on the library's bulletin board about a book sale for charity the coming weekend. This is just a way for the library to communicate with visitors, which may result in a coordinated event.

A.3.7 Planning a Trip

Collaboration
While planning a trip, Charles usually takes over booking the flights and hotels, whereas his wife Claudia starts researching the places they are going to visit, includ-ing food, attractions, and entertainment. They have particular interests and skills for both of these areas and each one accepts the other person's authority in their areas (cooperation). They both have the same goal, which is accomplished by coordinated

efforts that help each one work independently, and solve some sub problems (contribution). Often they consult each other before finalizing a decision (communication).

Cooperation
If we just look at the sub problem each of them is working with, they are getting the other person's cooperation. It is bringing these sub problems' solutions together and working toward a common goal that creates collaboration.

Coordination
Both Charles and Claudia need to coordinate their efforts as there is no point for Claudia to book concert tickets if their flight does not reach there before the concert starts. The very act of Claudia verifying with Charles that they would reach to their destination in time for the concert, so that she could book the tickets, is simply an act of coordination. There are no rules set by one party that the other has to follow in order to solve a higher level problem.

Contribution
Both Charles and Claudia contribute to the common project by doing their own tasks.

Communication
Throughout their project of planning a trip, Charles and Claudia exchange a number of messages face-to-face, through email or phone. Most of these messages are used for further coordination or collaboration, but some of them are simply for sharing some interesting information such as a link to the website with the history of the place they are going to visit.

A.3.8 Discovery of SARS Virus

Collaboration
When in early 2003, the SARS breakout was reported in Hong Kong, the WHO started a project involving a number of groups around the world. The WHO called this a "collaborative multicenter research project". Every day various labs around the world met through teleconference (communication), where they shared their work (contribution), discussed directions for further investigation (coordination), and agreed to take on responsibilities as well as to help each other out (cooperate) on various aspects of the project. In only about a month's time, the labs were confident enough to announce that the coronavirus was the virus that caused SARS. Achieving such a remarkable feat could have been an extremely difficult task, if not impossible, for a single lab.

Cooperation

All the groups combined as a single entity agreed to work in the project that the WHO started. The WHO, as an organization, was interested in good outcome of this project, but other than organizing collaboration among various labs (coordination), it did not have an active role to play in solving the problem. All the labs that participated cooperated with the WHO and collaborated with each other, not the WHO.

Coordination

This is the role that the WHO played in the whole project coordinating the collaborative efforts among various groups. That way, the WHO played a vital role (contribution) in approaching labs around the world (communication) and bringing them together (coordination).

Contribution

During the project, scientists at Hong Kong University isolated a virus that seemed like a likely candidate. That same day, scientists at the Center for Disease Control in the US separately isolated a virus, which looked liked what's called a coronavirus. Both of these labs, thus, made their contributions, which were later coordinated for a better understanding of the problem at hand, and thus, helping the collaborative goal.

Communication

One of the keys to the success of this project in terms of finding a solution in such a short duration was the ability to effectively communicate with each other almost instantly. Some of the communications were used to coordinate events, and some were for simply sharing information of various kinds.

A.3.9 Factory Line

Collaboration

Akamai Motor Company has several groups working on different aspects of automobiles. One of these groups is responsible for creating more fuel efficient and environment friendly combustion system. The group consists of IC engine designers, mechanical engineers, and environment specialists. They are working toward the same goal with their individual skills (contribution) that need to be brought together in an organized manner (coordination). None of them can solve the complete problem by themselves, and so they are working by helping each other in their sub problems (cooperation), which will result in a collective solution. Throughout this collaboration, the group members maintain an active interaction (communication).

Cooperation

The project manager of Internal Engine Technologies asks the fuel efficiency group to provide a new version of design specifications for the combustion mechanism of the engine that could make fuel consumption more efficient. The group agrees to deliver this project (contribution) by certain time in the specifications given (coordination), thus cooperating with the project manager. The group is working for, and not with, the project manager. Another interesting point to note here is that in order to cooperate, the group does collaboration internally. In other words, the group is cooperating with its superior by delivering a product that is a result of a collaborative effort.

Coordination
One of the factory lines in Akamai Motor Company is responsible for putting a set of parts together to create a wheel bearing system. There are several individuals working on this line, each responsible for their own small parts (contribution). All the parts need to be combined in a specific order (coordination). When one individual finishes his work, he hands it over to the next person in line (communication). Why aren't these people in collaboration? Because they can all work on their individual parts under set rules without explicitly working with each other with the intention of creating a common solution.[3] In other words, each individual is interested in working on his own small problem only and somebody higher up puts things together to create the final product. Similarly, these individuals can be said to cooperate with their supervisor, but not with each other directly.

Contribution
If we discount the portion of bringing all the individual parts together in the above example, the individuals are simply doing their jobs (contribution).

Communication
On an assembly line, one individual communicates with another one. This communication could be for passing one's contribution to the other person or to coordinate events, but it could also be simply passing some information or instructions.

A.3.10 May Day Parade

Collaboration
In Halifax, Nova Scotia, I participated in the May Day parade. Several labor groups got together and marched from a town plaza to the city hall with banners and flags. Every group coordinated with one another in sharing responsibilities (contribution) for making this event as smooth and successful as possible. People gave speeches,

---

[3]A search engine company aggregates actions of many users for the same query or webpage and use that knowledge to produce a better search services, but those users were not in collaboration. The search engine company simply aggregated their actions (coordination). Good products can result from proper coordination also, and collaboration in many situations is just not feasible or advisable.

distributed pamphlets, shouted slogans, and marched in harmony. The success of this event took more than simply bringing people together (coordination) and making them follow a set of rules (cooperation). Since there was no defined leader, each group had to work with each other to distribute responsibilities and roles.

Cooperation

Each group in the parade obeyed general rules of public safely. In that case, these groups were cooperating with the authorities to maintain the harmony. The law enforcement authorities present there were only interested in making sure that the crowd cooperates; they were not there to take part in the demonstrations. In other words, they were not collaborators.

Coordination

Bringing people together on a certain day (May 1st), at certain time and place is an organizational problem. On top of that, all the groups present there also had to coordinate with each other as there was no predefined leader.

Contribution

One of the groups brought flyers with information about May Day to distribute among the general audience at the event. This was their contribution. Internally for this group, preparing the flyers could have been a collaborative effort, but what resulted from that effort was simply a contribution to the May Day event.

Communication

Several people gave short speeches at this event. These can be seen as simply diffusing the information (communication), which does not guarantee any form of cooperation or collaboration.

A.4 Conclusion

This Appendix presented two contributions: (1) proposing a model of collaboration, and (2) presenting a number of scenarios showing how the model helps in understanding some real life situations of collaborative acts. We do not claim to have provided a universally acceptable definition of collaboration. As noted earlier, the scenarios presented here are also meant to show how one can understand concepts such as collaboration, cooperation, and coordination in specific contexts.

Having admitted these shortcomings of the framework presented here, we believe we have given reasonably clear definitions of various concepts for the kind of collaboration that we are interested in studying. The definitions are also unambiguous enough to let us clearly state which process is or is not a true collaboration. For instance, if a patron walks up to a reference librarian and asks where she could find information on immigration laws, and if the librarian simply points her to the right section, this was not collaboration according to our definition. Collaboration between a patron and a librarian is possible as we showed in one of our scenarios, but the situation reported above is simply an act of cooperation, but not a true collaboration.

Another interesting fact to note is that while the model presented in Fig. A.1 indicates that collaboration encompasses other concepts, such as contribution and coordination, some times to make these concepts of inner circle possible, one may have to collaborate. For instance, Maggie wants to bake cookies for her school's charity sale, for which her mom works with her. Thus, Maggie and her mom are collaborating to produce something that can become Maggie's contribution to a fund raising event.

References

1. Peter J. Denning and Peter Yaholkovsky. Getting to "We". *Communications of the ACM*, 51(4):19–24, 2008.
2. Ellen Taylor-Powell, Boyd Rossing and Jean Geran. Evaluating collaboratives: reaching the potential. Technical report, University of Wisconsin-Extension, Madison, Wisconsin, July 1998.

Appendix B
Brief Overview of Computer-Supported Cooperative Work (CSCW)

Computer-supported cooperative work (CSCW) is an interdisciplinary field that encompasses elements of interface design, collective decision-making, system-mediated information exchange and usage, and organizational behavior. It brings together researchers and practitioners from a variety of fields, including social psychology, sociology, computer and information science, economics, organizational theory, education, and anthropology. According to Grudin [16], CSCW was first coined by Irene Greif and Paul M. Cashman in 1984 at a workshop attended by those interested in using technology to support people in their work. According to Carstensen and Schmidt [4], CSCW is about "how collaborative activities and their coordination can be supported by means of computer systems" (p. 620). Bannon and Schmidt [2] defined CSCW as "an endeavor to understand the nature and characteristics of cooperative work with the objective of designing adequate computer-based technologies" (pp. 3–5).

B.1 Organizing CSCW Systems and Environments

The classical way of organizing collaborative activities is based on two factors: location and time [30, 38]. Recently, Hansen and Jarvelin [19], Golovchinsky et al. [12], as well as Shah [34] also classified approaches to collaborative information seeking/retrieval using these two dimensions of space and time. Figure B.1 shows various collaborative activities and systems organized along the time and space dimensions, creating four distinct quarters to study them.

This matrix serves as a helpful tool in designing and evaluating CSCW systems. For instance, social information filtering or collaborative filtering is a process benefiting from other users' actions in the past; thus, it falls under asynchronous and mostly remote domain. These days, email also serves as a tool for doing asynchronous collaboration among users who are not co-located. Chat or IM helps to carry out synchronous and remote collaboration.

C. Shah, *Collaborative Information Seeking*, The Information Retrieval Series 34,
DOI 10.1007/978-3-642-28813-5, © Springer-Verlag Berlin Heidelberg 2012

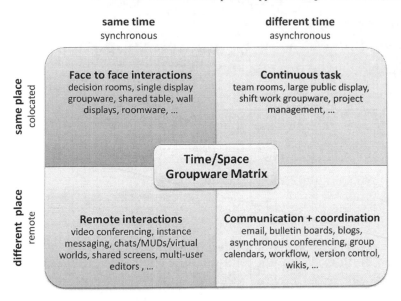

Fig. B.1 CSCW/groupware matrix showing how different collaborative activities and systems fit across time and space dimensions. Courtesy of Momo54 (http://en.wikipedia.org/wiki/User:Momo54)

The placement of a collaborative environment on this figure has implications for its implementation, functionalities, and evaluation. For instance, Adobe Connect[1] facilitates online meetings where the participants can share and discuss information. Such an environment will fall under Synchronous-Remote collaboration in Fig. B.1. Thus, this environment needs to have (1) a way to connect remote participants, (2) a shared space for exchanging information, and (3) a communication channel to provide real-time message passing among the participants.

B.2 Control, Communication, and Awareness in CSCW

Three components specific to group-work or collaboration that are highly predominant in the CSCW literature are control, communication, and awareness. In this section key definitions and related works for these components will be highlighted.

B.2.1 Control

Rodden [30] identified the value of control in CSCW systems and listed a number of projects with their corresponding schemes for implementing control. For instance,

---

[1]http://www.adobe.com/products/acrobatconnect/.

the COSMOS project [39] had a formal structure to represent control in the system. They used roles to represent people or automatons, and rules to represent the flow and processes. Roles of the people could be supervisor, processor, or analyst. Rules could be a condition that a process needs to satisfy in order to start or finish. Due to such a structure seen in projects like COSMOS, Rodden classified these control systems as procedural based systems.

Most of these systems were studied in office environments, where the subjects interacted with one another through personal conversations, group meetings, and phone calls. Several of the recommendations and findings of these studies were primarily based on observations.

To express control in a collaborative environment, early CSCW systems used various mechanisms to pass the messages around. These messages were often referred to as Structured Definition Language (SDL) messages. In the most basic sense, these were email messages that were sent back and forth among the participants of a collaborative project. However, for a collaborative project, an organization often needs more support than simply passing the information in messages. SDL provides this support by imposing a structure to these messages, and incorporating additional fields of information that can be used to filter and distribute messages appropriately.

For instance, Malone et al. [26] proposed the Information Lens framework, in which the messages carried additional information (some of which was automatically generated) that can later be used to filter and classify the messages to suit an individual's need in a group.

Let us see this with an example. Sam sends a message to circulate in the group, that he belongs to, asking for an opinion. At the time of sending this, Sam was not clear about who might be the right person in the group to inquire about that question, but since the system has additional information, such as user profiles and preferences, it can use it to redirect and distribute the message to appropriate individuals. This way, Sam does not have to worry about looking for the right people, and the receivers do not have to worry about getting the messages that are not right for them, even though they are useful for the group as a whole.

Looking at the above scheme with a different perspective, we are distributing the control between humans and automatons involved in the whole group process. Instead of explicitly deciding by himself who should receive the message, Sam is letting the system take charge of this process, thus relinquishing the control to the system. The system is driven by the rules that guide its decision-making. It is important to note that such a system is different than a traditional collaborative filtering system, where the system filters information based on similarities among the users. Here, the messages are filtered based on sender's intention (Sam choose to distribute his message this way), and receivers' intention to receive such messages that are relevant to them. Malone referred to such kind of filtering as *cognitive filtering*.

Later Malone extended the above framework to ObjectLens [27], in which the participants could create not only the messages to pass the information around, but any kind of objects. Each of these objects would have similar structure imposed on them that could guide further control and distribution processes. Object Lens also let people create links among those objects formed. Malone pointed out that this was similar to hypertexts on the World Wide Web.

B.2.2 Communication

This is one of the most critical components of any collaboration. In fact, Rodden [30] identified message or communication systems as the class of systems in CSCW that is most mature and most widely used.

It is interesting to note is that often, collaboration could begin by letting a group of users communicate with each other. For instance, Donath and Robertson [6] presented a system that allows a user to know that others were currently viewing the same webpage and communicate with those people to initiate a possible collaboration or at least a co-browsing experience. Providing communication capabilities even in an environment that was not originally designed for carrying out collaboration is an interesting way of encouraging collaboration.

Using four multidisciplinary design situations in the USA and Europe, Sonnenwald [37] came up with 13 communication roles. The author showed how these roles can support collaboration, among other aspects of the information seeking process, such as knowledge exploration and integration, and task and project completion, by filtering and providing information and negotiating differences across organizational, task, discipline and personal boundaries.

B.2.3 Awareness

Awareness is one of the most important issues that is identified and addressed in the CSCW literature. A clear definition and a methodology for providing awareness, though, are lacking. One of the often-asked questions about awareness in CSCW is *"awareness of what?"* Schmidt [33] argued that we should talk about awareness not as a separate entity, but as somebody's being aware of some particular occurrence. In other words, the term 'awareness' is only meaningful if it refers to a person's awareness *of* something. Heath et al. [22] suggested that awareness is not simply a 'state of mind' or a 'cognitive ability', but rather a feature of practical action which is systematically accomplished within developing course of everyday activities.

Several related terms and definitions are used in the CSCW literature to refer to awareness in collaborative projects. For instance, Dourish and Bellotti [7] defined awareness as "an understanding of the activities of others, which provides a context for your own activity" (p. 107). Dourish and Bly [8] suggested the following definition for awareness: "Awareness involves knowing who is "around", what activities are occurring, who is talking with whom; it provides a view of one another in the daily work environments. Awareness may lead to informal interactions, spontaneous connections, and the development of shared cultures—all important aspects of maintaining working relationships which are denied to groups distributed across multiple sites" (p. 541).

A set of theories and models for understanding and providing awareness emerged in the early works reported in the CSCW literature. Gaver [9] argued that an intense sharing of awareness characterizes *focused collaboration* in which people work closely together on a shared goal. He further claimed that less awareness is needed for division of labor, and that more casual awareness can lead to serendipitous communication, which can turn into collaboration. He proposed a *general awareness* model that incorporates and supports all such activities.

Bly et al. [3] also identified the importance of such general awareness by saying, "When groups are geographically distributed, it is particularly important not to neglect the need for informal interactions, spontaneous conversations, and even general awareness of people and events at other sites" (p. 29).

Some of the early works reported using ethnographic field studies in CSCW (e.g., [20, 21, 23]) identified the need to seamlessly align and integrate the activities of the participants of a collaborative project. While they did not refer to it as 'awareness', soon, the term 'awareness' was adopted to address such practices that support connecting collaborators without the activities of asking, suggesting, requesting, ordering, or reminding.

Several works argued that providing an audio–video communication channel could suffice for awareness [11, 28]. However, the use of communication as a substitute for awareness turned out to be very limited in its applicability [10]. Another line of research focused on providing awareness using *computational environments* based on 'event propagation mechanisms' for collecting, disseminating, and integrating information concerning collaborative activities. Some of the notable works in this stream of research include awareness models based on a spatial metaphor by Rodden [31], and Sandor et al. [32].

As we saw above, there are several ways of defining and implementing awareness. Various research projects have used their own taxonomy and interpretation of awareness for creating frameworks and systems. For instance, Gutwin and Greenberg [18] classified awareness in two types: *situational*, and *workspace*, and suggested that situational awareness underlies the idea of workspace awareness in groupware systems. Their definition of workspace awareness included how people interact with the workspace, rather than just awareness of the workspace itself. Simone and Bandini [36] identified two kinds of awareness: *by-product awareness* that is generated in the course of the activities people must do in order to accomplish their collaborative tasks; and *add-on awareness* that is the outcome of an additional activity, which is a cost for the collaborators to what they must do and is discretional in that it depends on collaborators' evaluation of the contingent situation. Chalmers [5], likewise, divided the awareness in two kinds: awareness of *people*, and of *information artifacts*. He suggested implementing activity-centered awareness tool, in that it focuses on presenting the ongoing appearance and activity of people.

Liechti and Sumi [25] identified four kinds of awareness as listed below. These are extensively used in awareness in collaboration work by Shah [34, 35].

1. *Group awareness*. This kind of awareness includes providing information to each group member about the status and activities of the other collaborators at a given time.
2. *Workspace awareness*. This refers to a common workspace that the group members share and where they can bring and discuss their findings, and create a common product.

3. *Contextual awareness*. This type of awareness relates to the application domain, rather than the users. Here, we want to identify what content is useful for the ⎯ . and what the goals are for the current project.
4. *Peripheral awareness*. This relates to the kind of information that has resulted from personal and the group's collective history, and should be kept separate from what a participant is currently viewing or doing.

B.3 Groupware Systems

Often CSCW systems are referred to as groupware systems. Some authors, however, disagree on these terms being used interchangeably and point out that groupware systems usually refer to real computer-based systems, whereas CSCW incorporates not just the groupware tools and techniques, but their psychological, social, and organizational effects as well. Wilson [40] clarifies that "CSCW [is] a generic term, which combines the understanding of the way people work in groups with the enabling technologies of computer networking, and associated hardware, software, services and techniques" (p. 1).

While most of the CSCW systems could be classified as groupware systems, there have been several specific groupware systems. Many of such systems were designed for viewing, sharing, and synthesizing information in group settings. For instance, *GroupWeb* [15] is a browser that allows group members to visually share and navigate World Wide webpages in real time. Its groupware features include document and view slaving for synchronizing information sharing, telepointers for enacting gestures, and "what you see is what I see" views to handle display differences. *GroupWeb* also incorporated a groupware text editor that lets groups create and attach annotations to pages. Similarly, *GroupScape* [14] was a multiuser HTML browser to support synchronous groupware applications and browsing of HTML documents on the web.

Yet another architecture to support multiuser browsing is *CoVitesse* [24], a groupware interface that enables collaborative navigation on the web based on a collaborative task model. This system represented users navigating collaboratively in an information space made of results of a query submitted to a search engine. In contrast to these systems, which are primarily designed for remotely located participants, *CoSearch* [1] is implemented to provide multi-device support for collaborative browsing among co-located participants.

Designing groupware systems is more challenging than one often realizes. As Olson et al. [29] suggested, "The development of schemes to support group work, whether behavioral methods or new technologies like groupware, should be based on detailed knowledge about how groups work, what they do well, and what they have trouble with" (p. 347). Grudin [17] recognized eight challenges for designing groupware systems.

1. *Bringing a balance in work and benefit*. More often, the users of a groupware system do not all get the same benefits for the amount of work they have to do. The designer has to address the needs and the work distribution for all the users.

2. *Building a critical mass.* If a groupware cannot achieve "critical mass" of users to be useful, it can fail as it is never to any one individual's advantage to use it.
3. *Entertaining to normal social processes.* A groupware system may sometimes hinder the social and political norms that its users have. A good system design adapts to an existing social structure rather than imposing one.
4. *Handling errors.* A system needs to be prepared to handle a wide range of exceptions and support improvisations that characterize much of the group activities.
5. *Providing unobtrusive accessibility.* Features that support group processes may be used relatively infrequently, and one needs to design a system that provides unobtrusive accessibility and integration of them with more heavily used features.
6. *Evaluation.* Due to its often-complex design, multi-faceted and multi-user interface, and a variety of user and system interactions, evaluating a groupware system can be a huge challenge.
7. *Addressing intuition.* Decision makers in a production environment rely heavily on informed intuition. Most product development experience is based on single-user applications, and transferring it to a multi-user groupware application can be a challenge.
8. *Adaptation.* Groupware systems require more careful implementation and introduction in the workplace than product developers usually confront.

B.4 Summary

While the field of CSCW has been around for a couple of decades and researchers have actively contributed to its various theories and applications, it is still an evolving domain. The recent years, especially, have seen a renewed interest in this multidisciplinary field, much of which could be attributed to the ease and effectiveness of using online social media and networking tools. Another factor that has fueled the ever-increasing development of CSCW systems is the notion of Web 2.0, where the Web users are welcoming and getting used to participating in creating content and working collaboratively—whether in their close circle of friends or with a wider community in an online world. On a theoretical side, new ground is being broken by going beyond the classical 'time' and 'space' dimensions of CSCW activities and systems. For instance, Golovchinsky et al. [13] presented a more comprehensive taxonomy that takes into account aspects such as intention and depth of mediation. Shah [34] presented 12 dimensions across which one could study, design, and evaluate CSCW systems.[2] With the inclusion of even more disciplines, such as information retrieval and library and information science, the field of CSCW is richer than ever and moving forward with great momentum.

---

[2]See Sect. 4.6 for a detailed treatment of these dimensions.

References

1. Saleema Amershi and Meredith Ringel Morris. CoSearch: a system for co-located collaborative Web search. In *Proceedings of ACM SIGCHI Conference on Human Factors in Computing Systems*, pages 1647–1656, Florence, Italy, April 2008.
2. Liam J. Bannon and Kjeld Schmidt. CSCW: four characters in search of a context. In S. Benford and J. Bowers, editors, *Studies in Computer Supported Cooperative Work: Theory, Practice and Design*, pages 3–16. North-Holland, Amsterdam, 1989.
3. Sara A. Bly, Steve R. Harrison and Susan Irwin. Media spaces: bringing people together in a video, audio, and computing environment. *Communications of the ACM*, 36(1):28–46, January 1993.
4. Peter H. Carstensen and Kjeld Schmidt. Computer supported cooperative work: new challenges to systems design. In K. Itoh, editor, *Handbook of Human Factors*, pages 619–636, 1999.
5. Matthew Chalmers. Awareness, Representation and Interpretation. *Computer Supported Cooperative Work (CSCW)*, 11(3–4):389–409, September 2002.
6. Judith S. Donath and Niel Robertson. The sociable web. In *Proceedings of the World Wide Web (WWW) Conference*, CERN, Geneva, Switzerland, 1994.
7. P. Dourish and V. Bellotti. Awareness and coordination in shared workspaces. In *Proceedings of the Conference on Computer-Supported Cooperative Work (CSCW)*, pages 107–114, Toronto, Ontario, 1992.
8. Paul Dourish and Sara A. Bly. Portholes: supporting awareness in a distributed work group. In *Proceedings of ACM SIGCHI Conference on Human Factors in Computing Systems*, pages 541–547, Toronto, Canada, 1992. ACM, New York.
9. William W. Gaver. Sound support for collaboration. In L.J. Bannon, M. Robinson and K. Schmidt, editors, *Proceedings of European Conference on Computer Supported Cooperative Work (ECSCW)*, Amsterdam, The Netherlands, 1991. Kluwer Academic, Dordrecht.
10. William W. Gaver. The affordances of media spaces for collaboration. In J. Turner and R.E. Kraut, editors, *Proceedings of the Conference on Computer-Supported Cooperative Work (CSCW)*, pages 17–24, Toronto, Canada, 1992.
11. William W. Gaver, Thomas P. Moran, Allan MacLean, Lennart Lövstrand, Paul Dourish, Kathleen Carter and William A.S. Buxton. Realizing a video environment: EuroPARC's RAVE system. In P. Bauersfeld, J. Bennett and G. Lynch, editors, *Proceedings of ACM SIGCHI Conference on Human Factors in Computing Systems*, pages 27–35, Monterey, California, 1992. ACM, New York.
12. Gene Golovchinsky, Jeremy Pickens and Maribeth Back. A taxonomy of collaboration in online information seeking. In *Proceedings of JCDL 2008 Workshop on Collaborative Exploratory Search*, Pittsburgh, PA, June 2008.
13. Gene Golovchinsky, Jeremy Pickens and Maribeth Back. A taxonomy of collaboration in online information seeking. *Search*, 32:1–3, 2009.
14. T.C. Nicholas Graham. GroupScape: integrating synchronous groupware and the World Wide Web. In *Proceedings of INTERACT*, Sydney, Australia, July 1997. Chapman and Hall, London.
15. Saul Greenberg and Mark Roseman. GroupWeb: a WWW browser as real time groupware. In *Proceedings of ACM SIGCHI Conference on Human Factors in Computing Systems*, pages 271–272, Boston, MA, November 1996. ACM, New York.
16. Jonathan Grudin. Computer-supported cooperative work: history and focus, 1994.
17. Jonathan Grudin. Groupware and social dynamics: eight challenges for developers. *Communications of the ACM*, 37(1):92–105, January 1994.
18. Carl Gutwin and Saul Greenberg. A descriptive framework of workspace awareness for real-time groupware. *Computer Supported Cooperative Work (CSCW)*, 11(3–4):411–446, September 2002.
19. Preben Hansen and Kalervo Jarvelin. Collaborative information retrieval in an information-intensive domain. *Information Processing and Management*, 41:1101–1119, 2005.

20. Richard H.R. Harper, John A. Hughes and Dan Z. Shapiro. The functionality of flight strips in ATC work. The report for the Civil Aviation Authority. Technical report, Lancaster Sociotechnics Group, Department of Sociology, Lancaster University, January 1989.
21. Richard H.R. Harper, John A. Hughes and Dan Z. Shapiro. Working in harmony: an examination of computer technology in air traffic control. In *Proceedings of European Conference on Computer Supported Cooperative Work (ECSCW)*, pages 72–86, Gatwick, London, 1989.
22. Christian Heath, Marcus Sanchez Svensson, Jon Hindmarsh, Paul Luff and Dirk vom Lehn. Configuring awareness. *Computer Supported Cooperative Work (CSCW)*, 11(3–4):317–347, September 2002.
23. Christian C. Heath and Paul Luff. Collaborative activity and technological design: Task coordination in London Underground control rooms. In L.J. Bannon, M. Robinson and K. Schmidt, editors, *Proceedings of European Conference on Computer Supported Cooperative Work (ECSCW)*, pages 65–80, Amsterdam, The Netherlands, 1991. Kluwer Academic, Dordrecht.
24. Yann Laurillau and Laurence Nigay. CoVitesse: a groupware interface for collaborative navigation on the WWW. In *Proceedings of the ACM Conference on Computer Supported Cooperative Work (CSCW)*, pages 236–240, New Orleans, Louisiana, USA, November 2002.
25. O. Liechti and Y. Sumi. Editorial: awareness and the WWW. *International Journal of Human–Computer Studies*, 56(1):1–5, 2002.
26. Thomas W. Malone, K.R. Grant, F.A. Turbak, S.S. Brobst and M.D. Cohen. Intelligent information sharing systems. *Communications of the ACM*, 30(5):390–402, 1987.
27. Thomas W. Malone and K. Lai. Object Lens: a spreadsheet for cooperative work. In *Proceedings of the Conference on Computer-Supported Cooperative Work (CSCW)*, Portland, OR, September 1988.
28. Marilyn M. Mantei, Ronald M. Baecker, Abigail J. Sellen, William A.S. Buxton and Thomas Milligan. Experiences in the use of a media space. In S.P. Robertson, G.M. Olson and J.S. Olson, editors, *Proceedings of ACM SIGCHI Conference on Human Factors in Computing Systems*, pages 203–208, New Orleans, Lousiana, 1991. ACM, New York.
29. Gary M. Olson, Judith S. Olson, Mark R. Carter and Marianne Storrosten. Small group design meetings: an analysis of collaboration. *Human–Computer Interaction*, 7(4):347–374, February 1992.
30. Tom Rodden. A survey of CSCW systems. *Interacting with Computers*, 3(3):319–353, 1991.
31. Tom Rodden. Populating the application: a model of awareness for cooperative applications. In *Proceedings of Computer Supported Cooperative Work (CSCW)*, pages 87–96, Boston, MA, November 1996. ACM, New York.
32. Ovidiu Sandor, Cristian Bogdan and John Bowers. Aether: an awareness engine for CSCW. In J.A. Hughes, W. Prinz, T.A. Rodden and K. Schmidt, editors, *Proceedings of European Conference on Computer Supported Cooperative Work (ECSCW)*, pages 221–236, Lancaster, UK, 1997. Kluwer Academic, Dordrecht.
33. Kjeld Schmidt. The problem with 'awareness': introductory remarks on 'awareness in CSCW'. *Computer Supported Cooperative Work (CSCW)*, 11(3):285–298, 2002.
34. Chirag Shah. A framework to support user-centric collaborative information seeking, 2010.
35. Chirag Shah and Gary Marchionini. Awareness in collaborative information seeking. *Journal of American Society of Information Science and Technology (JASIST)*, 61(10):1970–1986, 2010.
36. Carla Simone and Stefania Bandini. Integrating awareness in cooperative applications through the reaction-diffusion metaphor. *Computer Supported Cooperative Work (CSCW)*, 11(3–4):495–530, September 2002.
37. Diane H. Sonnenwald. Communication roles that support collaboration during the design process. *Design Studies*, 17(3):277–301, July 1996.
38. Michael B. Twidale and David M. Nichols. Collaborative browsing and visualisation of the search process. *Proceedings of Aslib*, 48:177–182, 1996.

39. S.B. Wilbur and R.E. Young. The COSMOS project: a multi-disciplinary approach to design of computer supported group working. In R. Speth, editor, *EUTECO 88: Research into Networks and Distributed Applications*, Vienna, Austria, April 1988.
40. Paul Wilson. *Computer Supported Cooperative Work: An Introduction*. Springer, Berlin, 1991.

Appendix C
Brief Overview of Computer-Supported Collaborative Learning (CSCL)

Computer-supported collaborative learning (CSCL) is an interdisciplinary field that refers to a pedagogical approach concerning learning that takes place through interactions among the students, mediated by technology. The roots of this field can be traced back to 1970s when researchers and educators realized that the emerging computational technologies could be used to facilitate constructivism and social cognitivism [5]. It is well-documented that the first use of CSCL appeared in a NASA-sponsored workshop organized in 1989 in Italy [2, 13].

C.1 Theories

Given that CSCL is highly interdisciplinary in nature, it is no surprise that it draws theories from several fields, including educational, cognitive and social psychology, instructional technology, and sociology. However, what has probably influenced CCL the most is a set of learning theories that acknowledge that knowledge can result from the interactions among the learners. The roots of such philosophy can be found in Vygotsky's Social Learning Theory [17]. He argued that there are tasks difficult to master by individuals, but possible using collaboration.[1] This is a similar concept to the notion of *synergy* that we discussed in Chap. 7. Vygostky called this "zone of proximal development", further arguing that when learnings thus work in collaboration, their learning cannot be measured using tests for individuals.

Moving further, in the late 1980s and early 1990s, Scardamalia and Bereiter [12] provided the theoretical foundation to four key concepts in CSCL: (1) knowledge-building communities, (2) knowledge-building discourse, (3) intentional learning, and (4) expert processes. It was around this time that the initial focus on artificial intelligence started becoming overshadowed by the development of collaborative

---

[1] Interestingly, and probably by no intended connection to CSCL, Minsky postulated that our minds are actually made of tiny elements that themselves do not appear to be smart, but it is through their interconnections that we achieve something useful.

technology for education. Emphasizing this, Koschmann [6] provided the sequence of related approaches as they historically followed: (1) computer-assisted instruction, (2) intelligent tutoring systems, (3) Logo as Latin, and (4) CSCL. Thus, it was around the mid-1990s that CSCL emerged as the field we know it today—exploring the support of computers to allow students to learn collaboratively in either small groups or in learning communities. And it was in 1995 that the International Society of the Learning Sciences established a biannual conference on CSCL.[2]

In the recent years researchers in CSCL have started realizing the need to create theories that are not simply borrowed from learning sciences, but rather tailored for collaborative learning that is computer-supported [14]. To address this, Stahl proposed Collaboration Theory [15], suggesting that knowledge is created through social interactions. The theory emphasizes that collaborative learning is a process of creating meaning, which frequently takes place within a group as the unit of analysis. To differentiate his theory from traditional learning theories and to situate it within the CSCL context, Stahl [15] incorporated four important themes: (1) collaborative knowledge building, (2) group and personal perspectives connected to create group understanding, (3) mediation by artifacts (e.g., computers), and (4) interaction analysis using extracted examples that can be analyzed as proof that the knowledge building happened.

Dillenbourg and Fischer enumerated 10 basic ideas of CSCL [4] as listed below.

1. More interaction balances less individualization.
2. Media effectiveness is a myth (just because new kind of media/technology appears in the market does not guarantee it will make learning better).
3. What matters is the effort required to construct shared knowledge.
4. A greater resemblance to face-to-face interactions in not necessarily better.
5. Task representations mediate verbal interactions.
6. Collaborative learning needs to be structured.
7. Interaction analysis can be partly automated.
8. Interaction is a substance.
9. Computing is more than computers.
10. Some virtual communities effectively share knowledge.

C.2 Practice and Applications

Most theories guidelines and methods/approaches developed under CSCL have direct implications to education. A number of situations and applications of CSCL in practice can be found from primary schools to graduate-level studies. One of the most common of such applications is collaborative writing. For instance, Olson et al. [10] developed *ShrEdit*, a shared text editor. To their surprise, they discovered that the groups working with *ShrEdit* generated *fewer design* ideas, but apparently

---

[2]http://www.isls.org/conferences.html.

better ones. They believed their tool helped the supported groups keep more focused on the core issues in the emerging design, to waste less time on less important topics, and to capture what was said as they went.

Studies of collaborative writing are often done with online community-based platforms such as Wikipedia and blogs [8, 11]. In fact, wiki-based environments are very ideal to study CSCL-based activities as they allow not only information synthesis and writing, but also discussions among participants/learners. For instance, using wiki-based platforms, Larusson and Alterman [8], and Asterhan and Schwarz [1] studied how technology-mediated discourse allow learners separated by distance to engage in discussions and collaborative knowledge building.

Recent developments and popularity of the online virtual world such as Second Life have enabled researchers to study CSCL using augmented reality in online environments, emphasizing how learners present and perceive identities, share knowledge, and communicate ideas.

Another common application of CSCL technologies can be found in problem-based learning [7, 9] or project-based learning [3]. For instance, Stahl [16, 18] has extensively studied how students work together for solving geometry and other math problems.

C.3 Summary

CSCL provides exciting opportunities to educators and technology developers to create and study solutions for enhancing learning through collaborative activities. Being computer-mediated, CSCL enjoys several benefits, but also faces challenges. Often teachers find it harder to monitor student progress in online environment that they do with face-to-face interactions. This could be solved with better implementation and integration of technology in existing learning environments.

Researchers, on the other hand, find it difficult to induce collaboration in CSCL studies. This may negatively affect various social, cognitive, and emotional aspects in CSCL processes that are necessary for real collaborative learning [2].

References

1. C. Asterhan and B. Schwarz. Online moderation of synchronous e-argumentation. *International Journal of Computer-Supported Collaborative Learning*, 5(3):259–282, 2010.
2. Liam J. Bannon. Issues in computer supported collaborative learning. In *Proceedings of NATO Advanced Workshop on Computer-Supported Collaborative Learning*, Maratea, Italy, 1989.
3. P. Blumenfeld, E. Soloway, R. Marx, J. Krajcik, M. Guzdial and A. Palincsar. Motivating project-based learning: sustaining the doing, supporting the learning. *Educational Psychologist*, 26(3/4):369, 1991.
4. P. Dillenbourg and F. Fischer. Basics of computer-supported collaborative learning. *Zeitschrift für Berufs- und Wirtschaftspädagogik*, 21:111–130, 2007.
5. C.E. Hmelo-Silver. Analyzing collaborative learning: Multiple approaches to understanding processes and outcomes. In *Proceedings of the International Conference of the Learning Sciences (ICLS)*, 2006.

6. T. Koschmann. Paradigm shifts and instructional technology. In *CSCL: Theory and Practice of an Emerging Paradigm*, pages 1–23. 1996.
7. T. Koschmann, P. Feltovich, A. Myers and H. Barrows. Implications of CSCL for problem-based learning. *Journal of Learning Sciences*, 21(3):32–35, 1992. Special issue on computer supported collaborative learning.
8. J. Larusson and R. Alterman. Wikis to support the "collaborative" part of collaborative learning. *International Journal of Computer-Supported Collaborative Learning*, 4(4):371–402, 2009.
9. J. Lu, S. Lajoie and J. Wiseman. Scaffolding problem-based learning with CSCL tools. *International Journal of Computer-Supported Collaborative Learning*, 5(3):283–298, 2010.
10. Judith S. Olson, Gary M. Olson, Marianne Storrø sten and Mark Carter. Groupwork close up: a comparison of the group design process with and without a simple group editor. *ACM Transactions on Information Systems*, 11(4):321–348, 1993.
11. J. Onrubia and A. Engel. Strategies for collaborative writing and phases of knowledge construction in CSCL environments. *Computers & Education*, 53(4):1256–1265, 2009.
12. M. Scardamalia and C. Bereiter. Higher levels of agency in knowledge building: a challenge for the design of new knowledge media. *Journal of the Learning Sciences*, 1:37–68, 1991.
13. G. Stahl, T. Koschmann and D. Suthers. Computer-supported collaborative learning: an historical perspective. In R.K. Sawyer, editor, *Cambridge Handbook of the Learning Sciences*, pages 409–426. Cambridge University Press, Cambridge, 2006.
14. Gerry Stahl. Contributions to a theoretical framework for CSCL. In *Proceedings of Computer Supported Collaborative Learning (CSCL)*, pages 62–71, Boulder, CO, 2002. Erlbaum, Hillsdale.
15. Gerry Stahl. Building collaborative knowing: Elements of a social theory of CSCL. In J.W. Strijbos, P. Kirschner and R. Martens, editors, *What We Know About CSCL: And Implementing It in Higher Education*, pages 53–86. Kluwer Academic, Boston, 2004.
16. Gerry Stahl. Computer mediation of collaborative mathematical exploration. In *Proceedings of the International Conference of the Learning Sciences (ICLS)*, pages 30–33, Chicago, Illinois, June 2010. International Society of the Learning Sciences.
17. L. Vygotsky. *Mind in Society*. Harward University Press, Cambridge, 1978.
18. Martin Wessner, Wesley Shumar, Gerry Stahl, Johann Sarmiento, Martin Mühlpfordt and Stephen Weimar. Designing an online service for a math community. In *Proceedings of the International Conference of the Learning Sciences (ICLS)*, pages 818–824, Bloomington, Indiana, June 2006. International Society of the Learning Sciences.

Appendix D
Brief Overview of Computer-Mediated Communication (CMC)

Communication has been recognized as a core component of coordination, cooperation, and collaboration [5, 8, 22]. We also saw that while communication is an essential element of collaboration, it is not sufficient, and that one could simply study communication without guaranteeing any higher level processes such as coordination or collaboration. Here we will review several theories related to computer-mediated communication (CMC), several of which can inform computer-mediated collaboration, whereas others stand on their own for explaining communication itself.

The widespread use of communication technologies has brought about new forms of collaborative work. Collaboration can be performed through various communication media (e.g., email, IM, audio, video), and vary on several dimensions including concurrency (synchronous vs. asynchronous) and location (co-located vs. distributed) [7, 17]. Literature suggests that collaborative work demands extensive information sharing, coordination, awareness [23], and division of labor and persistence [14]. Theories and studies within the context of CMC can explain how different communication media (e.g., email, audio, video) across varying dimensions (e.g., synchronous vs. asynchronous; co-located vs. distributed) can facilitate or hinder interaction and collaboration, and thereby performance of teams. This section outlines some of CMC theories to help understand such potential and shortcomings of various communication contexts within the framework of CIS.

D.1 Social Presence Theory

Social presence theory is one of the earliest theories in CMC, which can explain the kind of interactions during a collaborative work. Presence is considered an integral part of mediated environments. Social presence is defined as the degree to which a person is aware of another person in a mediate communication context [24]. This theory suggests that different communication media enables different levels of social presence experience. While face-to-face (F2F) communication has the highest level of social presence, CMC has a considerably lower level of social presence due to lack of nonverbal cues and reduced feedback. Since CIS requires extensive communication for information sharing and awareness, contexts with low social presence such as those in distributed and asynchronous dimensions may require extra efforts to compensate the limited affordances of these dimensions, or may call for additional system features to facilitate communication and awareness. Early research also suggests that social presence is related to increased satisfaction [9, 21], but there is also evidence that a misfit between the medium and a task's social need can negatively influence the experience of social presence [3] and communication performance [13]. Along these lines, there must be a fit between a CIS task and the degree of social presence to increase the outcomes of collaboration, and systems should support the necessary level of social presence. However, there is also evidence that a misfit between the medium and a task's social need can negatively influence the experience of social presence [3] and communication performance [13]. For example, simple tasks with unambiguous answers benefit from media which has only low social presence, while judgment tasks call for media which allow high social presence [3].

D.2 Media Richness Theory

Another theory in CMC is the media richness theory [4] which considers media according to their capability to provide feedback in terms of the number of channels they support (e.g., audio, visual). "Rich" media such as F2F communication allow excessive information whereas "lean" media like text allows little. The main argument in this theory is that there is a match between the equivocality of communication tasks and the communication media. More specifically, the more equivocal the communication task, the richer the media it calls for.

Early research has sorted out certain task categories in terms of their need for information richness [12, 20], and has showed mixed findings on the need for information richness with regards to a task in collaborative work. A recent literature review suggests that collaborative work demands extensive information sharing, coordination, and awareness [23], and significant amounts of coordination require richer media [26]. Past studies have found that F2F and audio-only interactions do not differ in terms of task outcome for problem-solving tasks, [2], but participants' performance on design tasks was significantly better in F2F, co-present than audio-only, remote conditions [16]. Other studies could not find any advantages for using video-mediated communication (VMC) in collaborative environments [1, 16, 30]. In contrast, social tasks, involving negotiation or conflict resolution, show some benefits of F2F or VMC [6] not for task outcome but for increased participant satisfaction [16]. More recent studies testing the effectiveness of CMC compared to F2F in collaborative working found CMC to be more effective (e.g., [10]), which can be explained by the task-oriented nature of CMC.

The task-oriented nature of CMC was also shown in early studies of CMC. Walther [28] investigated the effects of CMC on social relationships and found that the impersonal style of communication in CMC was reduced when participants had enough time to complete their task. Several studies in the CMC literature showed that certain personal communication was lower in CMC than F2F highlighting the task-oriented nature of CMC. For example, one study showed that task performance of CMC participants was initially poorer when compared to the performance of verbal interactions, but improved as they gained experience of the CMC context [15]. Participants in this study adopted a specific way of giving directions, where they were more precise compared to F2F interactions. Along with these lines, individuals working collaboratively on an information seeking task may find different ways for communicating awareness or search findings when encountered with communication constraints in contexts such as text chat.

D.3 Social Information Processing (SIP) Theory

The SIP theory of CMC interaction [29] assumes that communicators in CMC can reduce interpersonal uncertainty, form impressions, and develop affinity in online settings as they can do in F2F context and rejects the view that the absence of non-verbal cues restricts the communicators' capability to exchange information. SIP theory posits that communicators exchange social information through the content, style, and timing of online messages. The rate of information exchange is slower online due to instrumental and relational constraints as well as inefficiency in communicating online. When time is limited, interaction can be expected to be impersonal and task-oriented; and when not restricted communicators can reach levels of impression and relational development just like they would in F2F settings.

Some early studies considered the relative availability of higher-order information-seeking strategies in CMC and F2F. Studies of initial interactions in F2F settings have identified several distinct types and subtypes of information-seeking strategies. For instance, Tidwell and Walther [27] argued that, unlike F2F settings, online systems offer individuals only limited opportunities to observe others unobtrusively or to gain information about them indirectly. They further argued that if CMC users adapt available cues to perform interpersonal functions, then they would rely on interactive strategies to a greater extent in CMC than in F2F settings. They examined the information-seeking strategies of CMC and F2F dyads engaged in acquaintance and decision-making tasks. Their results support the adaptation view that CMC users employed a greater proportion of self-disclosures and questions than did F2F partners. Additionally, the correspondence between the frequency of the interactive strategies and partners' ratings of one another's communication effectiveness was significantly more positive in CMC than in F2F communication. Along with SIP theory, F2F partners seem to draw on visual, auditory, and verbal cues at their disposal and CMC partners adjust their strategies for effective interpersonal information acquisition. Later, the theory took also into consideration the variations in the motivation to reduce uncertainty across different types of media and anticipated future interaction in predicting interactions in CMC.

D.4 Social Identification/De-individuation (SIDE) Theory

SIDE theory assumes that CMC's lack of nonverbal cues filters out interpersonal and individual identity information [11]. CMC may promote de-individuation by reducing the number of channels that are used for personal interaction. De-individuation is defined as the process whereby submergence in a group produces loss of identity for individuals [18]. Communicating without nonverbal information, and in physical isolation, promotes greater group identification and self-categorization in line with social identity. CMC groups interpret the content of others' messages as signals for creating or reinforcing group norms [11]. When CMC context makes group identity salient, individuals overly attribute similarity and common norms, resulting in social attraction to the group and group members. A recent study revealed that the text-only users developed greater group-based self-categorizations, which affect group attraction which was indirectly affected through increased stereotyping of out-group members [19].

D.5 Hyperpersonal Communication Model

Walther [28] argued that four set of effects, namely sender, receiver, channel, and feedback, may create *hyper-personal communication* that goes beyond the interpersonal interaction in F2F context. Receiver and source effects come from the roles individuals play in the communication process. The channel facilitates goal-enhancing messages by allowing greater control over message construction than is available in F2F context. A CMC user may take his/her time in reviewing and editing message and may take advantage of an asynchronous channel to effectively consider responses. Asynchronous channels also allow individuals to exchange social comments more easily in task-oriented settings. Finally, hyper-personal feedback may allow receivers to send selective messages.

Numerous empirical studies in CMC literature demonstrated that the use of email and computer conferencing reduced interpersonal affect and group solidarity. Experiments with groups with no history working on a task in a limited time showed that CMC was more task-oriented than were F2F meetings. CMC was significantly higher than F2F on certain social categories of conversation, leading to conclusions about the task-oriented nature of CMC. Walther [28] suggested that within the context of group decision making, reduced socio-emotional communication and increased task orientation can enhance group work. In addition, impersonal communication can lead group members to use a greater proportion of their work time for instrumental tasks. As socio-emotional concerns such as conflict take time and effort away task resolution, any mechanism that reduces the need to expend effort should enhance the efficiency of a group's efforts. A study on a problem-solving discussion confirmed this notion with a finding of an inverse relationship between the frequency of personal remarks and decision-making success in CMC [25]. In other words, groups do not accomplish as much work on a task when they generate great amounts of conversation over the communication medium [25].

D.6 Summary

CMC theories present different perspectives towards the benefits of collaborative information seeking in CMC. Team members can benefit from varying affordances of media at different times of a CIS task. On one hand, team members may especially desire a rich media with high social presence, at the beginning of a task when they perform brainstorming and decision making on strategy and division of labor. In that sense, initial synchronous and collocated or audio-supported media context may foster such interactions. After the strategy is determined and responsibilities are shared, on the other hand, individuals may gain the advantages of lean media with low social presence as impersonal communication generated by CMC allows group members to focus most of their time and efforts on instrumental task increasing efficiency. Therefore, distributed and asynchronous contexts may generate affordances that would be advantageous for team members working separately on their assigned parts of the task. However, since awareness is an integral part of a CIS task, the communication context should still enable members to exchange information so as to know each other's steps. Altogether, theories of CMC can inform us on the guidelines to design better systems that would improve the outcomes of teams working on a CIS task.

References

1. A. Anderson, A. Newlands, J. Mullin, A. Mariefleming, G. Dohertysneddon and J. Vandervelden. Impact of video-mediated communication on simulated service encounters. *Interacting with Computers*, 8(2):193–206, 1996.
2. A. Chapanis, R.B. Ochsman, R.N. Parrish and G.D. Weeks. Studies in interactive communication. I—The effects of four communication modes on the behavior of teams during cooperative problem-solving. *Human Factors*, 14(6):487–509, 1972.
3. S. Chou and H. Min. The impact of media on collaborative learning in virtual settings: the perspective of social construction. *Computers & Education*, 52(2):417–431, 2009.
4. Richard L. Daft and Robert H. Lengel. Information richness. A new approach to managerial behavior and organization design. *Research in Organizational Behavior*, 6:191–223, 1984.
5. Peter J. Denning and Peter Yaholkovsky. Getting to "We". *Communications of the ACM*, 51(4):19–24, 2008.
6. Robert S. Fish, Robert E. Kraut, Robert W. Root and Ronald E. Rice. Evaluating video as a technology for informal communication. In *Proceedings of the SIGCHI Conference on Human Factors in Computing Systems CHI 92*, pages 37–48, 1992.
7. Gene Golovchinsky, Jeremy Pickens and Maribeth Back. A taxonomy of collaboration in online information seeking. In *Proceedings of JCDL 2008 Workshop on Collaborative Exploratory Search*, Pittsburgh, PA, June 2008.
8. Barbara Gray. *Collaborating: Finding Common Ground for Multiparty Problems*. Jossey-Bass, San Francisco, 1989.
9. Carol Hostetter and Monique Busch. Measuring up online: the relationship between social presence and student learning satisfaction. *Journal of Scholarship of Teaching and Learning*, 6(2):1–12, 2006.
10. Ann Lantz. Meetings in a distributed group of experts: comparing face-to-face, chat and collaborative virtual environments. *Behaviour & Information Technology*, 20(2):111–117, 2001.
11. M. Lea and R. Spears. Computer-mediated communication, de-individuation and group decision-making. *International Journal of Man–Machine Studies*, 34(2):283–301, 1991.

12. J.E. McGrath, H. Arrow, D.H. Gruenfeld, A.B. Hollingshead and K.M. O'Connor. Groups, tasks, and technology. The effects of experience and change. *Small Group Research*, 24(3):406–420, 1993.

13. Brian E. Mennecke, Joseph S. Valacich and Bradley C. Wheeler. The effects of media and task on user performance: a test of the task-media fit hypothesis. *Group Decision and Negotiation*, 9(6):507–529, 2000.

14. Meredith Ringel Morris and Eric Horvitz. SearchTogether: an interface for collaborative web search. In *ACM Symposium on User Interface Software and Technology (UIST)*, pages 3–12, Newport, RI, October 2007.

15. A. Newlands, A.H. Anderson and J. Mullin. Adapting communicative strategies to computer-mediated communication: an analysis of task performance and dialogue structure. *Applied Cognitive Psychology*, 17(3):325–348, 2003.

16. J.S. Olson, G.M. Olson and D.K. Meader. What mix of video and audio is useful for small groups doing remote real-time design work? In *Proceedings of CHI '95*, Denver, CO, pages 362–368. ACM, New York, 1995.

17. Jeremy Pickens and Gene Golovchinsky. Collaborative exploratory search. In *Proceedings of Workshop on Human–Computer Interaction and Information Retrieval*, pages 21–22, MIT CSAIL, Cambridge, Massachusetts, USA, October 2007.

18. T. Postmes, R. Spears and M. Lea. Breaching or building social boundaries?: Side-effects of computer-mediated communication. *Communication Research*, 25(6):689–715, 1998.

19. Tom Postmes, Russell Spears and Martin Lea. Intergroup differentiation in computer-mediated communication: Effects of depersonalization. *Group Dynamics: Theory, Research, and Practice*, 6(1):3–16, 2002.

20. Ajaz R. Rana, Murray Turoff and Starr Roxanne Hiltz. Task and Technology Interaction (TTI): A theory of technological support for group tasks. In *Proceedings of the Thirtieth Hawaii International Conference on System Sciences*, pages 66–75, 1997.

21. Jennifer C. Richardson and Karen Swan. Examining social presence in online courses in relation to students? Perceived learning and satisfaction. *Journal of Asynchronous Learning Networks*, 7(1):68–88, 2003.

22. Chirag Shah. Toward Collaborative Information Seeking (CIS). In *Proceedings of Collaborative Exploratory Search Workshop at JCDL 2008*, abs/0908.0, 2009.

23. Chirag Shah. Collaborative information seeking: a literature review. *Advances in Librarianship*, 32:3–33, 2010.

24. J. Short, E. Williams and B. Christie. *The Social Psychology of Telecommunications*, volume 7. Wiley, New York, 1976.

25. Mark W. Smolensky, Meghan A. Carmody and Charles G. Halcomb. The influence of task type, group structure and extraversion on uninhibited speech in computer-mediated communication. *Computers in Human Behavior*, 6(3):261–272, 1990.

26. Susan G. Straus and Joseph E. McGrath. Does the medium matter? The interaction of task type and technology on group performance and member reactions. *Journal of Applied Psychology*, 79(1):87–97, 1994.

27. Lisa Collins Tidwell and Joseph B. Walther. Computer-mediated communication effects on disclosure, impressions, and interpersonal evaluations: getting to know one another a bit at a time. *Human Communication Research*, 28(3):317–348, 2002.

28. J.B. Walther. Computer-mediated communication: impersonal, interpersonal, and hyperpersonal interaction. *Communication Research*, 23(1):3–43, 1996.

29. Joseph B. Walther and Judee K. Burgoon. Relational communication in computer-mediated interaction. *Human Communication Research*, 19(1):50–88, 1992.

30. S. Whittaker and B. O'Conaill. The role of vision in face-to-face and mediated communication. In *Vision-Mediated Communication*, pages 23–49. Erlbaum, Hillsdale, 1997.

Glossary

Information retrieval (IR) It is the area of study concerned with searching for documents, for information within documents, and for metadata about documents, as well as that of searching structured storage, relational databases, and the World Wide Web.

Information seeking (IS) It is the process or activity of attempting to obtain information in both human and technological contexts. IS, in this book, is seen as incorporating IR (see Chap. 1).

Information behavior/human information behavior It is the study of the interaction between people, information, and the situations (contexts) in which they interact.

Sense-making or sensemaking It is the process by which people give meaning to experience.

Coordination This is a process of connecting different agents together for a harmonious action. This often involves bringing people or systems under an umbrella at the same time and place. During this process, the involved agents may share resources, responsibilities, and goals.

Cooperation This is a relationship in which different agents with similar interests take part in planning activities, negotiating roles, and sharing resources to achieve joint goals. In addition to coordination, cooperation involves all the agents following some rules of interaction.

Collaboration This is a process involving various agents that may see different aspects of a problem. They engage in a process through which they can go beyond their own individual expertise and vision by constructively exploring their differences and searching for common solutions. In contrast to cooperation, collaboration involves creating a solution that is more than merely the sum of each party's contribution. The authority in such a process is vested in the collaborative rather than in an individual entity.

Information need This involves fact finding, exploration of a topic, content consumption (e.g., read a document, view a video, buy a product), negotiations (e.g., auctions), etc.

C. Shah, *Collaborative Information Seeking*, The Information Retrieval Series 34,
DOI 10.1007/978-3-642-28813-5, © Springer-Verlag Berlin Heidelberg 2012

Explicit collaboration When various aspects of collaboration are clearly stated and understood. For instance, a group of students working on a science project together know that (i) they are collaborating, (ii) who is responsible for doing what.

Implicit collaboration When collaboration happens without explicit specifications. For instance, visitors to Amazon.com receive recommendations based on other people's searching and buying behavior without knowing those people.

Active collaboration This is similar to explicit collaboration with the key difference being the willingness and awareness of the user. For instance, when a user of Netflix rates a movie, he is actively playing a part in collaborating with other users. However, since he did not explicitly agree to collaborate with others; he may not even know those users.

Passive collaboration This is similar to implicit collaboration with the key difference being the willingness and awareness of the user. For instance, when a user visits a video on YouTube, he passively contributes to the popularity of that video, affecting the ranking and popularity of that video for others. The key difference between active and passive collaboration is user's willingness and control over the actions. In case of active collaboration, user agrees to do it (rating, comments), whereas in case of passive collaboration, user has very little control (click-through, browsing patterns).

Timeframe A short slot of time. Two events happening in the same timeframe do not need to be happening exactly at the same time, but they do take place not too far from each other in temporal context. For instance, this morning's online discussions on a breaking news story is considered in the same timeframe. If one is commenting on a news story from the last week, that is out of that news story's timeframe.

Personalization System configuration for a given user based on his profile, preferences and/or behavioral patterns.

Groupization System configuration for a given group based on its profile, preferences and/or behavioral patterns.

Recommendation System configuration for a given user based on his matched profile, preferences and/or behavioral patterns with other users in the network.

Agent An entity—user or system—in a collaborative environment. A computer network is made by connecting agents that are computers. A focus group consists of agents that are humans.

Users Refers to the humans. In some cases, they may be using a system, but not be a part of a collaborative.

Participants Refers to the humans that are parts of a collaboration. In some cases, they may not even use a system. With respect to a user study, this refers to the subjects who participate.

System Refers to machines or automated mechanism.

Environment A set of objects and attributes that may include users, systems, and their context.

Symmetric roles When all the users in the group are given the same powers and responsibilities, they are playing symmetric role.

Asymmetric roles When each user in the group has different powers and/or responsibilities, they are said to be playing asymmetric roles.

Synchronous collaboration This refers to the situations when collaborators are working in the same time (co-located or remotely). Example includes collaborating using Diamond Touch.[1]

Asynchronous collaboration This refers to the situations when collaborators are working in different times (co-located or remotely).

Groupware It is computer software designed to help people involved in a common task achieve goals.

Computer-supported cooperative work (CSCW) It is a field that is concerned with understanding the nature and characteristics of cooperative work with the objective of designing adequate computer-based technologies.

Computer-supported collaborative learning (CSCL) It is an interdisciplinary field that refers to a pedagogical approach concerning learning that takes place through interactions among the students, mediated by technology.

---

[1] http://www.merl.com/areas/DiamondTouch/.

Index

A
Anomalous State of Knowledge, 63
AntWorld, 29
Ariadne, 27, 48, 51, 74, 93
ASK, *see* Anomalous State of Knowledge

C
Cerchiamo, 91
CIB, *see* Collaborative information behavior
CIR, *see* Collaborative information retrieval
CIRE, *see* Collaborative Information Retrieval
        Environment
CIS, *see* Collaborative information seeking
CIS systems, 89, 134
    system mediation, 50, 91
    user mediation, 50, 93
CiteSeer, 50
Cloud computing, 73
CMC, *see* Computer-Mediated
        Communication
Co-browsing, 25, 28
Co-search, 26
Coagmento, 51, 96, 142
    cognitive walkthrough, 100
    deployment, 109
    development, 104
    field study, 109
    laboratory study, 106
    participatory design, 102, 110
    pilots, 100
Cognitive filtering, 46
Collaboration, 4, 5, 11
    awareness, 16, 162
    C5 model, 13, 20, 61, 145
    communication, 162
    control, 160
    definitions, 11

limitations, 18
model, 145
models, 11, 61
phases, 17
principles, 16
process, 17
stages, 17
system-mediated, 50, 91
user-mediated, 51, 93
Collaborative exploratory search, 25
Collaborative filtering, 32, 44, 161
Collaborative information behavior, 4, 140
Collaborative information retrieval, 25–28, 44
    definition, 27, 28
Collaborative Information Retrieval
        Environment, 35
Collaborative information seeking, 28
    awareness, 46, 47, 142
    cognitive model, 74
    communication, 46, 142
    control, 45, 147
    definition, 25
    dimensions, 51
    frameworks, 41
    mediation, 50
    roles, 55
    scenarios, 6
    social dimension, 77
    space–time aspects, 41, 42
    user–source–time configuration, 42
Collaborative information synthesis, 25
Collaborative navigation, 25, 28, 44
Collaborative search, 25
Collaborative tie, 30
Computer-Mediated Communication, 9, 47,
        177

Computer-Supported Collaborative Learning,
        9, 169
    applications, 170
    practice, 170
    theories, 169
Computer-Supported Cooperative Work, 9,
        45–49, 75, 76, 116, 139, 142, 159
    matrix, 159
Concurrent search, 25
Cooperation, 12, 20, 61
Coordination, 11, 20, 61
CoSearch, 29, 30, 164
COSMOS, 45
CoVitesse, 29, 116, 164
CRUISER, 28
CSCL, *see* Computer-Supported Collaborative
        Learning
CSCW, *see* Computer-Supported Cooperative
        Work

D
Distributed IR, 73

E
Evaluation
    affects, 125
    awareness, 125
    case study, 126
    challenges, 115
    cognitive load, 124
    collaborative aptitude, 121
    coverage, 119
    diversity, 121
    effectiveness, 120
    emotions, 125
    engagement, 124
    F-measure, 118
    likelihood of discovery, 120
    precision, 118
    qualitative, 117
    recall, 118
    system measures, 118
    system-based training-testing, 117
    task or application based, 117
    usability, 123
    user measures, 121
    user studies, 116
Exploratory search, 8, 134

G
GAB, *see* Group Asynchronous Browsing
GIM, *see* Group Information Management
Group Asynchronous Browsing, 44
Group Information Management, 66

Group Unified History, 116
Groupization, 66
GroupScape, 29, 164
Groupware, 19, 97, 139, 164
    matrix, 159
GroupWeb, 29, 164
GUH, *see* Group Unified History

H
HCI, *see* Human–Computer Interaction
HeyStaks, 35
Human–Computer Interaction, 9, 65, 120, 143
Hyperpersonal communication model, 176

I
I-Spy, 26, 35, 117
Information retrieval, 4, 6, 26, 116, 139
Information search process, 26, 74–78, 81, 82,
        140
Information seeking, 4, 5, 21, 26–28, 30, 32,
        33, 35
    models, 63
Information Seeking Strategies, 71
InformationLens, 45
Interaction, 15
    ISS, 71
    models, 68
    Stratified model, 70
IR, *see* Information retrieval
IS, *see* Information seeking
ISP, *see* Information search process
ISS, *see* Information Seeking Strategies

M
Media richness theory, 174
Meta-searching, 44
MovieLens, 34
MUSE, 27

O
ObjectLens, 46, 161

P
Personal Information Management, 65
Personalization, 65
PIM, *see* Personal Information Management

Q
Querium, 92

R
Recommendation
    collaborative, 34
    content-based, 32
Recommender systems, 44

ReferralWeb, 35
Relevance feedback, 64

S
S^3, 27
SDL, 45, *see* Structured Definition Language,
    see Structured Definition Language
SearchTogether, 22, 27, 48, 49, 51, 95, 99,
    116, 142
Sense-making, 4, 63
SIDE theory, *see* Social
    identification/de-individuation theory
SIP theory, *see* Social information processing
    theory
Social identification/de-individuation theory,
    176
Social information processing theory, 175

Social media, 139
Social network analysis, 31
Social networking, 139
Social presence theory, 173
Social search, 25, 30
Social tie, 31
Social Web, 29
Strong tie, 31
Structured Definition Language, 161

T
TLX, 124

W
Weak tie, 31
WebTagger, 29
WebWatch, 44